THE COLLAPSE
OF HONOR

How Greed Led
to the Destruction
of a Young
Lawyer Caught-up
In a Law Firm's
Epic Battle Over
Compensation

LARRY L. HINES

Scriba Publications
5941 Terra Bella Lane
Camarillo, CA 93012

ISBN: 0692751025
ISBN 13: 9780692751022
Library of Congress Control Number: 2016910995
Scriba Publications, Camarillo, CA

Dedication

This novel is dedicated to the lawyers all over America who see the legal profession as something more than just a way to make a living. They are the lawyers who know that being a lawyer is something special, who will still represent a client in need even if they can't pay, and who measure their worth not by how much money they make but instead by what they can do to promote our justice system. They are the lawyers who love being lawyers.

The courthouse in Los Angeles is real, but otherwise all characters and dialogue in this novel are fiction. Any resemblance of the imaginary characters to actual persons is coincidental.

Prologue

Practicing law within a partnership, large or small, can be a wonderfully rewarding experience. A "partnership" is not just a legal title. It involves a feeling – a happiness to be together and to support each other. In many ways it is like a family where the partners spend their entire working career together in one firm. Without this, it is just a group of lawyers making money.

But the idea of firm loyalty and camaraderie is becoming antiquated. There are partnerships now where the lawyers unfortunately do not have this special feeling. To use an old phrase, the beast in the belly of these lawyers is to make as much money as possible. They can be ruthless and crush anyone who gets in their way. The Collapse of Honor tells the story of such a firm.

The Baukus & Johnson partnership has outstanding lawyers who are known to be some of the best lawyers in the Los Angeles area. But it has a weakness. It has a complex formula for dividing income at the end of each year – what lawyers call "splitting the pie" – and they have an annual fight over how much each partner will receive. It is a fairly typical formula for large firms. Some firms handle it well; others, like the Baukus & Johnson firm, do not.

When the Baukus & Johnson partners attend the annual meeting to determine compensation, it is fraught with tension and a belief by each partner that he should be paid more. Egos, normally large on a good day, puff out another inch or two; lawyers who are known as rational and logical become irrational and emotional. This can flow naturally from the adversarial nature of our legal system, or it may just be old fashion greed. Whatever the explanation, it makes for a contentious and often nasty occasion that is not for the faint of heart.

This is the story of the fictitious Baukus & Johnson law partnership and how some partners are willing to destroy the career of a brilliant young associate solely because they wanted to make more money. It is a classic case of greed in action.

Only you, the reader, can judge whether justice was done in the end.

The Los Angeles County Superior Court system is the largest unified court in the United States with forty-seven separate branch courts; over six hundred courtrooms; and over four hundred judges and numerous commissioners. The setting for this story is the main central court located in downtown Los Angeles.

CHAPTER I

It was 7:15 a.m., a few days before Christmas, and Mark Austin was sitting in his office drafting changes to a trust when he saw on his computer screen a red light blinking indicating that he had received an urgent email. "Who the hell is sending me an email at this time of the morning?" he thought to himself. His client expected his will and trust to be ready to sign that afternoon and he was trying to finish the first draft so his secretary could make the changes. He decided whoever it was could wait an hour for a reply.

As Mark Austin continued dictating corrections to the trust, he absent- mindedly reached over and touched the Outlook button on his computer to open his emails. When he saw who the urgent email was from, he bolted upright in his chair with a frown on his face. The email was from Harlan Cross, the Managing Partner of the whole damn law firm.

With a law firm like Baukus & Johnson, with almost eighty lawyers, young attorneys rarely get an email from the head man, so Mark quickly opened it. It said, "Mark — Urgent that I meet with you asap. Drop whatever you are doing and come on up to the conference room. Cross"

Mark whistled softly and his heart began to beat rapidly as he contemplated what kind of assignment Harlan Cross was going to give him. He thought back over the last five years and could only recall meeting Harlan Cross once, and that was earlier in the year when he had been made a junior partner. Mark had actually been elevated mid-year, a full six months before the other members of his incoming group of associates were even considered. Harlan Cross and the other members of the firm's Executive Committee had invited him up to the firm's formal conference room and told him of his advancement. And he could remember Harlan Cross's words as if it were yesterday. "You're doing excellent work, Mark." Cross had turned to Wayne Bailey, the chair of the estate planning department, Mark's immediate boss, and added with a smile and wink of his left eye, "If you land any more clients like Gibbons, we might even give you Wayne's job."

Mark Austin was twenty-nine years old, about six feet tall and weighed close to two hundred and twenty pounds. He had black hair cut short Marine Corp style and, while a little overweight, he was in good shape considering that all of the young lawyers at Baukus & Johnson worked ten hour days at least six and sometimes seven days a week. He had been raised by his grandparents on a rural farm and had been given the nickname "Farmer Austin" by the other associates because he looked like he belonged on a tractor more than in a business suit. But it was a friendly nickname. Mark was a graduate of Stanford Law School and had been second in his class.

Mark had been hired by Baukus & Johnson as a law clerk after his second year of law school. The firm liked the quality of his work and he was offered a position after graduation. The firm assigned him to the corporate law department at first, but he then moved into the tax and estate planning area where he now worked.

The law firm of Baukus & Johnson is located in Century City near Santa Monica in southern California. The firm takes up five floors of one of the many towering office buildings on the Avenue of the Stars, the former Twentieth Century Fox movie back lot. The firm started in the mid-eighteen hundreds when Los Angeles was still essentially a pueblo town in the desert. Rufus Baukus started out representing local merchants and ended up as counsel for the early banks that sprouted in San Francisco and Los Angeles after gold was discovered. Stanley Johnson was a real estate lawyer and represented the early land promoters. The two joined together in eighteen ninety and as southern California grew from a rural setting to a major industrial economy, so did the firm.

Mark Austin had good reason to think he was about to get a special legal assignment from Harlan Cross. He had not only just been made a junior partner six month earlier, but he had been receiving glowing reviews from every partner he worked with. His clients loved him. They liked his coat off with shirt sleeves rolled up to the elbows casual style, which gave him a friendly guy-next-door appearance, instead of a stuffy lawyer sitting in an office.

The crowning moment had come a year earlier when he had been responsible for bringing in a new client that eventually hired the firm as general counsel for all of the client's corporate and litigation work. The client's name was Boyd Gibbons and he owned five companies in the southern California area that built specialty items for the large contractors, such as Boeing, Hughes and others companies, which built military equipment and worked with NASA on the space program.

Mark had skipped lunch and had been working in the library researching a tax issue when he got an urgent call from Sally, one of the firm's many switchboard operators. "Sorry to bother you, Mark, but I have a gentleman on the line who says he has an urgent labor question. His name is Sam Archer. I tried to reach someone in corporate who handles employment matters but there're all out at a seminar today. Can you help him?" Sally asked with an urgent plea in her voice.

"I had a little experience when I was in corporate, but I'm certainly no expert," Mark replied with a silent sigh. He hesitated briefly and then added, "But put him on. If it's important, we'll get him an answer."

When Sally transferred the call into the library, Mark said, "Mr. Archer, I'm sorry that our labor attorneys are out today. What's the question? I'll try to help if I can. I actually do estate planning now but I was in corporate for a while."

Sam Archer was a senior vice president of Space Age Manufacturing, one of the companies owned by Boyd Gibbons. "Thanks. I appreciate your taking the call. We kind of got caught in transition on this," he said. "We don't have labor counsel right now. Anyway, we're a union company and the shop steward came barging into my office this morning and demanded that we set up a binding arbitration hearing. One of our machinists screamed and cussed out the plant manager who then fired him right on the spot. The steward says he can't do that if the union wants arbitration. Can you help us here?"

Mark knew enough to know that union contracts usually cover things like this, so he said, "Mr. Archer, can you fax me over a copy of your union contract? I suspect this is covered."

Within the hour the union contract was faxed over to Mark. He had been waiting and when it arrived, he flipped through the pages until he found the disciplinary section. He saw right away that the contract had a clause that forced management into binding arbitration if the union requested it over any serious disciplinary action. And he didn't need to be a specialist in labor law to know that being fired certainly fell into that category.

When he called Sam Archer back, Mark explained what the union contract controlled and that it did require arbitration. He was not happy with the answer but said, "Mark, I appreciate your quick response. It's not what I wanted to hear, but we'd just get sued if I simply canned the guy after the union's protest. Anyway, thanks for your help. Give me your email address and I'll send over our address to give to your billing department."

It was a few months later that Mark got a call from Boyd Gibbons. "Mark, Sam Archer tells me you're a smart kid and you do estate planning. Is that correct?"

"Yes sir. I did some corporate work for a few years but now I specialize in estate planning," Mark replied.

"OK. I need my trust revised and I'd like to get it done fast. I'm leaving for China this weekend. Think you can handle that?" Boyd Gibbons bluntly asked.

"Yes sir. When can you come in?" Mark asked.

"Well, that's the problem," Boyd Gibbons said. "I'm in Washington D.C. right now and can't get back to Los Angeles until just before I leave. Can we do this by phone?"

It is always best for an attorney to personally meet with clients when doing a trust so the attorney knows the client isn't being pressured by someone, and Mark almost said no until he recalled that he only wanted an amendment. "If you only need an amendment, Mr. Gibbons, I think we can help. Can you get me a copy of your trust and the asset schedules?" Mark asked.

"Yes. Of course," Boyd Gibbons replied. "Sam can get it out of the safe at the office and email it over today."

"What changes do you want?" Mark asked.

"The beneficiaries are all OK. Everything goes to my kids," Boyd Gibbons replied. "But I just got remarried and I want to set up a trust for my wife. The kids will get all of the businesses, but I want her protected. So my assets that are outside of the companies, meaning my home, our ranch in Montana and my brokerage accounts, I think there're three of them, they should all be put into the trust for Kathy, my wife. I'll write this out and email it to you."

"That's no problem, Mr. Gibbons. I'll need your wife's full name and copies of the deeds for the house and ranch and your stock accounts. We can transfer these into a new trust. The deeds will have to be recorded and the one in Montana may take a few weeks. But an assignment into the trust now will be good enough until you return from your trip," Mark explained.

"I'll have my stock broker call you and work out the transfer of those accounts. When can you get this done for me to sign?" Boyd Gibbons asked rather demandingly.

"Well, if I get everything by tomorrow, I can have everything ready to sign by Thursday. Will that work?" Mark asked.

"That's perfect," Boyd Gibbons replied. "When I email the instructions, I'll include my hotel address here in DC. Overnight the originals. And Mark, thanks for jumping right on this."

Mark Austin could tell that Boyd Gibbons was in a hurry so he quickly asked, "Mr. Gibbons, one more thing. Since you just got married, do you have a prenuptial agreement?"

There was instant laughter from Boyd Gibbons. "Hell no! I actually asked her about that when we got engaged and she, well, she got real angry. I love her dearly, but she does have a temper. She said 'It's me or your fucking money. You choose.' And, well, you know what I did." He laughed again and added, "You'll have to meet her someday."

When Mark hung up the telephone, he realized he hadn't asked Boyd Gibbons what his assets were worth. "Oh well. I can figure that out when I get the stock account," he mumbled to himself.

A copy of Boyd Gibbon's trust was delivered to Mark's office that afternoon. As he was looking over the trust provisions, he also received emails from Sam Archer with the deeds attached. He also received a fax from Gibbons' stock broker which included three account statements.

Mark was impressed with how quickly Boyd Gibbons had arranged for him to receive the needed documents. He buzzed his secretary to print out the attachments and when she brought them in to his office, he felt a rush of excitement when he saw the stock account. It had a current value of eighty-five million! "God, I wonder how big the ranch in Montana is?" he asked himself.

Mark spent most of that evening at his office drafting the new trust amendment to hold the assets going to Gibbons's wife. When he finished the task and sent all of the legal documents off to Gibbons's hotel in Washington D.C. for signature, he heard nothing more for several months. But then out of the blue he got a call from Sam Archer.

"Mark, this is your lucky day," Sam Archer said cheerfully. Gibbons liked what you did for him. We haven't been happy with our law firm now for some time and we checked out Baukus & Johnson, and they seem to have what we need. So we'd like to transfer over all of our matters, both business and litigation. Can you set up a meeting with your corporate and litigation departments so we can meet?"

It was hard for Mark to hide his enthusiasm. His pulse quickened and his breath caught in his throat for a second. Chances to land a major client rarely happen to a young lawyer and he knew this would end up making him a partner. "Of course, Mr. Archer. When do you want to meet?"

"We have some existing lawsuits that need immediate action, so how about tomorrow?" Sam Archer asked.

After he checked with the heads of the corporate and litigation departments, Mark arranged for a meeting in the firm's main conference room. When he ran the company names through the firm's computerized conflict system, he noticed that Jerry Keller, the chair of the corporate department, had done a lease for one of the Gibbons's companies seven years ago, but nothing since.

When Sam Archer arrived at the reception area of Baukus & Johnson the next day, he was met by Harlan Cross's secretary, Shirley Samuelson. She was short, about five feet four inches tall, and on the chubby side. Her grey hair was cut short so it sort of framed her round pinkish face. It was her smile and accent that caught everyone's attention. She was very British and said with her beaming friendly smile, "Welcome, Mr. Archer. Mr. Cross and the others are waiting for you in the conference room."

When Shirley Samuelson escorted Sam Archer into the firm's conference room, Harlan Cross rose and walked over to greet him. "Good to meet you, Mr. Archer. I'm Harlan Cross, the firm's Managing Partner." He waived his arm in the direction of the others standing at the conference table and said, "This is Jerry Keller. Jerry's the chair of the corporate department. And Derrick Warner here is the chair of litigation."

When they were all seated, Harlan Cross said, "Mr. Archer, we understand that you're interested in retaining our firm as your primary outside counsel, is that correct?'

San Archer looked around the room as he started to reply, but then asked with a slight quizzical expression, "Where's Mark Austin?"

Before he answered, Harlan Cross quickly made brief eye contact with Jerry Keller, cleared his throat and replied, "Well, he's down in his office. I assumed you wanted to talk with the heads of each department."

"Yes, of course," Sam Archer said with a raised inquiring eyebrow. "But it was Mark who did the work for Boyd Gibbons, so he's really the one who got us to consider your firm. Frankly, I expected him to be here. I think I can safely say that Gibbons would be seriously disappointed if Mark were not involved."

"Of course, Mr. Archer," Harlan Cross said with some urgency. "I'll get him up here."

Harlan Cross stood and walked over to a credenza that was along the wall at the end of the conference room. He picked up the telephone and buzzed his secretary. "Shirley, give Mark a call. We'd like him to join us in the conference room, right away."

It only took a few minutes for Mark to reach the conference room. When he walked in, it was Sam Archer who rose to greet him. "Mark, I'm Sam Archer, Boyd's Executive Vice-President. We talked on the phone once about a labor matter. Glad to finally meet you in person. Boyd thinks a lot of you. You did a fine job for him on quick notice. I expect we'll see a lot of each other."

"Thank you, Mr. Archer," Mark replied with some embarrassment.

There was a few long seconds of silence before Harlan Cross again cleared his throat and said, "Well, Mr. Archer, we're all here to help you as a team. Jerry here will be responsible for any of your corporate matters and Derrick will supervise any litigation."

"As I explained to Mark, Sheri Taylor is our inside counsel and she has the details. She's in New York this week, but I'll get her over here as soon as she returns. While she's our counsel, it's my job to select the lawyers and to keep track of how things are going and that's why I'm here."

The conference with Sam Archer lasted about two hours as he outlined what litigation the companies were currently involved in. Mark said very little during the meeting, but when it was over, Sam Archer stood and as they were leaving, he walked over and shook Mark's hand. "You know, Mark, old man Gibbons is not easy to please. Good job," as he slapped him on the back.

They were all standing next to the elevator outside of the conference room when Sam Archer turned to Harlan Cross and said as an after-thought, "I almost forgot. Gibbons told me specifically that he wanted Mark to be the billing attorney on his accounts. I know that's a bit unusual, but that's what he wants." He paused for a second and while looking directly at Harlan Cross added, "Will that pose a problem?"

Harlan Cross glanced over at Jerry Keller and he could tell he was about to object so he jumped in and said, "No problem at all. Mark will do a good job."

Sam Archer laughed and said, "Gibbons has hired hundreds of law firms over the years. He knows that the billing attorney is seen within the firm as being in charge of the account and will get well rewarded. I think he just wants to reward Mark for what he did." Turning to Mark, Archer smiled and added, "I assume you're OK with doing the billings?"

Mark's insides had been doing flip-flops during the entire meeting and he was having difficulty controlling his emotions. He knew that what just happened at the meeting would guarantee his success at the firm. He swallowed hard, looked over at Harlan Cross who nodded ever so slightly in consent, turned back to Archer and said, "Of course. We're here to do whatever Mr. Gibbons wants."

No one realized it at the time, but the companies owned by Boyd Gibbons were collectively worth over five billion dollars and the work they did for the government was huge. The fees for the current half-year were going to slightly exceed two million dollars and would no doubt double or even triple in the future because of the litigation matters and the securities work the firm would be handling.

And Wayne Bailey, the chair of the estate planning department and a member of the firm's Executive Committee, was ecstatic when he learned what Mark had done. Based on his recommendation, Mark was promoted to junior partner in the middle of the year.

When Wayne Bailey met with Mark to inform him of his promotion, he said, "Mark, you did a magnificent job landing Gibbons for the firm. We're going to make millions in fees and you'll get a handsome bonus at the end of the year. As a junior partner, you're now entitled to a share of the firm's Tier Two profits and that includes origination credit. Since you got the client, you'll get ten percent of the billings collected and that might get you a hundred thousand or more. Just think. If down the road we collect say four million, that alone will get you four-hundred thousand dollars and that's over and above your regular income. Certainly enough for the down payment on the house you and your wife want," he said encouragingly.

Mark related the good news to his wife that night and they started looking for a home to buy. "Can you imagine," Mark told his wife with a smile and a hug, "we can actually get out of this damn apartment and get a real home."

In late November, Wayne Bailey reminded Mark to prepare a memo to the Executive Committee outlining what he did with Boyd Gibbons and ask for the origination compensation. "Everyone knows what you did already. It's just a formality," he explained.

A few days later, Mark Austin prepared the memo and emailed it to the Executive Committee with a copy to Wayne Bailey. It was the last business day of the month. Wayne Bailey had explained that the firm waits for the year-end numbers before they divide up the profits. "They usually do that in mid-January."

As the Managing Partner who ran the day-by-day affairs of Baukus & Johnson, Harlan Cross had a corner office on the twentieth floor with a view west, overlooking the Pacific Ocean. It was a long rectangular office with a large conference table that could seat at least twenty people at one end, and an antique library table covered with rich blackish looking red leather that he used as a desk at the other end. Although the room had recessed overhead lighting, there was an equally old Tiffany lamp on the library table where Cross did most of his work.

Harlan Cross was in his late sixties, a short man, about five feet four, with a thin wiry frame, grey hair and a dark tan even in winter. He was a graduate of the University of Southern California as an undergraduate and law school, and had been a member of the university's golf team, a game he still played at least once a week, if not more. His specialty was bankruptcy and he had been the lead lawyer on some of the biggest bankruptcies in southern California.

While Harlan Cross was smart, his real forte was his ability to mediate between fighting factions to resolve financial problems. In fact, it was this ability that led the partners to elect him as the Managing Partner. The other two members of the Executive Committee, fondly or otherwise, were called by the younger attorneys "The Scorpions." Unfortunately, the ability to mediate financial matters did not extend to frictions between strong-willed egocentric partners.

When Mark Austin read the email from Harlan Cross asking him to come to the conference room, he immediately grabbed his suit coat that he had thrown over the arm of a client chair when he arrived that morning. As he almost ran out the door of his office, he put on his coat, fidgeted with his tie to make it straight and headed for the elevator. It was still early when he reached the top floor and he noticed that Harlan Cross's secretary was not there. He walked down the hallway to the conference room, hesitated a moment, and then knocked on the door.

"Come in," Mark heard someone say. As he opened the door and walked in, he saw Harlan Cross sitting at the end of the conference table with two other partners that he knew well. One was Wayne Bailey, the head of the estate planning department and more or less his boss and a member of the Executive Committee.

When Wayne Bailey saw Mark enter, he said, "Come on in, Mark," and waived his hand indicating he should take a seat in one of the conference room high back leather chairs.

"Thanks, Wayne," Mark said as he walked over and sat down in one of the leather chairs. He could feel his pulse begin to increase again as he speculated on what great assignment he was going to get. "Boy, it's not often this group gets together to discuss a project!" he thought to himself.

Mark got along well with Wayne Bailey, and it was Bailey who had pushed for him to be a junior partner. He was in his early forties, close to five nine and about one hundred and eighty pounds. He hated the sun and had pale whitish skin and a plain sorrowful looking face, as if he was always unhappy about something. It didn't help that he had droopy eye lids and unusually black curly hair. But he had something extra. His eyes were as black as coal and when he looked at you, you sometimes felt like a black widow spider was about to leap at you. If he liked you, things were fine. But if you crossed him, he could be ruthless.

The other partner seated at the conference room table was Jerry Keller, the head of the corporate law department. Mark worked briefly with him when he first joined the firm. Jerry was in his late forties, tall at six feet six, light brown hair and brown eyes. And he was slender, almost gaunt like someone with an eating disorder.

He had also graduated from the University of Southern California Law School (half of the firm's partners came from USC) and was a top "rainmaker" for the firm. This title goes to those who are exceptionally good at bringing in new clients. He was out giving speeches two or three days a week to business groups, especially those run by female executives. He considered himself somewhat of a ladies' man and it paid off. He was the highest paid partner in the firm.

As Mark sat down, Harlan Cross sat up straight in his chair, took a sip of water from a half empty bottle of water sitting on the table in from of him and said with obvious empathy in his voice, "Mark, things haven't worked out very well. You've done some really good legal work, but the partners just don't think you'll make it to senior partner status." He hesitated a moment, shook his head slightly and continued in a stiff voice, "Damn it Mark, we think you should know it now so you can move on and get with another firm while you're still young."

It would be an understatement to say that Mark was stunned and he couldn't think of anything to say at first. He felt a wave of adrenalin shoot through his body almost like a bolt of electricity. His heart began to pound in his chest and his vision blurred for a brief second. He finally took a deep breath and in a hesitant shaky voice asked, "Why? I …I don't understand. I was just made a junior partner this year!

Harlan Cross had terminated dozens of associates during the time he had been the Managing Partner. He looked directly at Mark and without blinking said, "I'm sorry, Mark. But the decision has been made. I hope you understand. We think this is in your own best interest. We need you to go down and clean out your desk and turn in your cell phone and key card. We want you out of the building."

It took all of Mark Austin's strength to keep his hands from shaking. He turned to Wayne Bailey and said, "Wayne, what...what's happening? I thought things were fine. Am I being fired?"

"I know this is hard to understand," Wayne Bailey said with his black eyes staring directly into Mark's eyes, "but if you're not going to make partner, its best for you and us to make that decision early. You'll be fine, Mark. I'll be happy to give you a recommendation."

Mark was flustered and not able to think clearly and looked over at Harlan Cross and said in desperation, "Mr. Cross, I've done great legal work since I started here and, you know, it was my quick action to help out Boyd Gibbons that led to the firm getting all of his legal work."

Mark was beginning to calm down and he started to get angry. "You all know this is wrong. What are you not telling me?" he said as he glanced over at Wayne Bailey.

"Mark, we've made a business decision and it is final," said Harlan Cross. "Please. Go down to your office and leave. It's the best for both of us. You'll see that for yourself when you get settled somewhere else."

Mark stood, glanced at the three partners and walked out of the room.

Jerry Keller had said nothing the whole time.

When Mark reached his office, Patricia from personnel was there waiting. "I'm so sorry, Mark. I just heard. Can I help?"

"Thanks, Pat," Mark replied. He reached in his wallet and brought out his key card that allows attorneys to activate the elevators to enter the law firm's floors and handed it to her. "My cell phone and lap top are on the counter. I guess I just need a box to put my certificates in. Something like that," he said dejectedly.

It was like a vice had gripped his stomach and all Mark could do was stare at Patricia. Like anyone in her position, she was embarrassed and avoided eye contact. After a few seconds of silence, she said, "I'll get you a box," and she walked out of his office.

Patricia returned five minutes later with a large box and one of the young men who worked in office services. "This should do Mark," she said. "Tim here will help you take the box to your car."

"Oh yes," Patricia added, "here's your final paycheck."

By now the full staff of the law firm had arrived. When Mark finished packing the box and he and Tim started to leave, he saw his secretary, Marina Monroe, standing by her desk. It was only five feet outside his office and she was crying.

As Mark walked over to say goodbye, Marina said with tears dripping down her cheeks, "Oh Mark, I just heard. What happened? This must be a mistake."

"I don't quite know myself, Marina. But everything will be OK," Mark said in a soft sad voice. He gave her a hug and he and Tim walked down to the elevator. As the elevator descended to the garage level, he was still mystified at what had happened.

When Mark reached his car, he put the box in the back seat, told Tim he could go back to work and drove out of the garage onto the Avenue of the Stars. He turned right and drove up to Santa Monica Boulevard and turned left towards the ocean. He and his wife lived in an apartment in Santa Monica proper and he had intended to go home. But as he drove down the street, the full import of what had just happened hit him and he pulled over to the curb and just sat.

There are many adjectives that apply to how a person feels who has just been fired, especially for no particular reason. They include embarrassment, humiliation, shame, disgrace, dishonor and probably a hundred more hurtful emotions. But you can put them all together and they won't even come close to the fear and degradation a man feels when he has to tell his wife.

As Mark sat in his car, all of these emotions flooded across his mind and he began to feel dizzy when he thought about what he would say to his wife. Her name was Suzzi Austin and she was an elementary school teacher and would be at her school this time of day. And she was six months pregnant. But that was no comfort. "What will she think of me?" he kept asking himself over and over.

Suzzi and Mark had met through a mutual friend right after he had taken the California Bar Examination. They immediately fell in love and were married four months later. She was a petite brunette with long hair down to the middle of her back, fiery green eyes and a smile that won over anyone she met. Their daughter, Cheryl, had been born ten months later.

When Mark finally reached the apartment, he was numb. Nothing made sense and even though it was only ten a.m., he fixed himself a double Jack Daniels and sat down on the living room couch. What made things worse was the Christmas tree that was in the corner of the living room, all decorated. This was December 22, three days before Christmas. As he sipped his drink, Mark just stared at the presents that were all wrapped and ready for their daughter to open.

When Suzzi Austin finished teaching, she drove by the day care center and picked up their daughter. When they reached the apartment and Suzzi opened the front door, she could smell the odor of alcohol and saw Mark passed out on the couch. She hurriedly told Shirley to go into her room and watch television. When she was out of sight, she walked over to the couch and kneeled down and gently shook Mark's shoulder. "Mark, wake up. What's going on," she pleaded.

When Mark woke up and realized that it was his wife talking to him, he sat up and grabbed her in his arms and squeezed her hard. "God, I love you," he said with a slight slur.

"Mark, what…" Suzzi started to ask, but Mark pushed her back slightly, looked right into her eyes for what seemed like an eternity and said, "Honey, I've been fired. I'm so sorry."

Mark pulled her close again and they just held each other for several minutes. Suzzi could feel Mark's tears run down his cheek and down onto her neck as she held on even tighter.

After Mark left Harlan Cross's office that fateful day, the three partners stayed and talked. For the first time, Jerry Keller spoke. "Thanks Harlan. You know as well as I do that we can't have young lawyers who want to jump in and make big money when they've only been with us for five years. No firm can operate that way. The young ones should only get a salary and whatever bonus we give at the end of the year."

"But we lost a great lawyer," Wayne Bailey replied. "Mark was already one of the best of the young group. And you saw yourself how eager he was to land old Mr. Gibbons. That was great client getting. You of all people should appreciate that."

Jerry Keller understood. He was a good lawyer, but his best talent was attracting new business and he was a fanatic in demanding that he be paid for the money he brought into the firm. In the parlance of the legal profession, they call this a "book of business," meaning the total revenue that comes in each year from "his clients", even though other lawyers do the legal work.

When he heard Wayne Bailey's comment, Jerry Keller shook his head and just grunted and said, "He just got greedy. He showed his lack of maturity when he put in for a piece of the Tier Two money because of Gibbons and his companies. You know as well as I do, I worked for one of the companies seven years ago. That means the origination credit goes to me, and not to Mark Austin as he claimed. And to top it off, he actually does the Gibbons's billings every month. As corporate chair, that's my job and he damn well knows it."

"Well, I'm not so sure you're right on the Tier Two money Jerry," replied Wayne Bailey. "The partnership agreement, the way we revised it a few years ago, says that the junior partners can participate in our Tier Two profits just like all of the partners."

"Bullshit," said Jerry Keller. "The agreement was never intended to let junior partners make a half million dollars just because they bring in a good client. Anyway, the credit goes to the one who first represented the client, and that was me. Mark was entitled to nothing."

Harlan Cross stood and walked over to the window looking down on the Avenue of the Stars. He stared out of the window for a moment and then turned back and said, "Wayne, I think we better clarify the partnership agreement on this. Why don't you and Jerry take a hard look and come up with some language."

"I'll take a look," Jerry Keller replied, "but it's clear to me the partners never intended to let junior partners be paid as senior partners from Tier Two. That would frankly be outrageous. Take Austin, for example. Gibbons's companies paid us about two million dollars this year and it will most likely be twice that next year with the securities investigation going on. Our formula says that the partner who originated the client gets ten percent of all money collected."

Wayne Bailey shook his head in disbelief as Jerry Keller continued. "Hell, Harlan, Austin would have been paid two hundred thousand dollars on top of his regular salary just on Gibbons alone. And maybe even four hundred thousand next year. We would never ok something like that!"

"I understand what you're saying," Harlan Cross replied with a smile. "And this means a lot to you. As the originator of one of the companies, you'll now get that ten percent. That might even push your total income to over four million this year."

"Yes, of course," chuckled Jerry Keller. "But that's not the point. The point is we never intended for junior partners to get that type of percentage."

Wayne Bailey was nervously tapping his pen on the conference room table as he listened to the exchange. He finally said, "The problem is that the partnership agreement does say junior partners. And you might recall, we all sat around several years ago and discussed how we could motivate the young partners to go after new clients."

"No way in hell," Jerry Keller said as he slammed his fist down onto the table. "We meant the young senior partners, not the junior partners. The damn agreement may say junior Partners, but that was never the intent."

Harlan Cross said, "Ok, folks. Let's calm down. Austin is gone so we don't have to worry about him. No other junior partner has brought in a big client so we can cure this by revising the agreement. You two get a draft to me by the end of the week."

As the partners stood to leave, Harlan Cross turned to Wayne Bailey and said, "Wayne, it was a partner in your department that lost confidence in Austin. What went wrong?"

"I'm somewhat surprised myself," Wayne Bailey replied. "It was Alison Craft. She just doesn't want to work with him anymore. I asked her why and she said 'He's eager enough, but he's having trouble with the difficult tax issues that drive most of the big estates.' And as much as I liked him, we can't force someone on a partner."

The next day Jerry Keller pulled from his files his copy of the partnership agreement. He flipped through the pages until he found the section entitled "Allocation of Tier Two Profits." It read:

"Tier Two Profits (in excess of Tier One Profits)
shall be allocated to the partners as follows:

    a.   10% for origination credit;

    b.   20% for work given to others;

    c.   30% on the partner's own hours and fees collected; and

    d.   40% on the merits of each partner's contribution to the firm's success."

"Shit," Jerry Keller said to himself. He realized the agreement did not actually define the word "partners." He checked the index and found the section on junior partners but all it said was "Junior partners and non-equity partners may be affiliated with the Partnership at any time during the existence of the Partnership."

"How in the hell could we have let this slip by?" Jerry Keller asked himself in disgust.

When he saw that the partnership agreement was at best ambiguous, he walked down the hall to Wayne Bailey's office. When he stuck his head in the door, Wayne was seated at his huge round table where he did most of his work. Typical of most estate planning attorneys, his desk had not seen the light of day for years due to the files stacked on it. And his couch and most of the floor space was also covered in stacked files. It always puzzled Keller how someone could possibly work that way. "How could he possibly know what's on that floor?" he asked himself.

There was no empty chair so Jerry Keller just stood. "Wayne, the damned agreement just says 'partners' without defining them. I think we really should amend it right away. All we need to do is add a definition so only senior partners are eligible for Tier Two."

Wayne Bailey agreed and a short amendment was circulated among the senior partners to sign the following week. Wayne and Jerry decided it was best to have it dated December 31st so it would apply to any compensation for the current year. The amendment said:

> "The purpose of this amendment is to clarify the eligibility requirements for Tier Two compensation.
>
> The phrase "partners" means senior partners who have been admitted to the partnership as equity partners."

CHAPTER 2

The Angry Young Lawyer

When Mark Austin and his wife recovered from the initial emotional blow, they decided that if the Baukus & Johnson firm treated attorneys like Mark had been treated, they were really better off learning that now. But the question of finances crept into their conversation.

It was his wife Suzzi that broached the question. "Mark, you know we committed your bonus money as a down payment for our house. Will we still get that?" she asked.

With all of the wild up and down emotions that flowed from being fired, or being told "it's for your own best interest" to leave, if that makes a difference, it never occurred to Mark to ask about the Tier Two distributions. They were scheduled to be paid out in the middle of January. Once Gibbons decided to give the firm his work, Wayne Bailey had reminded Mark that he would get a handsome bonus for the good work.

"They never mentioned any bonus," Mark replied. "I'll give Wayne a call and ask."

Although they had in their minds committed the bonus money for a down payment, all they actually did was to start the house-hunting process. They had found a great three bedroom older home in the Santa Monica hills off of Sunset Boulevard that was within their budget, but they had not signed any papers.

When Mark called for Wayne Bailey, he was told that he was in a conference. Not knowing what to do, he asked for his voice mail and left a message. "Hi Wayne. Mark here. Just a quick question. Will I still get the bonus for bringing Mr. Gibbons to the firm? This is obviously important to us now that I'm out job hunting. Let me know. And thanks for your help."

When Wayne Bailey listened to Mark's voice mail later that afternoon, he knew in his heart that they had a problem. He called Harlan Cross and they met in Harlan's office that evening. The third member of the Executive Committee, Derrick Warner, was in Miami meeting with a client and Cross had asked Jerry Keller to attend since he had been on the Committee in prior years.

Harlan Cross played host before they discussed how to proceed. He walked over to the opposite end of the conference table and opened a sliding door that concealed a small bar. It had tiger oak paneling, a granite top with a small sink and refrigerator. When the sliding door was closed, it looked like a normal conference room.

When each had poured his favorite drink, they sat down at the table. Each swirled his drink a little to shake the ice around before taking a sip. Jerry Keller spoke first. "As Wayne knows, it was Alison Craft who questioned whether Austin would be advanced to senior partner status. She was the partner who worked directly with him and if she questions his merit, we had to take that seriously."

Harlan Cross sat tapping his pen on the conference table as he stared out of the window. Finally he said, "Jerry, you're missing the whole point. Austin has now asked for his share of the Tier Two compensation when we divide it up in a few weeks."

Jerry Keller's face hardened and turned red as he turned to Harlan Cross and said with a scowl on his face, "Hell, Harlan, I think you're the one missing the point. Once Alison opposed Austin as a partner, we could never keep him. And he proved her point when he submitted a written request for Tier Two compensation. He actually asked for origination credit on the Gibbons's accounts! That was a reckless thing to do by someone not even a partner."

Harlan Cross said, "Jerry, remember it was Wayne here that told him to send the memo, and I...."

Before Harlan Cross could finish, Jerry Keller interrupted him. With obvious agitation he said, "Harlan, you know as well as I do that we can't have young lawyers claiming something that is just for partners. That's why I jumped in and said we should get rid of him before the end of the year. The Tier Two compensation is a reward for what a partner does the prior year. By terminating him in December, he wouldn't qualify. He didn't make the whole year, so I just don't see the problem."

"Maybe yes and maybe no," Wayne Bailey replied with obvious concern in his voice. "As an employee, he might be entitled to a prorated payment and that would give him almost the full amount due for the year. Remember, we let him go on December 22nd."

After kicking the issue around for a while, and in the meantime refilling their glasses, no one had a real solution if Mark Austin made a claim. They had intentionally left out any input from the firm's employment law attorneys at Jerry Keller's suggestion. They all remembered Jerry Keller's words. "I want Austin gone right now. Those damn employment guys will just muck this up," he had said.

The three sat in silence for a while, each in their own thoughts. Finally Jerry Keller said with a small grim smile of satisfaction on his face, "I have the perfect solution. I'll take care of this."

Mark Austin received a letter in the mail from Baukus & Johnson a few weeks later signed by Harlan Cross. It read:

"Dear Mr. Austin:

Thank you for your inquiry through Wayne Bailey about bonus Tier Two compensation. Unfortunately, since you left the firm before the end of the year, there is no entitlement to any bonus Tier Two compensation.

This is determined after the close of the year looking back on what each senior partner contributed to the firm for the whole year. Best of luck. Harlan Cross"

The letter from Harlan Cross was not unexpected. Mark and his wife had already cancelled the escrow for their new home. Mark knew he had great credentials as a Stanford law graduate and he made up his mind to forget his experience at Baukus & Johnson and move on to another firm.

As he began putting together his resume, Mark remembered Wayne Bailey's offer of a letter of recommendation and he called but he was not in his office. His secretary, Marla Daily, answered the telephone. She actually shared a secretarial station with Mark's own secretary and they got to be friends.

"Hi Mark. Good to hear from you. Wayne's out of town this week but I can reach him on his Blackberry if you need something," Marla Daily said.

"Yes there is, Marla. Wayne said he would give me a letter of recommendation and I would like to get that to include in my packet that I'm sending around to other firms. Could you reach him and see if he could dictate it to you?" Mark Austin asked.

"No problem. He's in San Francisco and he calls me every day just before I leave," Marla Daily replied.

When Mark heard nothing from Wayne Bailey for over a week, he called again on Wayne's direct line and he answered.

"Mark. Good to hear from you. How're things going?" Wayne Bailey asked in a sheepish, almost embarrassed tone.

"I was just calling about the letter of recommendation. I need to include it along with my resume," Mark said with a little irritation.

There was a long pause on Wayne Bailey's side before he replied. "Yes. I did say that Mark, but I'm told by our employment guys that we don't give recommendations. All we do when we get an inquiry is confirm that the attorney worked for us and left on a particular day. Nothing more."

"Wayne, I..." Mark started to say but was cut off.

"I'm sorry Mark. My hands are tied. Good luck," Wayne Bailey said as he hung up the telephone.

Mark was alone in his apartment when he called Wayne Bailey. When the phone went dead, he walked into the kitchen and sat down at the table. As he reached for the cup of coffee he had been drinking, his hands began to tremble and he suddenly slammed his right fist down on the table with such force that the cup flew off of the table and shattered on the floor.

"Why me?" Mark shouted out loud as he flung his arms in the air in frustration. "I know I'm a good lawyer!"

Mark was now both confused and furious. In his eyes, his whole maleness was at stake. "What will Suzzi think now? Hell, I can't even get a recommendation," he muttered to himself. As he said this, his gut tightened and he felt blinding pain in the back of his head.

Mark knew immediately that the pain was the result of tension. He had similar episodes in law school whenever he thought he would flunk an exam. He never did, but that didn't matter. The fear of failure can be just as real as failure itself.

When Wayne Bailey told Harlan Cross of Mark's call, Cross called another meeting at his office. But this time he asked for the chair of the employment and labor law department to attend. His name was Dirk Canfield. He was in his early fifties, pole thin with dark curly hair that made you question how often he went to a beauty parlor.

"What in the world were you guys thinking?" Dirk Canfield almost yelled at Harlan Cross and the others in the room. "Do you realize how bad this looks? You wait until December 22 to fire the guy, just days before he would get a huge bonus if he stayed to the end of the year. And for what? Just because Keller here thinks he should get all of the origination credit!"

"Now just hold up there, Dirk," Jerry Keller said, visibly trembling. "It wasn't me who questioned Austin. It was Alison who didn't think he would make partner. And, yeah, I got irritated when he claimed some Tier Two compensation. That goes to the originator and we have a hard and fast rule that it goes to the first attorney who does work for the client. And that was me."

"Yes, we all know your feelings on that subject," Dirk Canfield replied with clear disgust on his face. "You'll do just about anything for the greenback, including risking the future of this firm."

Jerry Keller jumped to his feet, slammed his note pad on the conference room table and shouted directly at Dirk Canfield, "You can go to hell. We made that rule ten years ago and I think you've gotten your share of the origination money over the years. So don't lay a guilt trip on me," as he stormed out of the room.

As soon as Jerry Keller left the room, Dirk Canfield said in obvious disgust, "That son of a bitch is going to get this whole firm in trouble one of these days. And when he does, I'm going to sit back and applaud when he takes a fall."

"Easy everyone," Harlan Cross said. "We all know how Jerry feels. But he's right in part. We did make it a rule that the first one who works for a client gets the credit. The only exception is if someone appeals to the Executive Committee and we decide to share the credit."

Dirk Canfield took a deep breath, slowly blew out the air and said, "OK. Sorry, Harlan. The prick just makes me mad sometimes. Jerry's a classical 'I, me and my' type of guy that looks out only for himself and has an ego the size of a battle ship." He paused and then, looking over toward Wayne Bailey, he added, "But we've got to be careful, Wayne. No letters of recommendation. Just stick with the procedure in the personnel manual. And a few Hail Mary's might also help."

When the meeting broke up and as they all walked out into the hallway, Harlan Cross touched Dirk Canfield's elbow and quietly asked, "Do we have a problem here?"

Dirk Canfield looked Harlan Cross directly in the eye and said, "Let's just hope he doesn't go looking for a good employment lawyer."

While Mark Austin was putting together his resume without the promised letter of recommendation, he had called several of his former Stanford Law School professors. They all wanted to help and each wrote a spectacular review of his legal abilities and even offered to answer questions by telephone if any firm wanted to call.

As he circulated his resume, Mark got calls from every law firm he applied to and was given personal interviews with the chair of the estate planning department of each firm. They were all impressed with his credentials and promised to make a decision within a few weeks.

But the weeks turned into months with no call. Mark had applied to every major law firm in the greater Los Angeles area, but after being interviewed, he failed to get a single follow-up call. When he called back several of the firms, the answer was more or less the same. "Sorry Mark. We just don't have any openings right now. But we'll hang on to your resume."

One afternoon, out of desperation, Mark called Sam Archer, the VP for Boyd Gibbons' various enterprises, and he was put right through. "Mark, great to hear from you. Gibbons has asked what happened to you and all we get from Keller is that you left the firm."

"Well, to be honest," Mark replied, "they just asked me to leave one day."

"I'm sorry to hear that," Sam Archer said sympathetically. "What the hell happened? Is there anything I can do to help?"

"Actually, that's why I'm calling," Mark slowly answered. "I know Mr. Gibbons liked my work, so... I was wondering if I could tell a new firm that his work would come along with me. Any firm in town would jump at that chance."

There was a long pause before Sam Archer replied. "Mark, I'd like to help. I can even do a letter of recommendation. But Gibbons is finally happy with his lawyers at Baukus & Johnson. As you know, he's a realist and I think changing firms again is out of the question."

"I understand," Mark said in a sad defeated manner. "Please tell Mr. Gibbons 'hi' for me. Maybe I could at least do any estate planning he might need."

Being fired and forced to explain things to your wife is a painful and emotionally stressful experience, but Mark and his wife Suzzi were determined to survive that turmoil with confidence in the future. Reality though has a way of changing things. After six months of rejection by one law firm after another, Mark's confidence in himself began to diminish. The most damaging of all was that he believed in his heart that he had lost the respect of his wife. It was nothing that she said. It was the quick glances in his direction yet saying nothing that was far worse than any words she could have used.

Mark never spoke to his wife about his fear, but late at night, when she was sleeping, he would lie in bed and feel like he was almost paralyzed. He could not remember the last time he and his wife had sex. It was not that he didn't want to. He thought of it almost every day, but he just could not bring himself to initiate something. And she didn't either.

In the mornings Mark would focus on reading the newspaper so he would not make eye contact with his wife. And the reality of his dismal status just increased each day when Suzzi left the apartment to teach. Her teaching salary was their only source of income.

Mark eventually stopped applying to major law firms and took a job as an associate at a small husband and wife two-lawyer law firm in Encino that did a little of everything but mostly handled inexpensive divorces; the kind of divorce case that did not involve serious litigation. His salary was four thousand dollars a month. At Baukus & Johnson, his salary without a bonus had been fourteen thousand a month.

The only happy occasion since Mark was fired was the birth of their second child. Suzzi took off a month, but because Mark was not working, she started back teaching and he took care of the baby during the day. While this was a joyous occasion, when Mark started working, their child care expense jumped to a little over two thousand dollars a month and this, with all of their other bills, caused what little savings they had to disappear.

A few months after Mark starting with his new job, he got a call from one of his Stanford Law School professors. "How are things going Mark?" he asked. "Are you still doing estate planning?"

Mark was hesitant at first to let him know what had happened, but then the ugly story gushed out. "I just don't know what happened. One day I was the star associate and then bang. I'm out."

The professor expressed his concern and said he would make a few calls and see what he could find out. Stanford Law School is one of the premier law schools in the United States and it has alumni in just about every major law firm.

The professor's name was Joseph Shockley. He was in his late sixties and a legend in the area of constitutional law. He had asked Mark what firms he had applied at and called one of his old students at one of the main competitors of Baukus & Johnson.

His old student happened to be the Managing Partner and he at first was hesitant to comment. But when Professor Shockley explained how talented Mark was and still couldn't get a job, the Managing Partner said he would look into it and get back to him.

A few days later the Managing Partner called Professor Shockley and said, "You're right. My own firm interviewed Austin and the estate planning head really liked him. But when they called his old firm they were told, and I quote this exactly, 'Mark Austin is a troublemaker.' And, well professor, you know, no firm wants to take on someone with a bad reputation. And my guess is that's the reason the other firms said no, too."

When Professor Shockley called Mark and explained what he had found, Mark was almost as stunned as when he was first fired. His heart was pounding so hard in his chest that he was sure it could be heard over the telephone. His breathing grew harder and when he tried to speak his throat closed tight. After a long moment of silence he finally said in a hesitant voice, "Professor, I just don't..., I don't understand. I never said anything bad about anybody!"

"Mark, this whole thing is beginning to fail the smell test. I think you should see a good plaintiff's employment lawyer," Professor Shockley said in a soft understanding manner.

"Maybe you're right," Mark replied. "This whole thing is wrecking my family. We've used up our savings and, heck, we even had to sell the Audi I bought my wife." What he didn't add was that he had also returned his leased Mercedes and that cost $2,200 to pay off the lease.

There was a tense silence as Mark tried to regain his composure. Tears were starting to roll down his cheek as he fought for words. "I, ah, I got her a used Volvo instead."

After talking with Professor Shockley, Mark made a number of telephone calls to employment lawyers he knew in some of the major firms in the Los Angeles area, but he again had no success. The standard answer was, "Mark, if you were a secretary or almost anybody else, you would have a great case. But law firms have to have great discretion in making someone a partner. All it takes is one or two partners to say no, and the ball game is over. You just can't force partners to vote to make someone a partner."

After at least ten rejections, Mark's demeanor changed. When he and his wife Suzzi made the decision to pursue litigation, Mark at first took on the challenge as a fighter determined to win. But his tough guy image soon faded into just being scared. He began to think of himself as a mediocre simple divorce lawyer who may, if he is lucky, make eighty thousand dollars a year.

Mark was about to drop the whole matter when he ran into a lawyer friend of his at the main courthouse in down-town Los Angeles. They were both appearing before the same judge and when they finished, they took the elevator up to the top floor to the cafeteria. As they sat sipping coffee, his friend said, "Mark, I don't think you'll get any major firm to sue another major firm. They work too closely together to sue each other. But there's one top notch trial lawyer who is somewhat of a rebel. His name is Dillon Clark. He has a firm over on Ventura Boulevard somewhere. He hit it big a few years ago and from what I hear, he's not afraid of anyone."

When he got back to his office later that day, Mark sat down at his computer and went to the internet to see what he could find about Dillon Clark. What he learned he liked. Dillon was in his late sixties and had been included as one of southern California's "Super Lawyers" ever since that honorary title began. The site described his legal career and some of the high publicity cases he had tried and quoted another local lawyer as saying "Dillon Clark is one of those rare trial lawyers who is dedicated to making our system work so justice really prevails. There of course are others who are equally talented, but many of those do it as a job. If a client can't afford to pay, they stop representing him. In Dillon's case, I've never heard him ever ask to be relieved because he isn't being paid."

The internet site also directed him to newspaper stories about Dillon and some of his more famous lawsuits that he had won. He skimmed several newspaper articles and saw that one described him as one of California's finest trial lawyers. He printed out two of the articles to take home to show his wife.

That night after dinner, Mark told Suzzi about his conversation with his friend and his referral to Dillon Clark. As he handed her the two newspaper articles to read, he said, "Take a look at these articles. I think I'll call him."

When Suzzi finished reading the articles, she said, "He sounds great, Mark. One article talked about Dillon getting an award from the Trial Lawyers' Association a few years back for his dedication to "pro bono" representation of needy clients. What does that mean?"

Mark chuckled and explained, "This is a Latin phrase used among lawyers for doing legal work for the public benefit. It can mean helping individual clients who can't afford to pay an attorney's normal hourly rates, or sometimes taking on causes for free, like free speech issues you read about."

They sat together at the kitchen table for several minutes without talking. Suzzi knew Mark was hurting inside and she reached over and put her hands on top of his, stared directly into his eyes for a long moment, and quietly said, "Mark. Give him a call. He may be the answer."

The next morning when he got to his office, Mark called the Burnam & Clark law firm. When he explained to the operator that he wanted an appointment with Dillon Clark concerning a termination case, the operator said, "Just one moment Mr. Austin," and she put him on hold.

Almost immediately a young female came on the line. "Hello Mr. Austin. My name is Laurel Kennedy. I'm one of the partners here at Burnam & Clark. I understand you're looking for a lawyer to help you on an employment case. Is that correct?"

"Yes, it is," Mark replied.

Laurel said, "Mr. Austin, our firm has never been involved in a wrongful termination case. But I can give you the names of some really good lawyers who can help you."

"I understand, but you see, I'm also a lawyer. I worked for a large firm and the other firms who do employment work won't take my case. I think they just don't want to sue each other. Anyway, I was told that Dillon Clark might help," Mark hurriedly said almost as a plea.

After a slight hesitation, Laurel asked, "What firm were you with?"

"I worked for the Baukus & Johnson firm. I had just been made a junior partner and then, well, I still don't exactly know what happened. I was just told to leave. When I apply with other firms, they seem to like me at first but then, well, I never get an offer. A law school professor of mine at Stanford called around and apparently when a firm calls Baukus & Johnson, they say that I'm a trouble-maker. I just don't know what to do," Mark explained.

Laurel could almost hear the pain in Mark Austin's voice and she made a snap decision. "OK, Mr. Austin. Can you come in to-morrow morning?"

"You name the time and I'll be there," Mark said with obvious relief.

The law offices of Burnam & Clark are located on the twelfth floor of an office tower on Ventura Boulevard in Encino. When Mark arrived, he was met in the reception area by another young woman who introduced herself as Kelly Parks.

"Hello Mr. Austin. Laurel asked me to meet with you and get the history of your employment with the Baukus firm. She'll join us later. Let's go down to the conference room where we can have some privacy."

As Kelly Parks led Mark to a small conference room just off of the reception area, she asked, "Would you like anything to drink?"

"No thanks. I'm fine," Mark replied.

When they were each seated in one of the conference room leather chairs, Kelly explained, "Mark, I'm one of the paralegals here and I just need to get the whole story. So why don't you just start from when you first applied for a job at Baukus & Johnson. Just kind of go month by month. We can add things later if you miss something."

Mark liked Kelly Parks. She was short, about five feet six inches tall, pretty close to his wife's size. Her hair was brown and cut short and she was wearing blue jeans and a red long-sleeved blouse.

When Kelly saw Mark look at her blue jeans, she laughed and said, "We're pretty informal here. And I'm just finishing law school myself and have to study every afternoon, so Dillon lets me dress for class unless I have to be in court."

Mark felt a little embarrassed that he had been so obvious and said, "Sorry about that. We were always so formal at Baukus & Johnson. We even had to put on our suit coats when meeting with a client."

"No problem. Let's just start from the beginning," Kelly said with a big friendly smile.

It took the entire morning for Mark to tell his story. Laurel Kennedy joined them about an hour into the interview. After introducing herself, she just sat and listened as Kelly took notes.

By the time Mark told about his meeting with Harlan Cross and Wayne Bailey just before the Christmas holiday, expecting to get a new plum work assignment, but instead was told to leave the firm, Kelly and Laurel made eye contact and both subtly shook their heads in shock but said nothing.

"You know," Mark said with considerable agitation, "I probably wouldn't have done anything if they had just given me a recommendation and had not told lies about me!"

"Why do you say lies?" Laurel asked softly.

"Well, as I said to Ms. Kennedy when I called, it was Professor Shockley at Stanford that clued me in. When I told him I had received many great interviews and then no one called be back, he called around to some of his old students. One was a managing partner of a large firm with whom I actually interviewed. It turned out that they liked my background and would have hired me except when they contacted Baukus & Johnson, they were told I was a troublemaker. And that is just not true. I got along with everyone," Mark explained with growing intensity in his voice.

Lawsuits against any major employer are expensive and as the meeting was coming to a close, Mark wanted it made clear that he could not afford to pay a fee. "I sure hope you can help me," he said. "But it should come as no surprise that I need an attorney to take the case on a contingency. I've already gone through what savings we had."

Kelly looked over at Laurel and after a pause, she said, "We understand Mark. Dillon takes contingency cases all the time."

After Mark left later that afternoon, Laurel and Kelly talked about what he had said.

"I'm no trial lawyer," Kelly said, "but I doubt there would be a dry eye in the jury box when Mark describes his feelings as he had to go home and tell his wife he was just fired."

"I agree," Laurel said. "Like the professor said, this whole thing doesn't pass the smell test. There has to be something else going on to have the firm ask him to leave, especially since he was the favorite of their biggest client."

Laurel sat in silence for a minute or two with a frown on her face as if contemplating something unpleasant. She then stretched her arms out onto the conference table with her palms down flat on the table, and said, "I think we should take the case. The problem is to convince Dillon. He's never tried an employment law case but, heck, he's still the best trial lawyer in town so he can just learn like you and I are going to do."

Kelly looked relieved. Because Laurel said very little during the interview with Mark, she thought she was not interested. She stood and said in an excited voice, "OK. I'll prepare a memo of what Mark told us and will include some preliminary research into a wrongful termination."

Two days later, Laurel and Kelly walked down the hall and spoke with Dillon's secretary, Jeannie Davis.

"Hi Jeannie," Laurel said. "We need to talk to Dillon about a new contingency case. Can you set that up for us?"

Jeannie Davis, along with Laurel Kennedy and a number of other lawyers, decided to come along with Dillon when he and his partner and friend, Phil Burnam, decided to leave the twenty-eight-plus firm they had built. They were both fed-up with demands by other partners that Dillon stop taking contingency cases. The argument came to a head when the business law partners demanded that Dillon abandon a client just before trial because she could no longer pay her bill. It was the age old quarrel between lawyers who see the law as just a way of making money and those who also believe that a lawyer should never abandon a client.

Jeannie Davis started working for Dillon when she was just nineteen years old and was the first to volunteer to move with him when the old firm split. She was thirtyish something and had fiery red hair that she kept tied in a pony-tail. The fact that she wore no make-up made her freckles even more pronounced.

"Dillon's out right now, but I think he's open tomorrow morning if that works," Jeannie said.

"That works for us," Laurel replied.

Dillon's new firm was not large. There were just three partners, four paralegals and five associates and they all assisted Dillon in his trial work. The one exception was Phil Burnam, who was mostly retired but still came to the office almost daily. The speculation was that his wife didn't want him staying at home.

The firm was located all on one floor and Dillon's office was in the rear corner looking west towards the Pacific Ocean. It was not a high rise like in downtown Los Angeles, but he did enjoy a good view of the green hills that divided the San Fernando Valley and the ocean.

As Laurel and Kelly entered Dillon's office the next morning, he was busy talking on the telephone and he just pointed to the two chairs in front of his desk.

Dillon was fairly short, about five feet eight inches tall and, although he had a full bushy head of hair, the grey hairs far outnumbered the black hairs. After years of litigation, he had deep crow's feet wrinkles under his eyes that suggested a man of great experience. And, without getting into details, he still carried what his doctor called "an extra bowling ball" around his waist. It was no doubt a side effect of his enjoyment of Macallan single malt scotch.

As they each sat down, Dillon finished his call and asked, "Jeannie tells me you want us to take on a wrongful termination case. Is that right?"

"Yes, that part is true. But don't just say no," Laurel said as she held up her hands defensively. "The plaintiff is a young lawyer who was fired from the Baukus & Johnson firm and no one will take his case."

Kelly jumped in and said, "Dillon, just listen. We've interviewed him extensively and even his law professors at Stanford think the facts are, shall we say, suspicious." Leaning in toward Dillon for emphasis, she added, "Dillon, he had just been made a junior partner and then, bang, he was told he would not be made a senior partner and that it would be best to leave now and get settled somewhere else."

"And to boot," Laurel added quickly, "he was told he had thirty minutes to turn in his laptop and other stuff and leave the building."

Kelly was about to say more when Dillon raised his hands in surrender and said, "OK. OK. Let's hear the story. But you know we've never tried a wrongful termination case."

Kelly had prepared an extensive memorandum outlining the facts and handed it to Dillon. As he read the summary, she could tell he was skimming rapidly without much interest until he got to the part where Professor Shockley called one of his old students who happened to be the managing partner of a firm Mark had applied to, and learned that he was being labeled by his old firm as a "troublemaker."

"Did you find any basis for them trying to black-ball him?" Dillon asked with a questioning raised eye brow.

"None," replied Kelly. "His record is clean. And remember, on top of that, he had just been made a junior partner on the recommendation of the department chair he worked with."

"There's something missing here," Dillon said as he tapped his desk with his fingers in thought.

"That's what we all think. I like the professor's comment that it 'doesn't pass the smell test'" Laurel added.

After a moment in thought, Dillon asked, "What kind of damages can you get in these cases?"

"We still have a lot of research to do," Kelly replied, "but the jury instructions I looked at focused on lost wages. He went from almost fifteen thousand a month to four and, if we can show it was wrongful, we could include the lost income he would have earned as a senior partner. This could be big because he would be entitled to the origination credit for landing Gibbons as a client."

"Do we have any idea what Gibbons pays the firm a year?" Dillon asked.

"Nothing concrete, and least not yet," Kelly replied. "Mark did say that anywhere from five to ten lawyers were working full time on his matters when he left. At Gibbons's request, he reviewed all of the billings and he thinks last year's income was around two million. But that was only a partial year."

Dillon leaned back in his high back leather chair, cupped his hands together like a tepee and sat there pondering what he had read and been told. After a moment he said, "Taking on a big law firm is going to be a battle royale. You both know that, I presume?"

"Yes," Laurel and Kelly said simultaneously, with a big grin on their faces.

"From what you say, I think it's worth pursuing. But I want to talk to the young man myself before we commit. Get him in here in the next few days," Dillon said. "And tell him to bring his wife. She may be important in a case like this."

As Laurel stood ready to leave, Dillon added, "Because we're in an area we haven't tried before, I want you to work up a draft set of jury instructions at the beginning. I want to know the subtleties of the instructions before we start discovery. And also prepare a set of interrogatories and request for document production for me to review. If we file suit, I want to hit the deck running."

Even though Mark was a lawyer, he was still nervous when he and his wife met Dillon for the first time. They actually talked about this on several occasions. "It's not every day you give control of your life to a lawyer and a jury," he remembered telling Suzzi. "Now I know what a client feels like and may be thinking, but he never tells that to his lawyer."

When they got off the elevator and entered the firm's reception area, Kelly was there to greet them.

"Hi Mark. Dillon is anxious to meet both of you. He asked me to bring you right over to his office," Kelly said. She turned to Suzzi and added, "You must be Mrs. Austin. It's a pleasure to meet you."

Dillon met with Mark and his wife in his office. As they entered, he stood and walked over to greet them. He liked what he saw. They were holding hands as if to give each other support. "I know you must be nervous. I sure know I would be if I had to hire a lawyer," he said kiddingly. "Please, have a seat."

As Mark and Suzzi situated themselves in the two client chairs by Dillon's desk, Dillon said, "Both of you need to understand what is about to happen if we file a lawsuit. I know you're a lawyer Mark, but litigation can be brutal. And I mean brutal on both of you emotionally. I'm told we can sue for not only lost income, but also for emotional distress if it is intentional. This covers not only the humiliation of being fired, but what affect that has had on your marriage."

Mark and Suzzi quickly glanced at each other but said nothing.

"When we get into discovery and the defendants take your depositions, they will be asking about the emotional side," Dillon said. He paused for a second and added in almost a whisper, "And they will be entitled to know the details about how the firing has affected your sex life. Every detail if we pursue the issue. Can you handle that?"

Mark's face flushed with anger and he almost shouted, "That's none of their business. Why should we have to expose ourselves when they're the ones who caused this mess?"

Dillon had this conversation with many clients over the years and the answer is always the same. "I understand, Mark. But just stop and think back to your law school days. Our system of justice gave up years ago the idea of righting a wrong with dueling pistols or swords. The only remedy is to sue for money damages, and when you ask for damages, the plaintiff, that's you and Suzzi, have to come forth and prove how you were damaged. And unless you want to stipulate that your being fired has had no effect on your sex life, then we have to give the details. It's not fun and maybe not fair, but that is how the damage game is played."

Mark and Suzzi seemed dazed by what Dillon had said. Mark looked over at his wife and he saw her eyes turn red as she was fighting back tears. The hundreds of nights that he lay in bed wanting to approach his wife but some impassable barrier always stopped him, flooded through his mind. "What if this never changes?" he asked himself as he gripped the arms of his chair to steady himself.

Mark started to say something when Suzzi let out a stifled sob and got up and walked out of the room. Mark quickly went after her and caught up with her in the reception area. "Look, honey. We don't have to do this. To hell with a lawsuit. I'm doing fine and ..."

Before Mark could finish, Suzzi reached out and threw her arms around his shoulders and cried. They just stood there in the middle of the room and it was more than Mark could take. For the first time since the day he was fired, he also cried uncontrollably. "I am so sorry," Mark repeated over and over.

Dillon had followed Mark when he left his office and was standing in the doorway leading into the reception area watching Mark and Suzzi. If he ever had a doubt about taking Mark's case, those doubts flew out the window as his heart went out to his two new clients.

Dillon walked over and gently touched Mark and Suzzi on the shoulder and said in a soft soothing voice, "I know this is tough, and I'm sorry. But you have to be willing to have your life exposed if you want to proceed."

Mark let go of Suzzi, stepped back and turned toward Dillon, but before he could say anything, Dillon said, "Look. Why don't the two of you go home and give this some thought. Just know that it would be an honor to represent both of you. So give me a call tomorrow and let me know what you decide."

When Mark and Suzzi left Dillon's office, they rode the elevator down to the basement parking area where they had left their car. Neither said a word as Mark pulled out onto Ventura Boulevard and then onto the San Diego freeway heading back towards Santa Monica. When Mark took the off-ramp to Sunset Boulevard towards their apartment, Suzzi said in a whisper, "Mark, why don't we go down to the beach. We can talk while we're walking."

At the end of Sunset Boulevard where it stops at the Pacific Coast Highway, there are miles of public beach areas. Mark pulled into the first one and parked. As they both exited the car, the sun was just starting to sink behind the horizon and it cast a blood red glow on the ocean. They both stood there and watched as the sun slowly slid past the horizon and disappeared.

Suzzi turned towards Mark and said, "Honey, you know I love you and I want to help. I just wasn't prepared for what Mr. Clark said. This whole mess…well, you know. It never occurred to me that our sex life was involved. But when he said we were going to be asked, it sort of hit me. It really is involved! Can you remember the last time we had sex?"

When he heard Suzzi's question, Mark felt like he had been hit with a lightning bolt. His whole body stiffened and a feeling of helplessness swarmed over him. The same feeling he had almost every night since he was fired.

When Mark said nothing, Suzzi reached over and took his right hand between both of hers and said, "Mark, it's ok honey. We can work this out."

When Mark finally relaxed a little, he and Suzzi sat in the car at the beach and talked for hours. In the end, they agreed they needed some counseling and that they would hire Dillon Clark to file a lawsuit.

CHAPTER 3

Law Firm's Annual Splitting of the Pie
(Five Weeks After Mark was Fired)

The annual meeting of the Baukus & Johnson partnership to slice-up the compensation pie took place on the last Friday evening of January in the firm's main conference room.

As with most law firms, the decision on who is to be paid what was fraught with tension and a belief by each partner that he should be paid more than the number recommended by the Executive Committee. Egos, normally large on any occasion, puff out another inch or two when it comes to compensation; and lawyers who are known as rational and logical become irrational and emotional. This may just flow naturally from the adversarial nature of our legal system, or it may just be simple old fashion greed. Either way, it makes for a contentious and often nasty occasion that is not for the faint of heart.

When the forty-two partners were all settled in their chairs, Harlan Cross began the meeting. "As you all know, the partnership agreement calls for the Executive Committee to weigh each partner's contributions to the firm for the prior year. The factors involve origination credit, work given to others, a partner's own hours and fees collected and his overall contribution to the firm's success," Harlan Cross explained.

The partners had received the Executive Committee's report on what they had concluded each partner would be paid from the remaining Tier Two funds and Cross now had their full attention.

"The EC distributed to each of you yesterday our summary of what each partner should receive from the Tier Two profits," Harlan Cross said. "I know some of you think you should receive more and we are here to listen. But before you start, please understand that we're operating a partnership here, and that means to make good money, we all have to work together." He put emphasis on working together.

Looking at Jerry Keller, Harlan Cross continued. "We have to recognize each other's contributions and not just focus on ourselves. Many great law firms have destroyed themselves because some partners make extravagant demands and look out only for themselves instead of the firm as a whole. Don't forget the Barrett firm that shut down two years ago. That happened when a group of lawyers left and took many key clients with them. That not only affected the remaining fifty or so lawyers, but also over ninety staff members who also lost their jobs. All because some partners were greedy."

Harlan Cross made this same speech, more or less, every year. Some partners listened and some did not.

Jerry Keller was the first to speak. "Harlan, as far as I can see, you've clearly ignored the partnership agreement which requires that I get the origination credit for the Gibbons's work. I know he paid his last bill late, and there's a reason for that. But just taking the $900,000 he did pay last year, that would be $90,000 for me. What the hell happened?"

"Jerry, when we looked at the numbers and what really happened, we concluded that Austin was the one who really brought Gibbons into the firm. That was made very clear by Sam Archer when he insisted that Austin be the billing attorney," Harlan Cross explained.

"That's nonsense," Jerry Keller almost shouted. "The credit goes to whoever first brought the client to the firm, and that was me. I understand that was some years back and on a limited matter, but the partnership agreement makes no exceptions."

Harlan Cross knew what they did was going to make Jerry Keller furious and he thought back to the input they received from other partners over the past three weeks. A significant number of the partners had complained that Mark Austin had in reality brought the Gibbons accounts into the firm. And, while the firm had billed Gibbons around two million for the prior year, he actually paid only $900,000 before year end. A check for $1,200,000 and some change came in mid-January and many partners felt that should not be considered. One partner, who often clashed with Keller, had said in frustration, "Christ Al Mighty, Harlan. Jerry will do anything to manipulate the numbers so he gets more money. He'll make over $4 million dollars and that makes him the highest paid partner in the firm!"

James Curan, one of the partners handling the litigation work for Gibbons, had said, "Gibbons is a good example of what's wrong with fixed formulas. Most of the income from Gibbons last year came from the lawsuits we defended. I think that of the $1.2 million we billed his companies, over $800,000 was for the trial work. This is hard work by a whole lot of attorneys and has nothing to do with origination. Where does this fit in the EC's magic formula?"

"I agree," another partner had said. "Jerry's income is one of the highest in the Los Angeles area. It's only fair that his origination credit be held to a minimum. This spreads the wealth a little among the other partners."

The partners all turned and looked at Jerry Keller. They could see he was upset. He was gripping the edge of the conference room table and there were streaks of red on the side of his neck.

Jerry Keller sat silent for a moment and then looked up at Harlan Cross and angrily said, "You're making a big God-damn mistake, Harlan. Our agreement is clear. Whoever first brings the client in the door gets the credit. It makes no difference if another attorney does the work or even gets more of the client's work years later. I was the first one to work for Gibbons and that ends the debate."

"Jerry, I take exception to your statement," Harlan Cross replied. "The EC has the authority to divide origination credit if the circumstances warrant, and that's what we did in this case. Mark Austin clearly was the one who, as you say, 'landed' the client. Gibbons liked Mark because he did a good job for him. I know that ruffled your feathers some when Archer insisted that Austin be the billing attorney, but that's just a fact of life. So we cut your credit to two percent for origination purposes instead of ten percent. And since Mark is not here any longer, the other eight percent is treated as if the firm was the originator. This way, all of the partners share in the income."

"Harlan, that's…" Keller started to say before Harlan Cross interrupted.

"And don't forget, over one million was paid by Gibbons in January of this year and that doesn't even count. We'll decide next year how to treat this for origination," Harlan Cross added.

Keller's face was now turning red. He stood and said with steel in his voice, "Everyone in this room knows I'm getting screwed here. I think you all better get smart and remember how much money I bring into the firm each year. You know as well as I do that

THE COLLAPSE OF HONOR

there are dozens of law firms in the Los Angeles area that I could go to and they would jump at the chance of getting my client base."

One of the partners tried to calm things down and said, "Come on Jerry. Sit down and relax. You know that it was Mark Austin that really pulled in the Gibbons work. Don't get so..."

Before the partner could finish, Jerry Keller looked at him with a hard cold stare and shouted, "Are you calling me a liar? I was the first to work on any Gibbons business and that makes me the originator. Period. End of discussion."

"But Jerry, that was a tiny matter years ago," Harlan Cross replied.

"Harlan, if you want to change the partnership language, then make a proposal. But you can't do it yourself. The language is very clear. The attorney who first works for a client gets the origination credit unless the client was brought to the firm by someone else and the work passed on to others," Keller said as his face became even redder and his neck muscles began to bulge.

Harlan Cross had had several similar arguments with Keller over the years and knew there was going to be no good ending to this exchange. He sat silent for a moment looking directly at Keller, and then said in a business- like manner, "You're right Jerry. The agreement does say that. But it also says that it is the EC who decides if there are circumstances that would make it fair to give origination to another partner or to apportion it among several partners."

Harlan Cross paused and watched Keller for a moment to see if he was getting through to him. When Keller failed to respond, Cross shook his head slightly and said with a huge smile on his face, "Hell, Jerry. With Mark gone and the agreement clarified, you're gonna get the credit anyway. Just not this year. You have to concede that the agreement tells us to factor only fees brought into the firm in the prior calendar year."

The conference room was silent for a long thirty seconds waiting to see how Jerry Keller was going to respond. Eventually Keller looked up at Cross and said almost in a whisper, "You know damn well why they paid in January!"

With this exchange, Jerry Keller picked up his papers and as he stormed out of the conference room, he added, "You're all gonna regret this!"

When the conference room door closed behind him, one of the partners chuckled and said, "What a show! He's getting almost $4 million and he still complains."

"Jerry's never going to be happy," another partner said. "I keep thinking that someday he'll get some humility, but he keeps proving me wrong. I think he wakes up and looks in the mirror each day and rhetorically asks 'Mirror, mirror, on the wall, who is the finest lawyer of them all.' And, of course, he knows."

A number of the partners were laughing when Cross interjected, "Enough for now. We need a vote. Does anyone think the EC should go back and recalculate the Tier Two compensation for Jerry?"

The partners all looked around at each other but no one spoke. Finally, Allison Craft raised her hand and said, "Jerry is this firm's biggest rainmaker by far. Do you really want to make him angry over a few hundred thousand dollars? You know, he just might leave and then what?"

Most of the partners knew that Alison Craft and Jerry Keller had a thing going between them and so understood that she would take his side.

Alison Craft was a lateral hire by the firm and worked in the estate planning area. She had been a partner in another down-town

Los Angeles firm and was recruited by Baukus & Johnson so, when she agreed, she came in as a full partner.

Alison Craft was a blond, about five feet six inches tall, and in her early forties and decidedly plump around the hips with large breasts. This feature stood out because she often wore tight blouses that caused the material to stretch and pull at the buttons. Some in the office even took bets on how long it would be before the threads surrendered the battle and let the buttons fly!

But none of the other partners supported Keller's appeal. Maybe it was because they agreed with the Executive Committee or maybe they got lost in watching Allison's blouse, waiting for a button to fly across the room. Either way, they were tired of Keller's prima donna antics and Cross adjourned the meeting.

After the partnership meeting, Alison Craft took the elevator up to the next floor to Keller's office. When she entered, Keller was sipping on a drink and it was obvious to her that he was still agitated.

"Those bastards just don't get it," Jerry Keller snapped.

"I agree, but you need to control your anger," Alison Craft replied.

"Well, they may think I'm bluffing, but I'm not," Keller said. "What do you think? Why don't we leave this place and start our own firm. If we play it smart, I think we can take the Gibbons work with us. All we need is to convince ten or twelve associates that are doing most of the corporate work that I'm supervising, and the trial lawyers that are doing his litigation. I know my others clients would move if they knew I was leaving. We would have maybe ten million in income to start with if we play our cards right."

The whole idea of leaving Baukus & Johnson took Craft by surprise. With some hesitancy she asked, "You're talking about corporate and trial work. What would I do?"

"The same as you do here. All of our clients need estate planning. You can even head up the department," Keller replied with a smile.

When Craft joined Baukus & Johnson, she had been finishing a bitter divorce and that no doubt played a role in why she changed law firms. Her husband, also a lawyer with another firm, knew most of the partners of her old firm and she just wanted a change. As it happened, Keller was between marriages and he and Allison began a fairly serious affair. It was of course no one else's business, but they nevertheless kept it quite confidential within the firm. Or at least they thought they did.

"This makes me nervous," Craft said. "Aren't there professional rules that would keep us from soliciting the firm's clients?"

Keller laughed and said, "You let me worry about that. If done the right way, it's perfectly legal."

Craft knew that Keller was a smart and crafty lawyer, but something in her gut told her they were walking into murky waters. She had been standing in front of Keller's desk, but now she sat down in one of his leather client chairs. Keller could see the concern on her face and audibly heard her sigh.

"Look Alison, we deal with unfair business practices all the time. I know what I'm doing," Keller said.

Craft just sat without responding. She knew the firm was known for having aggressive litigators and she could just picture herself as a defendant in a future lawsuit that she wanted nothing to do with.

Keller watched Allison for a moment and then stood and walked over to a cupboard in the back corner of his office that contained a bar. He refilled his glass and poured Alison a double Johnny Walker Black Label scotch. This was one of the first things they noticed that they had in common. After dropping a few ice cubes into their glasses, he handed one to Alison and added, "Besides, the firm won't make a fuss anyway. Fighting over clients never makes for good PR. They may gripe and swear a lot, but they won't sue."

After a few more scotches, Keller and Craft went to dinner and celebrated the idea of a new firm called Keller & Craft. Somehow they found their way back to Allison's apartment to continue the celebration.

Over the next several months, Keller and Alison Craft spent hours talking and planning about their new law firm. Jerry took aside each of the associates he had been working with and, one by one, he took them to dinner. Each was sworn to secrecy and his pitch was the same to each.

"The Baukus firm is going nowhere," Keller urged. "They don't appreciate associates and even partners who bust their butts bringing in new business, and it takes what, six or seven years to become a partner? My clients will all move with me and I can promise you, if you work hard and bring in clients, you'll make partner in two or three years and that counts the time you've been with Baukus. And until then, you'll get a much bigger bonus at year end than Baukus would ever think of giving you."

With a few exceptions, Keller convinced all of the essential players at Baukus & Johnson to leave with him. He had carefully talked with each of his clients to be sure they would move and when he was satisfied he had them all, he prepared an email to the partners announcing his departure. In total, he took sixteen associates, Alison Craft and each of the litigation attorneys including one partner, who was handling the Gibbons's matters. One partner was hard to convince and he had to promise him double his current compensation and included that partner in the new firm's letterhead. The new firm was called Keller, Craft and Anderson. James Anderson was the lead litigation partner for the Gibbons's accounts.

When Keller announced that he and a group of attorneys were leaving to start their own law firm, Harlan Cross and Wayne Bailey were furious. Cross immediately called together the other members of the Executive Committee to meet in his office.

"What the hell does he think he's doing," Cross said as he waived his hands in the air in frustration.

"We need to deal with this in a business-like manner," Wayne Bailey replied cautiously. "Jerry knows the rules against soliciting clients. But he's clever and I know he has been involved with a number of clients who have had partners leave and solicit customers, so he also knows how to let his clients know he is leaving without soliciting."

Derrick Warner, the third Executive Committee member and the head of litigation, cleared his throat and said, "We all know that it violates the code of ethics for a law partner to leave and solicit clients. The proper way is for a joint announcement to be sent to all clients that just says so-and-so is leaving and giving them the new contact information. It is then up to the client to stay with the firm or go to the new firm."

"This all sounds nice and good," Bailey replied. "But Jerry didn't do that. Can't we sue him for tortuous interference or something like that?"

"Yes, we probably can," answered Warner. "But the real question is whether we want to or not."

"Why wouldn't we want to?" Bailey asked almost incredulously.

"I can answer that," Cross said. "If our clients think we're in the gutter fighting over who represents them that could cause a big back lash. Clients have a funny way of thinking that they get to pick who represents them. And in the business community, there's a lot of talking about law firms. We don't want the actions of, shall I say, one highly unethical partner, to taint the whole firm."

"You're probably right," Bailey said with obvious frustration in his voice. "I can't believe Jerry would do something like this. We've paid him more than any other partner for years and he's just never happy."

Cross had Keller's memo to the partners in his hand. He studied it for a moment and said, "Looking at those who are leaving with him, it seems fair to conclude that he is counting on Gibbons going with him. This will be a big loss for the firm, but he's also taking the attorneys who've been doing the work, so maybe it will even out."

As a way of testing how far Jerry Keller had gone in soliciting clients, Derrick Warner decided to call Sam Archer, the Executive Vice-President of Gibbons's holding company who supervises litigation with his inside counsel. And what he found out was not pleasant.

"I assume you've heard that Jerry Keller is starting his own firm and has left with a number of our lawyers," he told Sam Archer.

"Yes. Jerry called me three or four months ago and asked if we would move with him if he left", Archer replied.

Warner cleared his throat and asked, "Sam, we've done a great job for all of the Gibbons's companies, so if you don't mind saying, why the decision to change?"

Sam Archer knew this question was coming and decided to just tell it straight. "Derrick, we've liked working with your firm. But we were put in a bind. Jerry told us which lawyers were coming with him and, well, it was almost every attorney that has been working on our matters. Jerry didn't actually say this, but it was obvious that if we stayed with Baukus & Johnson, we would be starting almost from scratch with new attorneys, and that includes trial lawyers. He told us Anderson was going with him and he had done most of our litigation. It just made no sense to start over."

Sam Archer paused for a second and then added, "Derrick, I know this is awkward, but you really had a coup going on. We just couldn't change again."

There was a long pause before Warner said anything. This type of conduct is exactly what is forbidden by the ethical rules and he knew they could sue Keller and Craft as well, and no doubt win. "Thanks for being square with me Sam. I hope we can work together again someday."

As the weeks went by after Derrick Warner reported back on what he learned from his call to Sam Archer, the EC members discussed their options. There are some excellent appellate decisions in California on holding departing partners liable in damages for soliciting clients. Derrick was all for suing, but it was Harlan Cross who counseled caution.

"No one comes out a winner in these kinds of lawsuits," Cross said. "I agree we are likely to win, but there would be no way to keep it out of the newspapers. Hell, I can see it now. One of the premier law firms in LA had to sue to keep their clients? We just can't afford to do that."

Ultimately the partners met and decided not to file a lawsuit. It was agreed that the firm would send a nice diplomatic letter to every client who any of the departing attorneys had ever worked for, wishing Jerry Keller and the others well and stressing the firm's broad based expertise. The letter would include a statement that if any client went with Keller, they would most certainly be welcome to return at any time.

Before the partnership meeting ended, one of the more senior partners said what was on all of their minds. "What ever happened to the idea of partners being loyal to the firm and to each other? Is it now just a matter of who can make the most!"

Another partner replied, "Let's be realistic. The idea of loyalty is now antiquated. Next time you read about it, it will be an article in the Smithsonian magazine."

CHAPTER 4

The Wrongful Termination Lawsuit

Once Dillon Clark decided to take on the representation of Mark Austin, Laurel Kennedy and Kelly Parks immediately drafted a complaint for wrongful termination and for intentional infliction of emotional distress. The designated defendant was the law firm of Baukus & Johnson. The title of the complaint read: "Mark Austin and Suzanne Austin, Plaintiffs v. Baukus & Johnson, a law partnership and Does 1 through 25, Defendants."

Since lawyers rarely know the full facts in advance, if there is any question, the allegations are normally made "On information and belief" so they can't be later faulted for relying on incorrect information. And this applied to Mark's situation because all he knew was that someone at Baukus & Johnson had labeled him as a troublemaker.

By mere coincidence, the complaint was filed with the Los Angeles Superior Court and served on Baukus & Johnson the week after Jerry Keller, Alison Craft and the others left the firm.

When Harlan Cross read the complaint, he was not surprised to see the claim for wrongful termination. The employment lawyers had already anticipated some type of claim. But he was surprised to see the allegation that someone from the firm had called Mark a troublemaker and the claim that the firm intended to cause Mark emotional distress as a result.

Cross again assembled the Executive Committee to his office to review matters along with Karl West, the lead employment lawyer in the firm. When they were all seated, Cross asked in a not so friendly way, "Is there any truth to this troublemaker claim?"

The others just sat and starred at each other awkwardly. Finally Wayne Bailey said, "I have no idea what this means. The only communication I had with Mark was over his bonus and that was it. No one from another firm called me and I just assumed it was because I told Mark that the firm gives no recommendations."

Derrick Warner, as a litigator, turned to Karl West and said, "Get me Austin's personnel file. I want to see any letters or whatever this firm sent out after Austin left."

Before the meeting broke up, Cross turned to Warner and asked, "Derrick, who is this Dillon Clark? I don't think I've ever heard of him."

"I've heard the name, Harlan, but let me call one of our former partners on the bench and get some details. I think he may have been named the trial lawyer of the year a few years back," Warner replied.

Later that day, Warner and Karl West returned to Cross's office. "Harlan, there's no letters at all except those sent by you and Bailey. But Judy in personnel said that she was instructed by Jerry Keller to send to him any inquiries about Mark Austin. So if she got a call, she directed it to Keller, but she has no idea what was said," Warner explained as he shook his head from side to side in disbelief.

Cross sat stiff in his chair and locked his eyes with Warner. "We need to know right now what the hell Keller was doing. Personnel must have some record of who called in about Austin. Right?"

"Hang on a minute. I'll find out," replied Warner.

Warner reached out and pulled the telephone from the center of the conference table and called down to personnel. "Judy, this is Derrick. Do you have a record of who called in to ask about Austin?"

When he hung up the telephone, Warner grimaced and said, "Sorry, Harlan. No record was kept of the callers. Jerry was the head of the corporate department and she did what she was told."

The partners sat in silence for a while before Cross said in a steely voice, "What a fucking mess! Derrick, I want you to be the lead trial lawyer in this case. Karl can work with you, but I want Austin and his lawyers to know we're damn serious in defending ourselves."

Cross fidgeted with his papers for a moment, raised an eyebrow and asked, "By the way, what did you find out about the attorney?"

"I actually called your old partner, Judge Bannerman, and he said Dillon Clark is one of the best trial lawyers he's ever seen in his courtroom. He asked why I was asking so I told him about the lawsuit. You know Dale and his gruff voice. He sort of snorted and said 'You better take him seriously. I've seen him crush witnesses in cross examination.'"

In was plain to everyone in the room that Harlan Cross was angry. He looked at Warner with a stony-face and said, "We're going to have to go great guns on this Derrick. No mistakes. Understood?"

"Of course, Harlan," Warner replied. "Clark has a small firm in the valley. We can run them ragged with discovery."

"Wayne, we have to talk to Keller and get the fucking straight scoop on anything he said. You were probably closest to him. Would you give him a call? Let him know of the lawsuit. In fact, send him a copy of the complaint. But whatever you do, find out what he said to other firms," Cross instructed.

"Incidentally, how much are they asking for?" Cross asked as the meeting ended.

"They don't say," Warner answered. "It's the usual sob story about emotional distress and lost earnings."

As soon as the wrongful termination complaint had been filed and served, Dillon scheduled a meeting in his office with Laurel Kennedy and Kelly Parks to discuss the strategy on discovery. It was a Friday, which was a casual dress day for the firm. Dillon was wearing tan slacks and a blue dress shirt open at the neck with the sleeves rolled up to his elbows. Both Laurel and Kelly were in blue jeans with white firm t-shirts. The firm ordered up dozens of t-shirts for a picnic the year before with the firm name emblazoned in red and they became popular with the attorneys and staff.

When they were all seated, Dillon asked, "Ok, where are we at this point?"

Laurel handed Dillon a memorandum and said, "This is a draft memo that Kelly and I have worked up that lists what we need to do for discovery."

Discovery is the way lawyers are able to find out from the lawyers on the other side what they assert to be the facts. This includes subpoenas to produce documents, interrogatories which are written questions that defendants must answer under penalty of perjury, and depositions. Depositions are by far the most important because the witness must go to the lawyer's office and submit to vigorous questioning with a court reporter present. The reporter takes down all questions and answers and types it into a transcript that the witness must eventually sign. In general, the lawyer taking the deposition can ask almost any question that involves an issue in the case or that might even lead to other relevant evidence, like the names of other witnesses or documents.

As Dillon read over the draft memo, he noticed that Laurel and Kelly had been very thorough. It said:

"Recommended Discovery
Austin v. Baukus & Johnson

A. Notice to Produce Documents by Defendants:

1. Personnel file for Austin

2. All internal firm communications regarding Austin including work evaluations, work assignments, commendations and criticisms.

3. All communications from the firm to any person outside the firm regarding Austin from the time Austin was terminated to the present, whether letter, email or other form of communication.

4. Notes, memos, emails or other forms of recording information about what was told to any person outside the firm about Austin's conduct while at the firm, including whether he was a troublemaker.

5. Records of Austin's compensation while at the firm.

6. Copy of the firm's policies on bonus compensation for senior and/or junior partners in effect while Austin was employed (goes to damages).

7. Records of what senior partners have earned for the past three years including base earnings and what is called bonus or Tier Two compensation (goes to future damages).

8. Copies of any liability insurance policies that cover wrongful termination and/or emotional distress.

B. Interrogatories:

I. We have not yet drafted a set of interrogatories, but here are some obvious questions:

i. Why was Austin terminated and what documents exist that confirm the reason?

ii. Was Austin told he would be entitled to participate in the firm's Tier Two bonus compensation by Wayne Bailey?

iii. Did Wayne Bailey remind Austin to prepare a memo requesting Tier Two compensation based on the Gibbons account?

iv. Was Austin responsible for bringing in Boyd Gibbons and his companies as a client for the firm?

v. Has anyone at Baukus & Johnson ever told prospective employers of Austin that he was a troublemaker?

vi. Name each person at Baukus & Johnson who ever spoke with a prospective employer of Austin from the time he left to the present.

vii. Identify by name and position of anyone in the firm who ever discussed the reasons for Austin's termination (including partners).

viii. Identify by name and position anyone in the firm who was in any way critical of Austin that played any role in his termination.

C. Depositions:

1. Wayne Bailey as Mark's boss and EC member;

2. Harlan Cross, managing partner and EC member who asked Mark to leave the firm;

3. Derrick Warner the 3rd member of the EC

4. Others???

This is just a start on discovery. Once we see the firms answer to the complaint we can add more requests.

We can anticipate an objection to any conversations between the partners over Austin's termination. But both of us have looked at the privilege issue and the law is really vague. Can the whole firm be treated as counsel for each other and protect what they say? This would allow them to protect almost anything."

After studying the memo for a few minutes, Dillon looked up at Laurel and Kelly and with a smile and a twinkle in his eye said, "Good job. The more I think about this case, the better I like it. If we find evidence of a real intent to harm Mark, we might even get punitive damages."

"From what I've seen so far, the damages for a termination are really based on contract law and so punitives aren't recoverable," replied Kelly.

Dillon leaned back in his leather chair and thought for a moment and asked, "But does that apply if it was done maliciously? Either way, I want you to add to the document request and interrogatories all financial records that show the firm's net profits for the past five years. If we can get punitives to the jury, they are entitled to know the defendant's wealth."

Laurel laughed and added, "Boy, this is going to be quite a donnybrook!"

"Yes, indeed," Dillon replied. "But that's what makes litigation fun, especially when you're representing the good guys."

When Wayne Bailey called Jerry Keller, his secretary told him he was not in. He called back several more times, and when he got the same answer, he sent him an email with a copy of the complaint attached. This apparently got his attention because Keller called back the same day.

After some tense perfunctory conversation, Bailey jumped in and asked the key question. "Jerry, Judy in personnel tells us that you had all calls that came in asking about Austin sent to you. Is that correct?"

There was a long pregnant pause before Keller answered. "Yes, I think I did do that," he said hesitantly. "Estate planning fell under the corporate department so I thought I should be the one to give answers to any questions."

"Jerry, you know as well as I do that I was Mark's superior. Why didn't you pass them on to me?" Bailey said with tension in his voice.

"I just didn't think of it," Keller said.

"Well, as you can see from the complaint, Mark is alleging that someone in the firm told other firms that he was a troublemaker. For God's sake Jerry, did you say that?" Bailey asked in obvious exasperation.

"I never called him a troublemaker," Keller replied defensively. "I only said I thought he had acted immaturely in seeking a share of profits reserved to the partners. Nothing more."

"Why the hell did you say that," Bailey demanded. "You knew I was the one who told Mark to apply for the origination credit."

"Yes, and that was your mistake," Keller said abruptly and hung up the telephone.

When a lawsuit is filed, what happens next typically falls into several distinct stages. The first stage is the discovery; next comes trial preparation and efforts at settlement; and finally a trial. In the case of Austin v. Baukus et al., that meant that the defendant had to turn over the list of documents requested in the Notice to Produce Documents that Laurel and Kelly had prepared.

When the defendant's response came in the mail, it was given to Kelly and she excitedly took the bundle to her office. For trial lawyers, it is always energizing when you get the oppositions first discovery responses. They always said a lot about how the case was going to proceed. Some lawyers were forthright and turned over the information required. Others were the exact opposite. They fought tooth and nail to hide information and usually only honored the discovery rules when ordered to do so by a judge.

When Kelly looked more closely at what was provided, she noticed right away that it contained only a few pages of paper. The law firm had included Mark Austin's personnel file but it only contained the papers when he was first hired, stuff about medical insurance and W-2 forms and other routine information. She did note that the file reflected Mark's advancement to junior partner status.

As Kelly flipped through the papers, she frowned and could feel her heart begin to beat more rapidly. The only evaluation for the years that Mark had worked at Baukus & Johnson, was the one critical memo written by Alison Craft. And when she read the formal written response, the firm objected to all of their requests for communications among the partners as well as the earnings of the partners, claiming it was protected under the right of privacy in California and also protected under the attorney client privilege. "Damn," Kelly said to herself. "They'll probably do the same with conversations among all of the attorneys. That can't be right," she said to herself, somewhat alarmed.

Kelly pulled the memo from Alison Craft and the written objections from the package, and walked down the hallway to the firm's central office area where the firm had two large copying machines. She made three copies and walked down to Laurel Kennedy's office. When she entered the office, Laurel, who was busy reading depositions from another case, looked up and said, "Come on in, Kelly. I need a break anyway."

Kelly handed Laurel a copy of the memo and said, "This is the only evaluation that they produced. There's not one single evaluation for the five years Mark worked there!"

"Nothing when Mark was made a junior partner?" Laurel asked.

"Only his change in status. Nothing about why. He got good bonuses and those show on the W-2 forms, but otherwise it was like he wasn't there," Kelly explained.

"Let's take this down and show Dillon. As the professor at Stanford said, this whole thing doesn't pass the smell test," Laurel said with a skeptical look on her face.

When they got to Dillon's office, he was leaning back in his leather swivel office chair with his feet propped up on his desk talking on the telephone. Laurel and Kelly sat down in the client chairs in front of his desk and waited for him to finish.

When Dillon finally hung up the telephone, he smiled and asked, "Well, what do I owe the privilege of getting you both at the same time?"

Kelly handed Dillon the memo and written objections and said, "Dillon, in the five years Mark worked for Baukus & Johnson, this memo from Craft is the one and only evaluation he got. Nothing at all about why he was made a junior partner. They have to be holding something back."

Dillon read the memo from Alison Craft. It said:

To: *Executive Committee*
From: *Alison Craft*
Re: *Mark Austin*
Date: *November 15, 2011*

As you all know, Mark has worked closely with me on a number of high income/high asset estate plans. While Mark works hard and is good at drafting trusts and wills, I have noticed that he has a clear lack of understanding of the sophisticated tax issues that someone doing work involving millions of dollars must know.

I no longer have confidence that Mark will be able to continue doing high end tax planning and as such, I don't want him assigned to any further of my clients. I also seriously question whether Mark should ever be considered for senior partner status. I suggest we start looking for a replacement. Mark can do well in a firm that does more routine estate planning."

When he finished reading the memo, Dillon quickly glanced at the written objections and said, "The objections were predicted. I want you two to research whether partners can claim a privilege when they talk among themselves about a lawsuit against their own firm. I really doubt that a firm can just clam up by saying they are each other's attorneys. But I honestly haven't seen that before."

"Dillon, remember Mark's law professor who said the whole thing didn't pass the smell test? Well, this single memo has to be what the firm used to terminate Mark. Can they get away with this one single criticism?" Kelly said in frustration. She was still feeling apprehensive and was looking for some words of encouragement.

"I agree," Dillon replied. "But the tough part here is that the issue is whether Mark would become a senior partner when one partner has lost faith in him. Would you like me to force you to work with someone who you don't trust to do the work right?"

Laurel and Kelly exchanged glances with each other but said nothing. The silence deepened as they all stared at each other. Finally Laurel said in a low soft voice, "No."

Kelly's expression tightened as her heart began pounding with her increased frustration. "Dillon, that's not the point here. Mark was a superb lawyer, landed a huge client for the firm and it's just not right to fire someone because one partner doesn't want to work with him!"

"Easy, Kelly," Dillon said. "I understand how you feel. And your point is a good one, but that's what the case is all about. Remember what your research said. There is a covenant of good faith in all employment relationships. If an employer breaches this covenant and fires someone maliciously, that can be a wrongful termination. We just have to start digging and see what everyone says when we take their depositions."

While Laurel and Kelly were in his office, Dillon saw Phil Burnam, his partner and close friend of almost thirty years, walk by his office. Phil had also lived through the tragic untimely death of Dillon's wife.

When Laurel and Kelly left his office, Dillon walked down to Phil's corner office.

"You old son-of-a-bitch, what're you doing here?" Dillon asked with obvious affection in his voice. "I thought you only came in to give us working slobs a bad time."

Phil Burnam was independently wealthy and they both knew that Dillon was now also wealthy as a result of winning a huge jury award in a trust lawsuit in Santa Barbara a few years back. It was a close call for Dillon. If he had lost the case, he would have been bankrupt, but he stayed with the client, Dani Germain, after the partners of his firm insisted he abandon her. This is why he and Phil Burnam left.

After a slight hesitation, Phil Burnam laughed and said, "Pretty close, Dillon. I heard through the grapevine that you'd taken on another contingency case and, well..." Turning serious, Phil added, "Hell, Dillon. You need to relax. You certainly don't need the money. Why don't you get serious with Dani Germain. You know she's been after you since you won her case up north?"

"No way, Phil," Dillon snapped with irritation. "A dinner or theatre once in a while is one thing. But ..." He then hesitated and slightly turned his head away.

Dillon had met his wife when she was a witness in one of his trials when he first moved to California. They married five months later and had been best pals until her death at a far too young age of fifty-four. And he still considered himself married.

Phil knew what was happening and he kicked himself for even raising the issue. It had been fifteen years since Jamie, Dillon's wife, had died unexpectedly, but his emotions were still raw whenever the subject of his wife came up. He also knew that Dillon had a tear in his eye and was trying to control himself to get by the moment.

"My friend," Dillon finally said as he turned back to face Phil, "I know you're just trying to help. But Jamie and I were, you know, partners for life. I could never imagine replacing her. I'm OK, Phil. I really am."

"I'm sorry, Dillon," Phil replied. "Please excuse my careless comment."

"Phil, you and I go way back. You could never say something to me that you had to apologize for. I probably should talk more about Jamie, but it's still hard. I think of her every single day. And you know what? I still write her letters and when something important comes up. I will sit down and tell her the whole story. Somehow, it helps. I think she has a way of reaching me from that far-away place where good folks go. It may sound silly, but it really does help. So she's still my wife and partner and that's the way I want it."

"Dillon, I'm..." Phil started to say but Dillon interrupted him.

"No apologies, Phil. You don't have to say anything more. Look, why don't you join me for dinner tonight? We can go to one of those French-Italian places on the Avenue," Dillon asked.

Anxious to put the awkward episode behind him, Phil hurriedly replied, "You're on. I'll make the reservation and let your secretary know the place and time."

When he left Phil's office, Dillon walked down to his own office, shut the door and walked over to the bookcase that filled the wall on one side of his office. There were several photographs of him and Jamie and he stood there looking at them, thinking back to the good times they had together. He knew she was in a good place, but he still felt that God had somehow made a mistake by taking her and leaving him behind.

As Dillon stood there remembering, tears ran down his cheeks. He was never embarrassed about the tears. They were part of their relationship. For him they showed love and caring. After a few minutes he finally said in a sad whisper, "Love you, kiddo."

CHAPTER 5

Discovery – What Really Happened?

When the Baukus & Johnson firm failed to produce any meaningful documents, Kelly Parks and Laurel Kennedy worked up a list of key partners in the firm for depositions. "If they want to play games, let them do it under oath," Dillon had instructed them. A good trial lawyer can make life miserable for a witness who later decides to change his story.

When Kelly met with Dillon a few days later to get his approval of the witness list, she was in a much better mood.

"You know, Dillon," Kelly said, "I wish I could be the one taking a few of these depositions. These guys are really hard-balling us and I'd love to ask old man Cross to explain why he fired Mark."

Dillon laughed and said with a smile, "You'll get to do one soon enough, Kelly. And when you do take your first deposition, I may even come and watch!"

"By the way, Kelly, when do you take the Bar exam?" Dillon asked.

"It's set for early August. They're giving it at the convention center in Santa Monica this year, so I got lucky. I could almost walk from my apartment," Kelly answered.

It's endemic to the legal profession that whenever lawyers talk about the dreaded "Bar exam," they can all recall their own experience like it was just yesterday. Many can recall the exact questions even after forty years, and Dillon was no exception.

Dillon leaned back in his leather chair, cupped his hands behind his head and said, "You know, Kelly, when I took the Bar it was all essay questions. There were two sessions a day over three days. I got either lucky or unlucky and was put up on the stage at the auditorium in Pasadena. There were six tables with four at each table. The rest were down on the floor sitting at long tables. I think there were about six hundred in the auditorium," Dillon said reflectively.

"Did you type or write your answers?" Kelly asked.

"I could type pretty well, but the noise bothered me, so I did everything by hand," Dillon replied. After a moment he added, "Even if you hand write, the noise can be a killer. God forbid you sat next to someone with a fountain pen. It may only be your imagination, but all you hear is the scratching sounds. It can drive you crazy, so be careful."

"What was amazing," Dillon added, "is that by the third day of the exam, there were only fifteen of us left out of the twenty four that started up on the stage. I've never understood how someone can spend three years in law school and then just give up! What do they have to lose by just finishing the thing and see what happens?"

Kelly laughed nervously and said, "Yeah, I've heard the stories." She paused and then said, "But I think those that quit just didn't prepare. But that won't happen to me."

"I have no concerns about you, Kelly," Dillon said encouragingly. "Just take a good bar review course. You're going to a good law school and you'll be surprised that you already know the stuff. You'll see what I mean when they mail you the outlines they expect you to study. A stack, by the way, that is about two feet thick. It scares the hell out of you when you see the monstrous amount of law they want you to study, but you really will know it."

Kelly exhaled slightly and said, "I hope you're right."

Of the several paralegals in his firm, Kelly was Dillon's favorite. He had been asked to represent a desperate woman in an ugly divorce two years ago, and he agreed to take it on a contingency but only on the condition that Kelly came to work for him. She had been working for a small firm in Santa Monica when she met the client and she quickly saw that the woman had been mistreated by the divorce court. When her boss said she couldn't afford to take the case, Kelly talked to one of her law professors who ultimately asked Dillon to meet with them.

After chatting with Kelly about her graduation, they discussed in what order Dillon wanted to take the depositions. "I want to start out with Harlan Cross, the managing partner. Like you, I want to see what he has to say about why Mark was fired."

Dillon turned sideways in his leather chair and looked out of the window pondering the other witnesses. After a moment he said, "I think I'll follow-up with Alison Craft. Cross must be basing his decision on her memorandum, and there must have been some conversation between the two of them. And then we'll take Wayne Bailey and Jerry Keller."

"What about the missing documents on Mark?" Kelly asked.

"I think we'll let them decide who to name as the most knowledgeable. And schedule that one at the end. It will be interesting to see who they produce after we get the key players pinned down," Dillon explained.

"Oh yes," Dillon added as an afterthought, "notice two separate depositions for the most knowledgeable. One for the personnel records relating to Mark, and the second for the firm's financial records. We'll get into a real donnybrook over the privileges, but better now than later."

"I love the idea that they have to produce whoever they think is the most knowledgeable," Kelly said with a little mischievous look on her face. "This puts them on the spot, especially on Mark's performance."

It was Dillon's practice to have important depositions video tape recorded as well as using a court reporter for a written transcript. This tends to make the witness, as well as the attorneys, take things a little more seriously. And this would be especially true when the witnesses were attorneys. Also, if a witness is not available for the trial, the video can be played so the jury can actually see the witness testify as if he were in court.

It was also Dillon's policy to have his client present at all depositions, so he had asked Mark to attend. They had discussed whether his wife should also attend, but that was vetoed. Her emotions were still running hard and Mark wanted her protected as much as possible.

The deposition of Harlan Cross took place in Dillon's main conference room. By this time, Dillon had learned all about Cross and his bankruptcy reputation along with his personality quirks.

Harlan Cross arrived with Derrick Warner, the head of the firm's litigation department. Cross was wearing a black three piece vested suit and looked every bit a law firm managing partner. Dillon wondered to himself whether this was because he was going to be on camera.

Derrick Warner was tall, about six foot five, and was way overweight and already almost bald. Dillon knew him by his reputation as a hard-nosed trial lawyer who lost few cases. Warner, perhaps also for the camera, was wearing a light tan suit with a blue shirt and stripped maroon tie. Unlike Cross, Warner introduced himself and shook Dillon's hand. "Sorry we have to meet under these circumstances," Warner said.

Mark was seated next to Dillon on the opposite side of the conference table from where Harlan Cross and Derrick Warner were seated. They had talked about what Mark should wear and settled on blue jeans, tennis shoes and a casual short sleeve shirt.

Dillon wanted them to see Mark relaxed and willing to go the full course to a trial if necessary.

Harlan Cross looked over at Mark but said nothing. After a few pleasantries, the video photographer had Cross swear he would testify truthfully and Dillon went directly to the core questions. "Mr. Cross, would you please explain, in your own words, why Mark Austin was terminated by Baukus & Johnson?"

"Certainly," Harlan Cross replied. "But I take exception to the word terminated. One of the senior partners had lost confidence in Mark and his ability to do the sophisticated tax planning needed for our clients and she questioned if he would ever become a senior partner. Once that happens, we let the attorney know so they can find a better fit with another firm."

"You can use whatever word you want, Mr. Cross," Dillon replied. "But you were the one that told Mark to leave the firm that day. Correct?"

"Yes, that's correct," Harlan Cross replied.

"Going back to the word terminated," Dillon said, "if Mark was not terminated, are you suggesting he could have stayed on as a junior partner or maybe an associate?"

Harlan Cross fidgeted slightly before he said, "Not really. When the decision is made that a young attorney won't become a partner, it is dangerous to keep that person around. He may be unhappy and cause who knows what problems. So I did ask him to turn in his cell phone and other things and leave that day. If Mark had not agreed and said 'I refuse' or something like that, I don't know what we would have done. Maybe we would have fired him. But that's not what Mark did. He agreed to leave."

"He left after you told him to vacate his office and the building. Right?" Dillon asked with slight disbelief.

"Yes," Harlan Cross answered with a coldness in his voice.

"OK, Mr. Cross, let's get back to my question. Why did you ask Mark to leave?"

"You have the memo from Alison Craft. As the managing partner, once I got that memo, I knew we had to do something. You know as well as I that you can't force other partners to make an attorney a partner if they are opposed, especially in the same area of practice. Mark would have had to work with Alison in estate planning and that obviously would not have worked. This is why I met with Mark and asked him to leave," Harlan Cross explained.

"Did you meet with Alison Craft to discuss her concerns?" Dillon asked.

"No," Harlan Cross said.

"Didn't you at least try to see if things could be worked out between her and Mark? He had just brought in one of the firm's biggest accounts, right?" Dillon asked a little incredulously.

"No," Harlan Cross said.

"Did you meet or talk with any of the other partners about letting Mark go?" Dillon asked.

"Objection," Derrick Warner said. "Conversations between Mr. Cross and any of the other lawyers about Mark Austin are confidential under the attorney client privilege. I instruct Mr. Cross not to answer."

"Mr. Warner, I seriously doubt whether any judge would agree that every lawyer in a firm is in effect the attorney for the firm in Mark's lawsuit, certainly when the issue concerns why an associate attorney was fired," Dillon said with a sharp tone to his voice.

"I understand your position," Derrick Warner replied, "but in this case we, meaning the firm, are representing ourselves and I think the privilege applies."

Dillon paused for a moment and said, "Mr. Warner, we can let the court decide this issue, but I think there is no privilege to conversations among the partners or even associates leading up to the decision to fire Mark Austin. We are entitled to know who said what and to whom so we can understand the reasons for the termination."

"I respectfully disagree, Mr. Dillon," Derrick Warner replied. "Again, I instruct Mr. Cross not to answer any questions about what the attorneys said among themselves."

Dillon knew he was in for a dog fight and decided to go on with other questions. "Laurel and Kelly can prepare a motion to compel answers and ask for sanctions and I'll just take Cross's deposition again when the court forces him to answer," he thought to himself.

"Mr. Cross, we'll let the court decide this dispute, so I'd like to move on to other questions," Dillon said. "Are you aware of anyone in the Baukus & Johnson firm telling other firms where Mark applied for a job, that he was a troublemaker?"

Harlan Cross and Derrick Warner had discussed the possibility that this question would be asked, and they agreed that this was a dangerous issue and that they would assert the attorney privilege here as well.

"Objection," Derrick Warner said. "This is the same attorney client privilege. Anything learned by Mr. Cross in investigating the issues raised in Mr. Austin's complaint are protected by the attorney client privilege and the attorney work product privilege. I instruct Mr. Cross not to answer."

Dillon was well aware of what trial lawyers call the "scorched earth" defense. It is to throw up every objections and road block possible to make the case prohibitively expensive and to demoralize the opposition. And he knew this is the tactic being taken by Derrick Warner.

"One word of caution," Dillon said. "In my judgment you are making frivolous objections and unless you change and let the witness answer the questions, we will seek an order that he answer and ask the court to order your firm to pay monetary sanctions. This said, are you still instructing the witness not to answer?"

"Proceed, Mr. Clark," Derrick Warner snapped. "Our objection stands."

Dillon could tell that Mark was finding it difficult to sit and listen to the defendants stone-walling every question, so he took a recess and he and Mark walked out into the hallway and into Dillon's office. As soon as the door was shut, Mark blurted out, "God damn it Dillon, is this the way this whole case is going to go?"

"I know it's tough to just sit, but we have to take this one step at a time. We'll file a motion to compel answers and seek sanctions, and Cross will be right back here in a month or so. Then we'll get the truth."

When Dillon and Mark walked back to the conference room to finish Cross's deposition, Dillon changed the subject.

"Mr. Cross, was Mark Austin entitled to receive an origination bonus because he brought in Sam Archer and his companies as clients?" Dillon asked.

"No," Harlan Cross answered. "The origination credit is limited to the partners. Also, Mark did not work the full year. All Tier Two compensation is based on looking back on what a partner did for the full year. In Mark's case, he left in early December."

Dillon was now truly incredulous to hear such words from such a distinguished attorney. With one eyebrow raised suspiciously he asked, "But Mr. Cross, Mark left in December because you fired him, right?"

"We asked him to find another firm," Harlan Cross said.

"Let me ask this another way. If Mark Austin had stayed the entire year, would he have been entitled to a bonus, part of what you call Tier Two compensation, for bringing in Archer and his companies?"

"I already answered that. Tier Two is limited to the partners," Harlan Cross replied.

"Isn't it true, Mr. Cross, that Wayne Bailey advised Mark to submit a memo asking for Tier Two compensation because of the Archer companies and revenue?" Dillon asked.

"Yes, that is true," Harlan Cross answered. "But Wayne was mistaken. The issue had never come up before and we clarified the partnership agreement on that before the end of the year. And, while I hate to repeat myself, it wouldn't have applied to Mark because he did not finish out the year."

Dillon stared at Harlan Cross for a long moment and then asked with some irritation, "Mr. Cross, when did you get the memo from Alison Craft?"

Harlan Cross leaned over and whispered something to Derrick Warner and then turned back and said, "I don't know the specific date, but it was not long before we made the decision to let Mark go."

"Was it before or after Mark sent you his own memo requesting a Tier Two bonus for bringing in Mr. Gibbons and his companies?" Dillon asked still staring at Cross.

"They could have been about the same time frame. You have both of the memos. What are the dates?" Harlan Cross said with some frustration.

"Yes, we should do that," Dillon replied as he reached over to a stack of papers sitting on the conference room table next to him.

After thumbing through the papers for a second, he handed two of them to the court reporter and said, "Please mark the memo from Mark Austin as Exhibit 10 and the memo from Alison Craft as Exhibit 11."

After the memos were marked, Dillon handed Exhibit 10 to Harlan Cross and asked, "Do you recognize this exhibit as the one from Mark Austin asking for a bonus?"

"Yes. This is the memo he sent to the Executive Committee about the bonus. It is dated November 20 so I assume that is when I got my copy. We don't have a system of stamping internal documents when received," Harlan Cross explained.

"What was your reaction when you got this memo?" Dillon asked.

"As I explained before, Mark was not entitled to a Tier Two bonus," Harlan Cross replied.

"What specifically did you do?" Dillon asked.

"It came somewhat out of the blue, so I called a meeting of the Executive Committee to discuss the matter. I also called Jerry Keller because he had done work for Gibbons some years back. Anyway, we met and it was agreed that the Tier Two was for senior partners only. Wayne was not so sure, so he and Keller looked into the matter. As it turned out, the phrasing in the partnership agreement was a little vague, so we amended it right away to make it clear only senior partners were entitled to Tier Two. This was always the intent," Harlan Cross explained.

"Mr. Cross, was the agreement amended just because of Mark's memo?" Dillon asked.

"No," Harlan Cross said, "the partners all thought it applied only to senior partners. And besides, Tier Two is a look back at what a partner does for the entire year. Mark never finished the year."

"Yes, we know he didn't finish the year. But even Wayne Bailey, Mark's boss and your fellow Executive Committee member, thought Mark was entitled to the bonus, correct?" Dillon asked.

"Mr. Clark, all I can say is that Wayne was wrong. He jumped to a conclusion and once the partners talked about it, we all agreed it was always intended for senior partners only," Harlan Cross explained.

By now Dillon was getting a little fed-up with the technical mumbo jumbo. "Mr. Cross, I asked you to bring the law firm's financial records. These are relevant on damages. Did you bring them?"

"Mr. Clark," Derrick Warner interjected, "we believe our records are confidential under the privacy clause of our state constitution. If you disagree, that will have to be taken to the court to decide."

"OK," Dillon said, "I will go on to another issue. Mr. Cross, to your knowledge, did anyone at Baukus & Johnson ever tell another law firm where Mark Austin was applying for a job, that he was a troublemaker?"

"Not to my knowledge," Harlan Cross answered.

The deposition took the better part of the day, and when Dillon finished with Harlan Cross, he said, "Mr. Cross, I think we'll see each other again when the court orders you to answer my questions. Until then, I am keeping this deposition open."

After Harlan Cross and Derrick Warner left, Dillon and Mark walked back to Dillon's office and Kelly Parks joined them.

Kelly could see that Mark was discouraged. He sat in the guest chair in front of Dillon's desk with his head down just staring at the floor. "Mark, are you OK?" she asked.

Mark straightened up and, looking at Dillon, said, "You tell me. As far as I can see, we got stone-walled!"

"I agree with Mark," Dillon said. "But we have to file a motion to compel Cross to answer the questions. They're claiming all conversations between the partners are protected by the attorney-client privilege. And the financial records they claim are protected by the right to privacy. I think it is bullshit but I want you and Laurel to research this and prepare a draft as soon as possible."

The deposition of Alison Craft was set for the next week. But this time Mark's wife Suzzi decided to attend. She had been following the discovery and knew that it was Craft's memo that the firm was using as an excuse to ask Mark to leave. They actually fought over her decision to go.

"Suzzi, there's absolutely no reason for you to put yourself through the emotional turmoil of listening to Alison say whatever she is going to say," Mark insisted.

"I know you're just trying to protect me," Suzzi replied, "but if she is the one who cost you your job, I want to sit there and listen. I want her to see my face."

"Suzzi, I just…" Mark started to say.

"No way, Mark," Suzzi said as she interrupted him. "Woman can sense sometimes when another woman is hiding something. It can just be a feeling that men may not have. Anyway, I'm going even if I have to drive myself!"

Mark and Suzzi arrived early for Alison Craft's deposition and were in the conference room chatting with Laurel Kennedy and Kelly Parks when Dillon entered the room.

Dillon smiled as he said, "Mrs. Austin, I for one am glad you're here today. I think your presence is going to make Alison a little uneasy. Let me know how you react to her when we're done."

When Alison Craft and Derrick Warner arrived for the deposition, Mark and Suzzi were seated next to Dillon on his right. When they were all seated, the video photographer provided each with a small microphone, focused his camera on Alison and the deposition began.

"Ms. Craft, you already know Mark, but you may not know his wife. She is one of the plaintiffs in this case." As he said this, Dillon waived his hand in Suzzi's direction.

"Actually, we have met. I think it was at a firm summer barbecue," Alison Craft said with more than a little nervousness in her voice.

As soon as the reporters were ready, Dillon handed Alison Craft a copy of her memo. "Did you write this memo?" he asked.

"Yes, I did," Alison Craft answered.

"Why did you write it?" Dillon asked.

Alison Craft looked over at Derrick Warner for a brief second and said, "Mr. Clark, in any law firm, it is important that the partners have confidence in the abilities of those who they work with. In Mark's case, he is very bright and knows a lot about trust and wills, but he has no sophisticated tax background. When I was still at Baukus & Johnson, and even now with my own firm, we do work for very wealthy individuals and taxes often drive the type of estate plan we do for them. Mark was just weak in this area. I had no time to train him, so I thought it best that he find another firm."

"OK. The memo is dated November 15. Did you give this to the Executive Committee that day?" Dillon asked.

"No. I knew this would result in Mark leaving, so I kept it for a few days. I don't know how many, but I wanted to think about it before I sent it on," Alison Craft replied.

"Who did you eventually send it to?" Dillon asked.

"Well, it is addressed to the Executive Committee, but since I work for Wayne, I gave it to him. I think he sent it on to the Committee. I told him I had sat on it for a while, but was sure this was the right thing for the firm and for Mark," Alison Craft explained.

"Do you know when you gave it to Wayne Bailey?" Dillon asked.

"I've thought about this and I'm pretty sure it was around December 10. I say this because Wayne said he passed it on to Harlan Cross the same day."

"Did Harlan Cross or any other partner talk to you about this memo before they fired Mark Austin?" Dillon asked with anger in his voice.

"No," replied Alison Craft.

"Did Wayne Bailey, the head of your department, talk with you about the memo and what it would do to Mark?" Dillon asked.

"Objection," Derrick Warner said. "We have the same objection as with Mr. Cross. We're going to have to have a judge decide if conversations between partners are discoverable or protected."

Dillon spent another hour with Alison Craft going over Mark's legal work, but the only problem she could describe was his lack of tax training.

When Dillon finally finished with Alison Craft, he asked Mark and Suzzi to join him and they walked back to his office. He buzzed his secretary, Jeannie Davis, and asked, "Jeannie, call Kelly and Laurel. If they're free, have them come down to my office."

While he was waiting for Kelly and Laurel, Dillon turned to Suzzi and asked, "So, Suzzi, what do you think?"

Before Suzzi could answer, Kelly and Laurel both walked into Dillon's office and almost simultaneously asked, "How did it go?"

"That's what I was just asking Suzzi," Dillon replied.

Suzzi looked over at Mark as if asking permission to speak. "Go ahead. I think she's a bitch, but then I guess I'm a little tainted," Mark said.

After taking a deep breath, Suzzi straightened her shoulders and said, "It was pretty clear she didn't want to make eye contact with me. I could see her sort of furtively look at me a few times, but that was it. Anyway, you can all see that on the tape."

At this point, Suzzi's hands began to shake and she was trying desperately to hold back the tears. Mark reached over and said quietly, "It's OK honey, you don't have to say anything. Dillon can figure this all out."

Everyone in the room wanted to help her, but there was not much that can be said. Dillon cleared his throat and said, "Mark's right, Suzzi. You two go home and we can talk about your reactions later."

Suzzi shook her head and in a low whisper said, "No, I'm OK. It's just hard. That woman has ruined our lives over what?"

As Suzzi's heart began to pound heavily in her chest, she felt herself getting angry. With tears dripping down her cheeks, she blurted out, "I think she's lying! And I think she knew that is exactly what I was thinking. That's why she wouldn't look at me."

The room was silent for a long minute before anyone spoke. Finally Dillon slowly rose from his chair and walked over to the counter and poured a glass of water from a container and gave it to Suzzi. "I know this is hard, and it will probably get even harder. But for whatever its worth, I agree with you. I think she was lying. But with the objections to my questions, we're just going to have to wait until the court makes a ruling on the attorney client privilege claims."

"What about Wayne Bailey?" Kelly asked. "His deposition has already been set."

Dillon looked over at Kelly and Laurel and said, "We're just wasting our time. With Craft's deposition done, at least for now, we need to file the motion to compel. Once the court makes an order, we can get back to the depositions. When can you get this ready to file?"

Laurel Kennedy replied, "We already have the draft motion prepared and the legal research done. All I need to do is fill in the specific refusals. I think I'll just file the deposition transcripts and give the judge the page and line numbers for the key points."

"OK," Dillon said. "I'd like to get it filed tomorrow. We can then get this to a judge for a hearing in three weeks." He paused and then added, "Incidentally, with the new system, we won't know who the judge will be until the motion is filed, so let me know immediately who it gets assigned to."

When the motion to compel was filed, it was assigned to the Honorable Elton Reynolds. He had been a judge for some thirty years and most lawyers thought he was way past the day when he should have retired. While he had at one time been a good judge, in the past few years he would fall asleep during trials and, by reputation at least, rarely read the lengthy legal briefs filed by attorneys.

When Judge Reynolds was handed the file with the motion to compel, he noticed right away that the defendant was the Baukus & Johnson law firm. He chuckled a little to himself as he thought of Judge Dale Bannerman, the current Presiding Judge of the Los Angeles County Superior Court. Judge Bannerman was a former partner at Baukus & Johnson and still a close friend of the firm's managing partner, Harlan Cross. "Boy, oh boy," Judge Reynolds said to himself, "Bannerman is going to love to hear about this one."

In fact, Judge Dale Bannerman already knew of the lawsuit by Mark Austin. When Derrick Warner told Harlan Cross about the attorney-client privilege issue, Cross had called Bannerman and discussed the issue.

"Dale, we've taken a hard look at this privilege issue and the law seems to be against us," Harlan Cross told Bannerman. "Have you run into this since you've been on the bench?"

"I haven't seen it personally," Judge Bannerman replied, "but I can ask around with the judges to see what they think."

"Thanks, Dale. I think we're clean on the lawsuit anyway, but I don't want to take any chances," Harlan Cross said. "And Dale, please say hello to your lovely wife for me."

"Will do, Harlan. Good to hear from you again," Judge Bannerman said.

After talking with Harlan Cross, Judge Bannerman asked his secretary to get him a copy of the motion and the firm's reply brief. When she brought it to his office later in the day, he frowned when he saw that Dillon Clark was representing the plaintiffs. He had been the trial judge on half a dozen cases where Dillon had been on the winning side and he could still recall how prepared he was on the slightest detail. And he recalled one ruling he made where Dillon had appealed and his ruling was reversed.

Judge Dale Bannerman wanted to help his old firm if possible, but it had to have a good legal basis. After reading the briefs, which he knew Judge Elton Reynolds was not likely to do, he typed a short memo on how he would rule on the issues to give to Judge Reynolds. It said:

> *"The attorney -client privilege is one of the most sacred rules in the legal profession. It exists so a client can feel free to tell his lawyer the honest truth without being afraid the lawyer would be obligated to tell the authorities or the opposition. And I find no exception for law firms.*
>
> *A law firm, like any other defendant, has the right to counsel and to have those conversations protected.*
>
> *But the protection applies only to communications between counsel and the client. So here, the question is how far does the concept*

of counsel go? Without question, it applies to the attorneys actually representing the firm. This gets complex when the firm is representing itself. So a balancing test must be applied. The privilege would apply as to those attorneys who have actual responsibility in the handling of the case, which would be those whose names appear on the pleadings and those assisting them. In this case, that means Derrick Warner and the associates assisting.

The second factor to consider is who constitutes the client? Clearly it is not all of the firm's lawyers. But on balance, I think it would include the members of the Executive Committee responsible for conducting the litigation.

With the above factors in mind, the final inquiry is what communications would be privileged? And here is where the court must weigh the privilege as against the right of the plaintiffs to conduct proper discovery of the facts.

The court concludes, on balance, that the privilege must yield to communications and facts that happened before the lawsuit was filed. Any other answer would deny the plaintiffs the right to find out what happened and why. So the court sustains the objections to communications after the lawsuit was filed, and overrules objections to communications before that date that are relevant to when and why, in this case, Mark Austin left the firm. Any steps by the Executive Committee to investigate what happened would be protected.

On the issue of damages and the firm's income, the court believes that this evidence is protected by the right to privacy until such time as a court or jury finds liability."

The court denies the request for sanctions. The legal issues here are complex and it is reasonable for any counsel to want a court ruling before going forward."

Dillon decided to argue the motion to compel himself. Motions on discovery are often handled by the associates but he knew about Judge Elton Reynolds reputation for not reading legal briefs, and thought his presence might make a difference.

When Dillon arrived at Judge Reynolds's courtroom, he walked up to his clerk and handed her his business card. The clerk, a pole thin gray-haired lady in her late fifties, looked at the card and said, "Mr. Clark, Judge Reynolds is not here this morning. But he took the motion under submission and asked me to tell counsel that he would issue his ruling in a few days."

What the clerk did not say was that when Judge Reynolds got Judge Bannerman's suggested ruling, he handed it to her and told her to type it up as the order. And she had the final order in her desk drawer as she was speaking with Dillon.

Dillon was a little irked at not being told in advance, but he nevertheless smiled and said, "Thank you. Please give the judge my regards."

A week later, a copy of Judge Reynolds's order was received in the mail. Dillon's secretary, Jeannie Davis, had made copies for each attorney. When she saw Kelly Parks walking down the hallway, she said loud enough to catch her attention, "Kelly, the ruling came in on the motion to compel."

Kelly walked over to Jeanne's desk and quickly skimmed the order. As she was reading, she knew immediately that it was in their favor on some of the key issues, but raised a whole bunch of other issues. After a moment, Kelly said, "I'll give Dillon and Laurel their copies."

It was the next day when Dillon, Kelly and Laurel were able to get together. They met in Dillon's office.

"I can understand the judge sort of splitting the baby when a law firm is the defendant, but what about Jerry Keller and Alison Craft?" Kelly Parks asked.

"Good question," Laurel Kennedy replied. "Since they are no longer with the firm, they can't come within the attorney client-privilege except maybe as to Derrick Warner who, at least for now, is representing all of the defendants."

"The worst part of this ruling is that it slams the door shut on us asking about conversations between partners after Mark was fired," Laurel said with frustration. "I mean, what if by chance this was a big frame-up to get rid of Mark? There may have been dozens of conversations between the partners after we filed the lawsuit."

Dillon tapped his pencil on his desk as he thought about the ruling. After a pause, he said, "That part of the ruling is just an attempt to protect the firm. But we have to remember, Keller and Craft are not defendants. We sued the law firm only. So anything they have to say since they left the firm should be open game. And, of course, any conversation they may have had with anyone at the firm after they left would also be discoverable."

"It's still ambiguous," Laurel Kennedy said.

"Well, we're going to have to just see where this leads us," Dillon explained. "Set up a new round of depositions. We'll do Cross and Craft first, but this time lets include Wayne Bailey and Derrick Warner. I know he's the attorney, but he was part of the EC committee that made the decision to fire Mark. And he just may have had conversations with Alison after she left. I don't see any attorney client protection at that point since she is not a defendant."

Kelly laughed and said, "This is great. If they want to claim a privilege with Craft, there're going to have to say they were anticipating a lawsuit and were gathering facts or something that would allow them to ask questions that are protected."

"Interesting thought," Dillon said with a smile.

As the video photographer swore Alison Craft to testify truthfully, Dillon watched her closely. He saw that her hands were shaking slightly and she put them on her lap to steady them. Dillon did not want to add to Suzzi's emotional trauma so she and Mark both stayed away.

When the videographer was ready, Dillon asked, "Miss Craft, I assume you have read Judge Reynolds court order?"

"Yes, I have," Alison Craft answered.

Turning to Derrick Warner, who was still steaming when he learned that Dillon was planning to take his deposition, Dillon said, "Counsel, are we in agreement that I am free to ask any question relating to the issues in this case before the lawsuit was filed:"

Derrick Warner and Harlan Cross had argued over the meaning of Judge Reynolds order and had called Judge Bannerman to ask his understanding. When they explained the areas that were open for questions, Judge Bannerman explained, "Look guys. I wrote that order for Reynolds. God only knows what he would have said. But, yes, they can ask about things before the lawsuit was filed. If I had said no, Dillon Clark would have gone to the appellate court and you could be in real trouble if that happened. Pay attention. That order was written to keep your tit out of trouble. Only you and God know what was said and done after the lawsuit was filed, so be thankful."

"We are in agreement," Derrick Warner replied grimly.

"OK. Miss Craft, my questions today are centered on what happened before we filed this lawsuit and anything you may have said to anyone anywhere after you left the firm," Dillon explained. "Using that time frame, before the lawsuit was filed, did you talk to anyone at Baukus & Johnson about your unhappiness with Mark Austin?"

"No," Alison Craft said. "As I said before, I drafted the memo and sat on it for a while and then gave it to Wayne and the other EC members."

"Were you pressured in any way by anyone in the firm to write the memo?" Dillon asked.

Alison Craft had an odd bewildered expression on her fact as if Dillon was asking some bizarre question that she did not understand. But she then said somewhat hesitantly, "No. Why in the world would you ask something like that?"

Dillon ignored her question and asked, "Did you talk with anyone on the Executive Committee about Mark before they fired him?"

"No," Alison Craft answered.

"So I can be clear, this means the Executive Committee did not talk to you about Mark Austin at any time before the lawsuit was filed?" Dillon asked with growing intensity in his voice.

Alison Craft glanced over at Derrick Warner and replied, "No."

It made no sense to Dillon that the Executive Committee would act solely on Alison Craft's memo, but he decided to leave that subject for now and went on to other areas.

"Miss Craft, when I asked you about talking with anyone at the firm, did you understand that the question also included Jerry Keller, your current partner?" Dillon asked.

"Yes, I did," Alison Craft replied.

"OK. Let's turn to folks outside the firm. Did you talk to anyone outside the firm about Mark Austin before or after the lawsuit was filed?" Dillon asked.

"Mr. Clark," Alison Craft replied irritably, "let me make this clear. I spoke to no one about my views of Mark. I wrote the memo and that was the end of it."

Dillon found Alison Craft's statement incredulous and with intense eye contact asked, "Does that also include Jerry Keller? I mean, you surely at least chatted among yourselves once you learned that he had been fired. Right?"

Alison Craft was not used to being cross-examined and again looked over to Derrick Warner for guidance. He leaned over and whispered something to Alison who then straightened up and said, "Yes, of course we chatted about it. But we never discussed the merits of the firm's decision. And, frankly, I'm really guessing that we even chatted. I actually don't recall any conversation. Jerry and I mostly just talk about our own firm after we left."

When Alison Craft left Dillon's office after her deposition, she rushed back to her office. She tried several times to reach Jerry Keller on her cell phone, but all she got was his answering machine. "Damn," she said to herself. "This is way more than I bargained for!"

After parking her car in the underground garage, Alison Craft quickly walked to the elevator and anxiously punched the button for the sixth floor where she and Jerry Keller had leased space for their new firm. When the elevator door opened, she almost ran across the reception area and down the hallway to Keller's office. When she entered his office he was standing behind his desk packing some papers into his briefcase.

"Jerry, this whole thing with Austin is a mess," Alison Craft blurted out." She was breathing hard and there was tension in her voice.

"Easy does it," Jerry Keller said. "Sit down and tell me what's happened."

As Alison Craft sat down, she said with a slight sigh, "Well… hell I don't know. I just wish I'd never written that memo. I don't think Mark's lawyer believes me. He kept asking if I was pressured into writing it."

"Alison, there's no way he can find out what happened," Jerry Keller said with anxiety now in his voice as well."

"Jerry, what if he does?" Alison Craft asked.

"He won't," Jerry Keller snapped. "Just keep your damn mouth shut."

"Don't snap at me," Alison Craft said in a stiff defensive voice. "Remember, it was your idea that I write that damn thing!"

When Dillon took Jerry Keller's deposition, his testimony was as bland as that given by Alison Craft. He confirmed that he had been upset when Mark was made the billing attorney for the Gibbons accounts, but otherwise got on fine with him. And he confirmed that he and Alison had never spoken about Mark's termination before or after the lawsuit was filed.

But when Dillon asked questions about conversations he may have had with his former partners after he left Baukus & Johnson, things quickly changed.

"Mr. Keller," Dillon asked, "after you left Baukus & Johnson, did you have any conversation with anyone at the firm about Mark Austin's termination?"

"Mr. Clark," Derrick Warner interjected, "while I'm not technically Mr. Keller's counsel, I am objecting to any conversation he may have had after the lawsuit was filed. He may no longer be a partner, but he was when the decision was made and the firm is entitled to do their own in-house investigation in private, so I am advising him that any conversations are protected under the attorney-client privilege."

"Mr. Keller, as Mr. Warner said, he is not your counsel, so I must insist that you answer," Dillon said.

Jerry Keller was not pleased to even be in the deposition and, with lips half parted, he sort of growled his answer. "Next question. I'm taking Derrick's advice."

Dillon knew he was going to get nothing meaningful from Jerry Keller without going back to the court, so he moved on to another area. "Mr. Keller, before the firm terminated Mark Austin, did you talk to the Executive Committee about his termination?"

"Do you mean did I ask them to terminate him?" Jerry Keller asked.

"If you like. Did you?" asked Dillon.

"No. As I said, I got along with Mark fine."

"What about Mark's memo to the Executive Committee asking for a bonus for being the one who brought Gibbons and his companies into the firm?" Dillon asked.

He knew that his anger at Mark Austin for seeking origination credit was well known in the firm, so Jerry Keller decided to play it safe. "The odds are pretty good someone will talk about what I said," he thought to himself.

"You're correct. I was critical of Mark when he sent his memo to the EC asking for a bonus. The partners always intended that Tier Two compensation was for senior partners only. After he sent his memo, we met and decided the agreement was a little vague so we amended it to limit Tier Two to the senior partners," Jerry Keller explained.

Without alerting Jerry Keller that he was changing subjects, Dillon asked forcefully and with a grim expression, "Did you ever tell anyone outside the Baukus firm that Mark Austin was a troublemaker?"

Jerry Keller had read the complaint and understood the allegations and gave Dillon the same answer he gave to Wayne Bailey when he asked. "No. Any comments I made about Mark were limited to his immature action in seeking origination credit."

The deposition of Wayne Bailey was almost a waste of time. Bailey was a member of the Executive Committee that terminated Mark Austin and on virtually every question he asked, Dillon faced a barrage of objections asserting a violation of the attorney-client privilege. The Baukus firm was obviously trying, so far successfully, to hide behind Judge Reynolds's order applying the privilege to everything after the lawsuit was filed.

What Dillon did not know was that the order permitted the firm to stay silent on one critical event. He could never ask the question that would reveal Wayne Bailey's conversation with Jerry Keller about what he said to other law firms where Mark Austin had applied for employment. This conversation happened after the lawsuit was filed and protected.

After the deposition of Jerry Keller, Derrick Warner called a meeting to discuss the firm's strategy on defense. They were cautious about who should attend because Warner had alerted them in private that the ruling by Judge Reynolds might not stand if Dillon were to take it to an appellate court. So the meeting was limited to Warner, Bailey and Harlan Cross, each members of the Executive Committee.

"Harlan," Derrick Warner said, "I can sense that Dillon Clark thinks the termination of Austin was totally bogus. I suspect he also thinks that Keller was lying when he denied involvement."

Turning to Harlan Cross and Wayne Bailey, Derrick Warner asked almost pleadingly, "Did Jerry ever come to either of you and try to get Mark fired?" Looking at Harlan, he added, "I know you had him sit in when we discussed Alison's memo, but was there anything else?"

Harlan Cross hesitated a moment and then said, "I know he was angry about Mark seeking Tier Two money, but that was just about it. I can't recall him ever asking us to actually get rid of him.

As you know, it was Alison's memo that forced our decision. We just can't force someone on a partner."

Derrick Warner was visibly concerned and he got up and walked over to the window and looked out for a brief moment. He finally turned back and said, "We have another problem. Dillon is sharp and knows how much trouble he can cause if I end up testifying at the trial. It would be a joke. One minute I'm the attorney, and another I'm the witness. That would be the ultimate in dumbness, so we're going to have to get new counsel."

Harlan Cross had been thinking of the same problem from a different perspective. He had met with the firm's insurance agent and they agreed that their policy would require their insurance company to give them a defense. It was not the wrongful termination that would get them coverage, but the emotional distress allegation.

"I think you're right," Harlan Cross replied. "In fact, we should be able to get the insurance carrier to defend on the emotional distress issue. I know Austin is alleging intent, but it can arguably also be negligence. They may not pay anything on any judgment, but the cost of the defense would be covered."

Harlan Cross hesitated and then added, "They suggested Jason Haverley. Do you know him Derrick?"

Derrick Warner laughed and said, "Boy do I. He and I crossed swords several years ago. He is about as ruthless as you can find, and that's saying a lot considering the demeanor of most defense counsel."

"But is he good?" Harlan Cross asked. "It is one thing to be ruthless and another to be a good trial lawyer."

"He's both," Derrick Warner replied. "If he's available, I say go for it."

When Dillon received the substitution of counsel form in the mail, he didn't laugh. He too knew Jason Haverley from several skirmishes over the years. When he met with Kelly Parks and Laurel Kennedy, Dillon cautioned them both about what to expect.

"Jason is a tough in the trenches trial lawyer that is dedicated to only one thing and that is winning at any cost. He is exceptional in front of a jury but, more importantly, he cannot be trusted. You can't accept anything he says as true. And I mean that. Nothing. I don't know if he would have a witness knowingly lie, but he sure wouldn't go out of his way to find out."

Kelly and Laurel had never heard such strong words from Dillon describing another lawyer before and they both just sat in silence for a while.

Finally Kelly said, "The firm is already stone-walling us. How much worse can it get?"

"He will be our worst nightmare. So whenever they say something, always ask yourself 'what are they not saying.' I guarantee you will have to dig for every helpful fact," Dillon replied.

CHAPTER 6

On The Eve of Trial
(Monday, December 22)

The life blood of every trial lawyer begins to run faster as soon as the court sets a trial date. It was a slow Tuesday morning when Dillon received the formal notice from the court setting the trial of Austin v. Baukus & Johnson for Monday, December 18.

Dillon was sitting at his desk sipping a cup of coffee when his secretary, Jeannie Davis, came bouncing into his office and handed him the notice. "This is your lucky day, Dillon," Jeannie said with a big smile on her face. "The court set the Austin case for December."

When Dillon saw the date, he inwardly smiled at the coincidence. Mark Austin had been fired on December 22, just a few days before Christmas. He looked over to a photograph of his wife sitting on a book shelf and quietly thought to himself, "So, what do you think. Is this going to be a good Christmas?"

"Let Kelly and Laurel know," Dillon said as he looked back to where Jeannie was still standing. "And be sure to call Mark. They've been waiting a long time for this."

Dillon asked Kelly and Laurel to join him later that day to talk about what they needed to do to prepare for trial. The meeting was in the firm's conference room. Dillon and Laurel were waiting for Kelly when she threw the door open and in a rush of excitement said, "Guess what?"

Dillon was used to Kelly's exuberance but played along. "OK. Spill it. What is it this time?"

"You'll love it. Mark and I talked to Professor Shockley up at Stanford. The one who helped him find you. Anyway, we asked him to call his old student who now runs one of the major firms here in LA, and he agreed. He just called back this morning and gave me the name and telephone of the partner at Goldman and Forrester, who interviewed Mark," Kelly said quickly.

This was a key part of Austin's case and Kelly was deliberately stringing out the story. "Come on, Kelly. What did you find out?" Laurel asked.

"Yes, I thought you might want to know," she said kiddingly. "The man's name is Stanley Smart. I just spoke with him and he said the one who returned his call at the Baukus firm was none other than Jerry Keller. Can you believe that?" Kelly replied.

"So what did he say?" Laurel asked.

"Here's the best part," Kelly said. "Keller told him that Mark was a troublemaker. He described him as a good lawyer but not one to trust."

"Holy shit," Laurel blurted out. "That's retaliating against Mark. We've got them!"

Dillon, too, was excited. He sat upright in his chair, clapped his hands together and said, "Yes, I think you're right. I think you'll find that 'troublemaker' and 'not one to trust' are clearly words that would discourage anyone from hiring Mark." Looking towards Kelly, he added, "Did you ask if that affected their decision to hire Mark?"

"You bet," Kelly replied. "He said they would have hired him for sure if the comments had not been negative. But no firm wants someone who had just been fired and who has been labeled by his old firm as someone who is difficult."

The three sat in silence for a minute thinking over the repercussions of this evidence. Laurel finally said, "Keller was a partner at the Baukus firm when he made those comments, so the firm is on the hook no matter what. But we could now amend the complaint and add Keller as a personal defendant. And who knows, he probably said this to a number of the firms."

Dillon remained seated tapping his pen on the table in front of him as he stared out of the conference room window. He turned back and said, "I don't think it would add much to have him as a personal defendant. The jury instruction will make it clear that the firm is responsible, so we'll just get ready for trial. I do want you to speak with all of the other firms who Mark applied to. Find out if Keller said this more than once. He might even have used different words that make it even worse."

Before the meeting adjourned, Laurel Kennedy asked, "What about the judge? I've never appeared before Judge Harpman."

Dillon smiled and said, "He's a little crotchety, but a fine judge. You'll like him."

What Dillon didn't know was that the Honorable Gerald A. Harpman was also a friend of Jerry Keller.

When Mark Austin and his wife learned of the trial date and that it was Jerry Keller who had bad mouthed Mark, they were both furious, scared and yet anxious to finally see an end to what had been a terrible ordeal that was swamping their relationship.

Mark and Suzzi had been going to a marriage counselor once a week for the past five months. This was in part because Dillon recommended it because they would need expert testimony to show the emotional damages they had, and are continuing to suffer. But it was also for their own sake. After the first few weeks, they were able to open up to the therapist and to themselves about how bad things had become. Mark's ego and how he viewed himself had been devastated. He went from a scholar at Stanford Law School, to a major law firm bringing in a huge new client, to being fired and working for a small firm doing family law. The result was that Mark no longer felt like a man. Although they both thought about it constantly, sex was like a bridge that neither could cross for fear of failure. And in Mark's case, the psychologist explained why he felt so frozen. One more failure was something he could not face.

Dillon had given Mark an outline of what questions he would be asking them at trial and they were sitting at the kitchen table discussing the questions and what was about to happen with the trial.

"Mark, I know this has been hardest on you," Suzzi said in a soft loving voice, "but Dillon is right. What they did to you has for sure screwed up our life more than just financially. We, well, you know. It was over a year before we got back to a normal relationship. Even now, I can see you tense up whenever either one of us wants to get intimate."

They sat in silence for several minutes. It was Mark who found it difficult to talk about their personal life. He finally sighed and looked directly at Suzzi and said with a humorless smile, "I know honey. I, ah, just..."

"Mark, you can do this. Just get angry at what those creeps did," Suzzi said in an irritated voice.

Mark could feel his stomach tighten and little jolts of electricity shoot through his body. He finally took a deep breath and leaned over and whispered, "OK. I know your right. But God, I sure wish this whole thing was over."

The part about being a paralegal that Kelly Parks loved the most was when she was interviewing witnesses. She had a natural talent at putting people at ease when she asked them even difficult questions. And this talent was needed when she called the other law firms that Mark had approached for a position. Law firms, for obvious reasons, are hesitant to get involved with suing other law firms.

But Kelly persisted and five of the firms confirmed that Jerry Keller had one way or another, called Mark a troublemaker and were willing to testify. The other firms declined to talk and asserted that any conversions involved personnel issues and therefore private.

"They're a bunch of weaklings," Kelly told Dillon when she met with him to go over what she had learned.

Dillon was amused when he saw how upset Kelly was that so many of the firms refused to get involved. "Welcome to the big city," he said with a mischievous grin on his face.

Kelly bristled for a brief second and then laughed herself. "Yes, I know," she said. "We have five who will help and that's probably enough anyway."

"The biggest problem we have in this case," Dillon now said with a serious look on his face, "is damages. I've looked over the jury instructions, and unless we can prove bad faith, or some conspiracy to intentionally harm Mark, the jury might just give him a token award."

"That would be terrible," Kelly quickly replied with some alarm. "What about the emotional distress Mark and Suzzi have suffered?"

"This is the area that concerns me most. Mark and Suzzi are going to be on the hot seat on this. It must be intentional and this is tough to prove. We haven't seen any evidence yet that would fall into this category. It is one thing for our shrink to describe what they have suffered, but the jury will want to hear this directly from them. I can see how stressed the topic is for Mark whenever I try to discuss it with him. We're going to have to get him in here and practice his testimony. The last thing we need is for him to down-play what he has been going through."

"What about punitive damages?" Kelly asked. "Intentional in-fliction of emotional distress is a tort and if the jury decides Keller or the firm was malicious, they can make an award based on the wealth of the law firm."

"True enough," Dillon replied. "But malice is a tough standard. They would have to find that they willfully tried to harm Mark, or at least had a reckless disregard for what would happen. The bot-tom line is that a jury has to get really pissed off to award punitive damages," Dillon explained.

Dillon had been giving serious thought to how the defense would handle the trial. Putting himself in the shoes of Jason Haverley, it was not difficult to see a clear picture of what he would be doing. "He'll paint Mark as not being a team player by playing up to Boyd Gibbons and reviewing the billings. If nothing else, this was embarrassing to the partners in charge of the work. A jury just might buy this as showing a man that was a troublemaker. Maybe even not trustworthy. And the killer evidence is Craft's memo. He'll argue that the firm just made a business decision when it was clear Mark would not be a partner," he concluded.

The practice sessions with Mark and Suzzi really worked. Dillon set up a video camera and Kelly taped three different ses-sions so Mark and Suzzi could both watch themselves testify. After the second session, they were both laughing at how "frozen" they both were in the first session and thanked Dillon for his patience.

After the third session, Mark told Dillon and Kelly, "You know Dillon, being a lawyer is actually a negative if you're one of the litigants. We like to think we are so experienced and testifying is easy. But, boy oh boy, that's far from the truth."

Mark was now relaxed and added, "You can't imagine how fast my heart was beating when you first started asking questions?"

Seeing themselves on film was also the best therapy. When Mark and Suzzi left Dillon's office after the last taping session, they drove down to the Santa Monica pier for lunch. They ordered fish sandwiches from one of the fast food stands and walked out to the end of the pier to a bench to eat. Little was said at first, but Suzzi noticed that Mark for the first time since their ordeal started, had a half grin on his face.

"Mark, what are you thinking?" Suzzi asked.

Somewhat hesitantly, Mark replied, "I'm going to call the office and cancel the rest of the day. I think I'd like to just spend the rest of the day with you."

After Jason Haverley took over the defense of Baukus & Johnson, it took him only a few days to speak with every law firm that Mark had approached for a job and he got the same information given to Kelly Parks.

When Jason Haverley met with Harlan Cross and the other members of the Executive Committee, he was blunt and to the point. "You guys must have been drinking something strong to fire a young lawyer based on just one memo from a partner who didn't like him. How the hell do you think this is going to play out in front of a jury?" he said in a booming voice.

Jason Haverley was about six feet five and looked like he had been a line-backer for a professional football team. He had broad shoulders; hair cut short army style, and a voice that sometimes hurt your ears if he got carried away. And whether he was in court or just meeting with clients, as he was this day, he always wore the same tan colored suit, blue shirt and black shoes. The change was his bow ties. He must have had hundreds because no one saw him wear the same one twice.

Harlan Cross looked over and made eye contact with Wayne Bailey before he spoke. They had already had many hours of conversation with Derrick Warner on this same subject and were well aware of the risks.

After a moment, Harlan Cross said, "We understand your concerns. And we're particularly concerned about that prick Keller and what he may have said to other firms. What do you suggest?"

Jason Haverley was an outstanding defense lawyer and lost very few cases. And his wins came for a good reason. He was a master at cross-examining witnesses and could lead a jury to drink even if they weren't thirsty. "Harlan, like it or not, we're going to have to go after Mark Austin and show him up as an opportunist who tried to advance himself past the other associates. The real danger is what Keller told future employers. I don't know what he was thinking when he questioned Mark's trustworthiness, but that is the kind of thing a jury is not going to like. So we have to convince the jury that he really was a troublemaker, whatever that means. And the very ambiguity in the phrase is our best bet. Keller has already said in his deposition that he didn't use those words, but he did describe Mark as immature, which others may have interpreted as meaning a troublemaker. He was referring to his seeking a bonus reserved to the partners and how he insisted on doing the billings."

"But isn't this a two edged sword?" asked Derrick Warner.

"Yes, of course it is," replied Jason Haverley. "But it gives us a good chance with the jury. And we have more. We can show that Keller was justified to alert the other law firms. Remember, when the issue came up about Mark being the billing attorney for the Gibbons's accounts, he willingly stepped in. A responsible associate would have said 'Thank you, but I think someone more senior and experienced should do that.' But Mark didn't say that. He took advantage of the situation and reviewed all of the bills before they were sent out. Why? Because he wanted to be advanced faster than the other associates."

Each of the Executive Committee members sat back in their chairs and smiled. Derrick Warner, as a trial attorney himself, spoke first. "That's a great theme to play on, Jason. We can produce testimony about how huge mistakes can be made in the billing process and how critical it is to have an experienced eye reviewing them."

What Derrick Warner thought, but did not say, was that he never considered taking that approach. "Too damn close to the players," he mumbled to himself. "No one can be their own lawyer and I almost forgot that golden rule."

"That still leaves the memo from Alison Craft," Wayne Bailey interjected.

"I'm not too concerned about that part of the case," Jason Haverley answered. "I think a jury can understand that a partnership cannot force an attorney on a partner who doesn't want to work with that person, no matter how much others liked him. Partnerships are like a big family. Everyone has to trust each other and there has to be a keen sense of loyalty. And this won't be there if the relationship is forced. Fortunately, the evidence is clear that it was Alison Craft's memo that the Executive Committee relied on when they asked Mark to leave."

"What about the intentional conduct claim?" Wayne Bailey asked.

"I think they threw this in to make us nervous," Haverley replied. "I see no evidence of any intentional conduct."

Harlan Cross was normally a fairly cold calculating person, but as he listened to Jason Haverley, he looked irritated. At one point he slammed his pen down on the conference room table and said with considerable vehemence, "I've just been thinking back on Keller. He'd been with the firm for about fifteen years when he left.

And guess what? The two partners he took with him, both Alison and Anderson, were lateral hires just like Keller. And all three have one additional thing in common. Not one of them has any sense of loyalty!"

Wayne Bailey and Derrick Warner both stared at Harlan as the meaning of his words clicked in their heads. Each was thinking 'Yes indeed. Hiring attorneys from other firms, no matter how talented, can be a big mistake. They come without knowing and appreciating the firm's culture and history.'

Wayne Bailey nodded his head and said, "I agree, Harlan. We need to be more careful in how and who we hire in the future. Sometimes we get too fancy and try to hire experienced attorneys. But I think we'd be far better off if we stuck with young lawyers and let them grow within the firm. Just like each of us and most of the other partners."

The strategy session was in the firm's main conference room and when the session ended, Harlan Cross invited Jason Haverley to stay and join the others in a drink. When they each had their glasses filled, Cross offered a toast. "To our continued success!"

"Here, here," Wayne Bailey and Derrick Warner said as they clinked glasses.

Two days before the trial was due to start, Dillon was at his home in the hills overlooking Santa Monica. He had been working with Laurel Kennedy and Kelly Parks for most of the day getting their jury instructions ready and going over the final witness list and deciding when each witness would testify.

Dillon was sitting at his kitchen table looking out over the Pacific Ocean sipping his favorite Macallan single malt scotch. This happened to be the sixteen year old version and was a burnt brown in color and had a strong earthy taste. As he reflected on the day and the trial that was about to start, his mind wandered back to his deceased wife. A few days before every trial was to begin, he and his wife would talk over the issues and she had an uncanny sense of what a jury would like and not like. "This is going to be a tough one, honey. I sure wish you could give me some of your wisdom," he said to himself.

Dillon started to ask his wife a question when he caught himself and realized she was not there. "Damn," he said out loud in frustration as he walked over to the kitchen counter and refilled his glass.

Dillon had learned quickly after his wife's death that the brightness of life had somehow grown darker with her absence. Things that they had especially enjoyed doing together, he now avoided; and even the things he did do, he did without the joy that comes from sharing things with someone special. As he took another sip of scotch, his vision blurred slightly and with a sigh he said, "I sure miss you, partner."

CHAPTER 7

Judicial Interference
(Tuesday, December 23)

The courtroom of Judge Gerald Harpman is located on the sixth floor of the Los Angeles County Superior Court building adjacent to the Music Center and the new Walt Disney Concert Hall in downtown Los Angeles. It is getting on in years but it is still one of the busiest courthouses in the United States.

Dillon parked his car in the underground parking garage beneath the Music Center and walked through the tunnel that connects the parking area to the courthouse. Kelly Parks would be assisting him in the Austin trial and she had gone ahead earlier to help the court clerk get their exhibits marked. They had filed their trial brief two days earlier.

When Dillon reached the courthouse, he had to go through the typical security check which is set up at every entrance. He put his briefcase on the conveyor belt that took it through the x-ray machine, emptied his pockets into a bowl and sent it through as well and slowly walked through the scanner under the watchful eye of a security guard. He learned a long time ago not to walk fast. That was one sure way for the machine to go crazy and you had to start all over.

When Dillon successfully got through security, he took the elevator up to the sixth floor and walked down the hallway to courtroom 52 where Judge Gerald Harpman had his chambers. When he entered, he saw Kelly Parks standing next to the clerk's desk. She was talking with the judge's clerk.

When Kelly saw Dillon, she waved him forward. "Dillon, I'd like you to meet Charmaine Parker. Funny coincidence, but she's also going to Loyola Law School in the night program."

"My pleasure," Dillon said as he reached out to shake her hand. "Is the judge all set to start?"

"He is, Mr. Clark. We're just waiting for the other parties. When they get here, the judge wants to talk to the attorneys in chambers before he calls in a jury panel," Charmaine Parker explained.

As Dillon and Kelly were talking, Mark Austin and his wife entered the courtroom. Kelly took an involuntary gulp of air at what she saw. Mark, on a normal day, looked a little rumpled, but today he had gone over the line. He looked like he had literally slept in his suit coat. His tie was half undone and as he walked up the courtroom isle, the heels of his shoes scraped the carpet as if he did not have the strength to pick up his feet.

"Mark, what happened?" Kelly said somberly. The last time she saw Mark was at the end of the final practice session and he looked relaxed and confident.

When he heard Kelly, Dillon looked up from his notes and saw the same thing. "Mark, are you ok?" he asked with concern.

Suzzi Austin was holding Mark's hand and before he could answer, she said in a voice so low that she was almost whispering, "Mark hasn't slept in two days. All he does is think about this case and how embarrassing it's going to be to talk about what his firing has done to us personally."

"Kelly, you stay here and call me when the judge is ready," Dillon said quickly. "We're going next door to the attorney conference room." As he said this, he reached out and touched Mark's arm motioning for him to come with him.

When they got to the attorney conference room, Dillon had Mark and his wife sit down at the small conference table. There are dozens of these small conference rooms scattered throughout the courthouse where attorneys can meet and talk with a client or witness during a trial.

"Mark, I know this is a tough time, but you've got to get yourself under control. God only knows what a jury might think if they saw you looking like, well, like you do right now," Dillon said with firmness.

Suzzi Austin started to cry and as she reached into her purse for a handkerchief, she looked over at Mark, shook her head in frustration and said, "I've tried, Mr. Clark. But this whole thing about our sex life just pushed him over the edge. Our therapist has been working on this for weeks, but I think it may have just made things worse. Mark doesn't even want to talk about it with me!"

Dillon sat silent for a moment and then said with obvious concern on his face, "Mark, take Suzzi up to the cafeteria. It's on the top floor. I want you to get a grip on yourself. Go to the men's room and tidy yourself up and then just relax. I'll tell the judge you aren't feeling well and you can come back after we start picking the jury."

Mark's shoulders sagged as he reached over and squeezed Suzzi's hand. The paralysis that he felt kept him from saying anything and he just nodded his head as he and Suzzi stood and walked out of the courtroom.

While Dillon was talking with Mark and his wife, Judge Gerald A. Harpman was in his chambers talking with two fellow superior court judges about the Austin case. Judge Dale Bannerman was the Presiding Judge of the Los Angeles Superior County Court and a former senior partner at Baukus & Johnson. He was in his late sixties, had snow white hair cut short and was talking in an animated high-pitched voice.

"Jerry, you've got to be careful with this Austin case. One of the finest law firms in the city has its reputation at stake and we need to be absolutely sure they did something wrong before this case gets to a jury. We all know that juries can do crazy things even if the judge carefully instructs them on the law," Judge Bannerman said with concern.

Judge Harpman was sympathetic to what Judge Bannerman was saying. The Baukus & Johnson firm was one of the oldest firms in Los Angeles and had a sterling reputation. And he knew of course that Judge Bannerman had been a partner of the firm for many years before he was appointed to the bench. As he sat listening, he was thinking to himself about a jury that just came in last week with a verdict a hundred times what even the plaintiff had requested. "Being careful is an understatement," he thought to himself.

The second man was Judge Henry Paulger who also had been a partner at Baukus & Johnson. Judge Paulger was still in his early fifties and had been a last minute appointment by the former outgoing Governor five years back. He was short, about five feet six, had light brown hair, yellowy-brown eyes and skin that was almost white. He obviously did not favor sunshine.

"I agree," Judge Paulger said. "The critical issues in the case have already been ruled on by Judge Reynolds. I've looked over his rulings and he seems to be right on the law. Most of what Clark was trying to get in discovery is protected by the attorney-client privilege. If we're going to be consistent, the same rulings should control the trial evidence."

"I appreciate your concerns, gentlemen," replied Judge Harpman. "I've read over Reynolds's rulings." He paused and then added reflectively, "And I agree we need to be consistent. Exactly what is protected by the attorney-client privilege is fuzzy at best when a law firm is the defendant and one of the attorneys is also representing the firm. We'll have to see how the evidence plays out during the trial, but I think we can start with the premise that the attorney- client privilege protects any conversations once the lawsuit was filed."

The conversation between the three judges went on for a while. They all knew that they were breaking a number of ethical rules by talking about the case without the knowledge of the parties and their attorneys. But they also knew no one would find out.

Finally, as Judge Bannerman and Judge Paulger were about to leave, Judge Harpman leaned back in his leather swivel chair and said, "I suppose the best way to get the evidence flushed out early is to have the attorneys address the evidence in motions to exclude certain evidence before the trial starts."

Judge Harpman and Judge Paulger looked at each other and nodded their approval. What no one told Judge Harpman was that it was Judge Bannerman who wrote the order for Judge Reynolds.

After his conference with his fellow judges, Judge Harpman buzzed his clerk. "Charmaine, are the attorneys all here and ready?" he asked.

"Yes, judge," Charmaine Parker replied. "The defense counsel, Jason Haverley, just arrived. His client will be here later."

"Have them come in," Judge Harpman said.

When Dillon and Jason Haverley were escorted into Judge Harpman's chambers, they both walked up and greeted the judge and took seats in front of his huge black oak desk. Dillon mused to himself, "This must have come from his old law firm. Far too rich for a government desk."

"Gentlemen, I don't think we've had any prior dealings so we can skip that part. But I've been reading over the trial briefs and the orders by Judge Reynolds, and I think we can have a more efficient trial if we get some of the evidence objections sorted out before the trial starts. So I'm not going to pick a jury today. By tomorrow, I want each of you to file any motions you have to exclude evidence of any kind. I want to get this out of the way before we start so the jury doesn't have to sit and waste time. We'll argue the motions tomorrow morning at 9:00 a.m. Any objections?"

As he sat listening to Judge Harpman, Dillon realized his gut had tightened like a fist. "Damn it to hell, he's going to jam the rulings from Reynolds down our throat," he said to himself.

After the conference in chambers with Judge Harpman, Dillon and Kelly hurriedly left the courtroom and took the elevator up to the cafeteria on the top floor. As they approached the table where Mark and his wife were seated, they could see that Suzzi was very animated in whatever she was telling Mark. As they got closer, Dillon could hear her say, "Mark, you can't just quit. That's like, well, that's like saying those bastards were right in firing you!"

When Suzzi saw Dillon and Kelly, she stood up and said, "You talk to him, Mr. Clark. He won't listen to me. He just doesn't want to testify in front of the jury."

As Dillon and Kelly pulled up chairs and sat down, it was plain to see that Mark had not taken Dillon's advice. His hair was still a mess, his clothes looked rumpled and he just sat looking out into space but seeing nothing.

"Mark, I can't say I really know how you feel," Dillon said, "but what I can say is that you've never been a quitter your whole life and this for sure is not the time to start. You know as well as I that the firm treated you badly."

When Mark did not respond, Dillon hesitated and then leaned in closer and said, "Mark, my wife had a little sign that she always had hanging on her kitchen wall. It said, 'Snap out of it!' And it worked for her. Whenever she got down, she would look at that sign, sometimes chuckle at herself and the next thing I would see was a smile. It is amazing what happens when you just put things into perspective, Mark. Here we are at the start of your trial. And I say 'your trial' for a reason. This is your chance to show that the mighty lawyers over at Baukus and Johnson were wrong. Just take a deep breath and let the jury decide this thing."

Everyone sat in silence, each in their own way holding their breath to see how Mark would respond. After what seemed like an eternity, Mark looked up at Dillon and said in a shaky voice, "I'm sorry Dillon. I know you're right. It's not you asking me a question that scares me. It's that Jason Haverley and what he might ask."

Mark looked over at Suzzi and then at Kelly and back to Dillon. It was all that Kelly could do to not let a few tears flow seeing the pain in his face. Keeping her voice low she reached over and lightly touched his arm and said, "Mark, every woman and man on that jury will understand how you feel and why you don't want to talk about how these defendants have destroyed your sex life with your wife. They would feel exactly the same way. I know I would. But that will just add to the importance of what you will be saying. None of this would ever have happened if you hadn't been fired."

Kelly's words seemed to finally sink in. Mark reached over and took his wife's hand in his, took a deep breath and said, "I sure hope you're right."

Dillon cleared his throat a little and in a back-to-business sort of way said, "Mark, we need to take some of the anxiety out of this for you. The judge is not going to call the jury until the day after tomorrow, so that means we have some time. If you're up to it, I want you and Suzzi to both work with Kelly and Laurel back at the office. They will both play the role of Haverley and ask you over and over the worst kinds of questions they can think of about what has happened to your sex life. I want you to tell the story so many times that you can do it in your sleep. OK?"

"This whole thing makes me feel like a wimp," Mark replied in a soft low voice that was hard to hear. "Hell, I'm a lawyer. I shouldn't be this sensitive."

Dillon laughed and said, "Well, Mark, most folks may not think so, but the last time I looked, lawyers are people, too."

As expected, Jason Haverley filed a motion asking the court to exclude any questions that would violate Judge Reynolds's prior ruling that protected many conversations under the attorney-client privilege. This, for lawyers, is technically called a motion "in limine" which asks the court to make certain rulings before the trial starts.

After Dillon and Jason Haverley argued the issues, Judge Harpman said, "Gentlemen, I know this is just the start of a difficult trial. But we can't have inconsistent rulings. So I've decided to stay with the limitations that Judge Reynolds placed on discovery. This means, when the trial starts next week, no questions can be asked about conversations between members of the Executive Committee and any lawyer representing the firm once the lawsuit was filed."

Judge Harpman looked directly at Dillon as if to make sure he was listening and said, "Mr. Clark, do you understand the order?"

"Unfortunately, I do," Dillon replied. "But to be clear, I believe I am free to ask about conversations between members of the Executive Committee and anyone else in the firm that occurred before the lawsuit was filed as they may have relevance to the events that led up to the firm firing Mark Austin."

"Yes, that is correct, Mr. Clark," Judge Harpman agreed.

"But I have to respectfully object to any limitation on conversations between the Executive Committee members that involve the facts," Dillon argued. "And by that I mean conversations about why Austin was fired. If you don't let us pursue these questions, you are essentially blocking our ability to ask the witnesses why they fired him."

"Mr. Clark," Judge Harpman replied, "I'm not blocking you at all. You can ask any of these questions relating to conversations before the lawsuit was filed. At that point, no attorney-client relationship existed. But not later when you have attorneys on the Committee, namely Mr. Warner, representing the firm."

"Your Honor, I cannot disagree more," Dillon replied with a slightly raised voice. "They could easily be talking about the facts after the lawsuit. Any member of the Committee could, hypothetically, admit that they had no basis to fire Austin, or that Jerry Keller, for example, pressured them into firing him. Your ruling blocks us from even finding out if such valuable evidence exists. You know, in any other case, we would always be entitled to get to all of the facts at any point in time."

"You may be right in a normal civil case, Mr. Clark," Judge Harpman said, "but this case is unique. Mr. Warner was both a member of the Committee and the defense counsel."

"What about conversations between other members of the Executive Committee without Mr. Warner or other counsel present?" Dillon doggedly asked.

Judge Gerald Harpman looked at Dillon with a cold stare and said, "Enough, Mr. Clark. My ruling stands. Let's move on."

Jason Haverley had been quiet during Dillon's debate with the judge. But now he interjected, "Your Honor, I have one further question. The Executive Committee is the key contact with defense counsel. So I think that any investigation that they did after the lawsuit was filed would also be protected."

Judge Harpman knew the dangers of going too far in prohibiting what attorneys can ask during a trial before it even starts and, with a raised eyebrow he said, "Mr. Haverley, I'm not going to fine tune this any further. I'll address any other evidentiary objections as the trial progresses. My rulings apply only to the attorney-client privilege between those representing the law firm and their attorneys."

As Dillon and Jason Haverley were picking up their papers and getting ready to leave, Judge Harpman added with an irritable tone in his voice, "Gentlemen, the issue of liability in this case is, shall we say, up in the air. So I'm also going to bifurcate the issue of damages. The jury will first determine liability. Of course, if they find none, the case is over. If they do, we will then proceed to hear the evidence on damages. We'll start picking the jury tomorrow morning. Any questions?"

Dillon knew this was going to happen from prior conversation with the court, but it still grated on him. A jury can often find liability in a close case because they get agitated over the emotional damages that a plaintiff has suffered. Without hearing the damage evidence, the jury must determine liability just on the facts leading up to the termination, and nothing more.

As they were leaving Judge Harpman's chambers, he added as an afterthought, "Gentlemen, with Christmas coming up, we'll start the trial Monday, January 4. Enjoy the holiday."

By the time Dillon drove back to his office, he was good and mad. He quickly walked past the receptionist and into his office and slammed the door shut. His secretary, Jeannie Davis, knew his moods well and buzzed Laurel Kennedy. "You better go in and see what happened. He's madder than a hornet right now."

When Laurel got to Dillon's office and knocked on the door, Dillon snapped, "Come in!"

As Laurel entered, she saw Dillon standing next to the window looking out with his hands clasped behind his back. "What happened?" she asked apprehensively.

Dillon turned around and went back to his desk and sat down with an audible sigh. "The good news is we don't start now until January 4. The bad news is that Judge Harpman stuck with the rulings by Judge Reynolds. I half-expected this. But he then bifurcated damages. This could be serious. You know as well as I do that a jury might just think a law firm has a right to fire an associate if a senior partner says she doesn't want him as a partner."

Before Laurel could speak, Dillon slammed his fist down on his desk and with visible anger added, "Jason Haverley is no dummy. He'll play this to the hilt. I can hear him now. 'You can't force someone on a partnership that is not liked by every partner. This goes to the heart of a partnership. The very word 'partner' means they have trust and faith in each other.' Hell, we could just lose this case!"

Laurel had been with Dillon for a number of years and knew to just let him blow-off some steam. After a few minutes of silence, she said, "We still have a good case. Mark was doing excellent work and he landed a terrific new client for the firm. I don't see how the jury could find good cause for a firing."

Dillon looked up and smiled. He loved attorneys who saw the positive things in cases and didn't just dwell on the problem areas. "Yes, we do have a good case," he said, "but on a scale of one to ten, our case on pure liability is at best a six. This means the jury could go either way. If they could see how badly the firing has affected Mark's life, we would be at an eight or nine. A fifty-fifty chance is not goods odds in any case."

Laurel fidgeted a little in her chair before she replied. "I've been working up the jury instructions, and I think our strongest point is to argue that Baukus & Johnson violated the covenant of good faith and fair dealing. I'll give you copies later today in case the judge asks for the instructions early. The instruction makes it clear that an employer must treat an employee fairly, and I see no exception just because the employer is a law firm. In fact, that may even be to our advantage."

Dillon put up his hands in a manner of surrender and said, "You're right. Thanks for the reality check. This has always been a case of what is fair. The firm has one solid witness in Alison Craft and her memo to the Executive Committee. We'll soon find out if a jury thinks that the negative opinion of one partner is enough to justify firing a promising young associate."

Dillon, Laurel and Kelly met later that afternoon in the firm's conference room to finalize the jury instructions. When they moved into the new office space, Dillon had a cabinet installed which held various kinds of liquor, including his favorite Macallan scotch. The whole cabinet looked like an innocent coat closet to anyone who did not know what was hidden behind the fine paneled oak doors.

When Dillon entered the conference room, he saw that Laurel and Kelly had the instructions laid out on the conference room table. He walked over to the liquor cabinet and poured a little Macallan into a glass. He had an English friend that always berated him for putting ice into his glass. "Good scotch is to be consumed at room temperature. That's the way it was made," his friend said. So instead, he put only one small ice cube in the glass, swirled it around a bit and took a sip and walked back over to the table and sat down.

Laurel handed Dillon the instruction on the Covenant of Good Faith and said, "The law firm has no personnel manual that applies to associates, so I think the judge will have to give the jury this instruction. This is what we talked about this morning. As you know, the law is quite different if they had a manual that said the employment relationship was 'at-will.' This would have allowed the firm to fire Mark without any valid reason."

Dillon took the instruction from Laurel and carefully read the wording. It says:

> "*The plaintiff, Mark Austin, claims that the defendant law firm, Baukus & Johnson, violated the duty to act fairly and in good faith. To establish this claim, Austin must prove all of the following:*
>
> 1. *That Austin and Baukus & Johnson entered into an employment relationship;*
>
> 2. *That Austin substantially performed his duties unless his performance was excused or prevented;*
>
> 3. *That Baukus & Johnson terminated him which prevented him from receiving the benefits that he was entitled to have received under the contract;*
>
> 4. *That Baukus & Johnson's conduct was a failure to act fairly and in good faith; and*
>
> 5. *That Austin was harmed by the conduct of Baukus & Johnson.*
>
> *Both parties to an employment relationship have a duty not to do anything that prevents the other party from receiving the benefits of their agreement. Good faith means honesty of purpose without any intention to mislead or to take unfair advantage of another. Generally speaking, it means being faithful to one's duty or obligation."*

Dillon sat silent for several minutes as he pondered the evidence that would come out at the trial and he finally said thoughtfully, "This is the key, Laurel. The judge will have to give this instruction. The rest is up to the jury."

"We also have the emotional distress cause of action," Kelly interjected as she handed a copy of that instruction to Dillon. "I know the evidence is thin, but the jury just might not believe Alison Craft or Jerry Keller. We have several attorneys who will say Keller said Mark was a troublemaker and questioned his trustworthiness."

"I know," Dillon replied. "And thin may just be a wishful description. If I were Haverley, I wouldn't even question whether Keller said it or not. He's a very courtroom savvy guy and I'd bet my house right now that he's going to say this statement is actually true. He'll paint Mark as a troublemaker when he insisted on doing the billings for the Gibbons's accounts, knowing that a partner would have to go over them anyway."

Dillon took another sip of scotch and added, "This is at best another fifty-fifty shot with the jury!"

They all three now sat in silence, each contemplating how a jury would perceive the evidence. Dillon finally rubbed his hands together and said, "OK. Good job everyone. How is Mark holding up? Have you had a chance to grill him yet?"

"We had our first session set up for this afternoon, but we are now starting tomorrow morning," replied Kelly. "I get to be Haverley. Laurel and I had cooked up a set of pretty hard questions on what happened with their sex life. I only had a chance to check in with Suzzi, but she thought Mark was ready."

They all three stared at each other for a moment and Laurel then added, "Time will tell if Suzzi is right. And a few prayers might help."

After Dillon and Jason Haverley left his chambers that day, Judge Harpman reached over and picked up his telephone and dialed the number for the direct line to Judge Dale Bannerman. When Judge Bannerman answered, he said, "Just a short update, Dale. The damage phase is bifurcated so Dillon won't be able to put into evidence any of the emotional and financial damage testimony. Without this, he'll have a hell of a time convincing a jury on liability."

"Thanks, Jerry," Judge Bannerman replied. "Let me know how the case is going once you get started."

When Judge Bannerman hung up his telephone, he pulled out his Apple smart phone and called his old partner, Harlan Cross. Cross answered on the second ring. "This is Dale, Harlan. The trial starts on Monday, January 4 and Harpman bifurcated the damages. And he's sticking to what Judge Reynolds ruled on the attorney-client privilege. This is about the best we can do. Good luck."

Harlan Cross smiled and said, "Thanks, Dale. I owe you one."

After Harlan Cross hung up the telephone, he dialed his secretary and had her ask Wayne Bailey and Derrick Warner to join him in his office. When they arrived they saw that Cross was smiling.

"Have a seat, gentlemen," Harlan Cross said. "It must be five o'clock somewhere in the world. Anyone for a drink?"

Harlan Cross was an old time whiskey drinker and the bar in his office was stocked with some of the best money can buy. He also was not shy of letting clients know he favored old whiskies and those he did well by frequently bought some really old bottles. One was an old Crown Royal that had been bottled in the early nineteen-hundreds. But for some reason he never offered to share that bottle.

After they all were seated with their favorite drinks, Cross conveyed the good news. "I heard from Dale earlier today. He said

Judge Harpman bifurcated the Austin trial so the jury has to first find liability before damages evidence can even be heard. He thinks that without the emotional damages evidence, the jury should go our way."

Derrick Warner asked, "Don't get cocky, Harlan. Dillon Clark is an experienced and smart trial lawyer. We've checked him out in detail and he's won some major damage awards for his clients."

"I understand," Cross replied. "I read your report on him. But we have a clean and simple basis for asking Mark to leave. Once Alison raised her objections, we had no choice. And thanks to Dale, Judge Harpman will be running a tight ship in the liability phase."

"Are you going to attend the trial?" Wayne Bailey asked Cross.

"I'll be there most of the time. I have clients to deal with, but Jason said he can explain to the court and jury that I will be coming in and out. He's done this many times and everyone understands," Cross replied.

"Have you talked with Alison or Jerry about the case?" Derrick Warner asked.

"I've talked with Alison a few times, but Jerry is his usual self. If I call the firm, they just say he's not in. When I try his cell, he no doubt sees my name as the caller and lets it go to voice mail," Cross explained.

Derrick Warner paused before he added, "Well, we have the deposition testimony of both of them. So we know already what they will be saying when they testify, so I don't see any problems."

As the meeting ended, Cross, Warner and Bailey all raised their glasses and Cross said with a rapacious smile, "Here's to Mark Austin. May he enjoy what he is about to receive."

CHAPTER 8

The Trial Begins – Day One
(Monday, January 4)

A trial can be a scary thing for any litigant. You can huff and puff with lots of bravado during pre-trial proceedings, but when the trial judge brings in a panel of fifty or more prospective jurors, every person involved, including the lawyers, understand that their fate will be decided by the final twelve jurors who are fortunate or unfortunate to be selected. And this brings a fear factor into play. All lawyers know, even if they are not trial lawyers, that juries can do very crazy things and often decide cases on things that catch their attention but have nothing to do with the real issues. This is why a good trial lawyer will only go to trial when all other options at settlement have been exhausted.

When Dillon and Mark attended the final mandatory settlement conference, it lasted all of thirty minutes. Jason Haverley was adamant that Baukus & Johnson had done nothing wrong and offered zero to settle.

Dillon was thinking of this hard line defense tactic as he, Mark and Suzzi walked from the parking garage under the Music Center to the Los Angeles County Superior Court building across the street. It was Monday and Judge Harpman's clerk and told them he would be pulling in a panel of jurors at 9:30 a.m.

Dillon knew that Mark and his wife were nervous, but this was standard in any case. Both Laurel and Kelly had worked with them over the weekend for over ten hours going over their testimony and questions they thought Jason Haverley would ask, and they were as ready as they could be to testify.

As they approached the elevator to go up to Judge Harpman's courtroom, Dillon stopped, looked directly at Mark and said, "This is your big day, Mark. I know you're nervous. But this is a natural feeling. Just take a deep breath and relax." He paused for a second and added, "Actually, except when you're each testifying, just sit back and watch the jurors and witnesses like you would a good show on your television." Dillon hesitated and then, looking at both Mark and Suzzi, added, "And always remember, the jurors will be watching you as well, so relax and let them know you have absolutely nothing to hide. And take notes if you want. Either one of you may see something that I might miss. This is also why Kelly will be with us during most of the trial. She'll be watching the jurors as well."

As they approached Judge Harpman's courtroom, Dillon stopped and pulled Mark and Suzzi off to the side and said, "There's one final point. Don't let yourself get caught up staring at the jury. Most of the time I want you watching the witnesses, but you can casually look over at the jury to see how they are reacting to the witnesses when I'm the one asking questions. And especially watch and let me know if they take notes at any point. This usually indicates they think something is important."

Mark, while nervous, actually looked calm and ready. "Hard work in preparing for a trial often does wonders," Dillon thought to himself as they entered the courtroom. No one noticed that he had his fingers crossed.

When Dillon and the others entered the courtroom, Dillon saw that they were the only ones there except the clerk. Dillon walked up to the clerk and said, "Good morning, Charmaine. Are we ready to go?"

"Yes sir," Charmaine Parker replied. "The jury will be here in about thirty minutes. But the judge wants to see counsel as soon as you are all here."

Jason Haverley arrived a few minutes later and he and Dillon were taken back to Judge Harpman's chambers by his clerk. When they entered, Judge Harpman smiled and said, "Well, gentlemen. Are we all ready to pick the jury?

When both Dillon and Jason Haverley said yes, Judge Harpman nodded and said, "Good. Tell your folks we'll take ten minutes to use the bathroom or whatever and we'll start. I want to have a jury selected by noon if possible, so there will be no mid-morning break."

The jury selection process is at best a gamble. Trial lawyers often select or dismiss jurors based on a gut feeling that they will be fair or that they will favor their side of the case. But it for sure is not a science.

It actually only took two hours to pick the jury. The final panel, plus one alternate, consisted mostly of women. There were eight women and four men. The alternate was a woman. Alternates listen to the evidence but they only step in as a final juror if one of the other jurors gets sick or is dismissed for some reason.

Dillon liked the panel. They were all working folks or housewives with a working spouse and he thought they would be sympathetic to Mark's firing without a real cause. But no matter how confident he might be in the jury panel, Dillon knew the risks. The thing that always fascinated him in selecting a jury was the reality that his opposing counsel also liked the same twelve good citizens! "So who is going to be right?" Dillon thought to himself.

As the panel was sworn in by the clerk, Dillon leaned over and whispered to Mark, "This is as good a panel as we could have asked for. Any last thoughts?"

"Is it proper for me to tell you to 'break a leg'" Mark asked in a feeble attempt at humor.

Once the jurors were selected, Judge Harpman recessed the trial for lunch. Dillon and Mark joined Kelly and Suzzi and they took the elevator up to the roof top cafeteria. Once they had ordered and were seated with their food, Kelly said, "I think you have a good jury, but they seem to be looking at Mark more than Harlan. Is this good or bad?"

"No way to really tell," Dillon replied. "Jurors are funny. They sometimes think they can tell who is telling the truth by watching the witness's facial expressions, or if their hands are shaking, or their feet are tapping nervously. You just can't tell at this point."

Dillon turned and looked at Mark and said, "Remember Mark, lean back in your chair and try to relax a little and look at the witnesses when they are testifying. And look over at the jury once in a while so they know you feel they are important."

"I'll try, Mr. Clark. But I just keep thinking my whole life is at stake here and, well, I guess I'm afraid to look too closely," Mark explained with apprehension written all over his face.

When they all returned to the courtroom, Judge Harpman was already sitting on the judge's bench. When the jurors were all seated in their proper places in the jury box, he looked over at the attorneys and then the jurors and explained, "Ladies and gentlemen, this case has been bifurcated. This simply means you will be asked to determine the issue of liability first. If you find the defendant liable on either or both of plaintiff's two causes of action, one for wrongful termination and one for emotional distress, we will then move into the damage phase. So for now, counsel for each party will give you a brief summary of what they intend to prove."

Dillon had Mark seated with him at the plaintiff's table and Suzzi, by agreement, sat in the audience with Kelly.

Dillon was wearing his typical dark blue suit, white shirt and a pale yellow tie. And he had his good-luck suspenders that he had been wearing when in trial for over twenty years. When asked why, he would just shrug his shoulders and say, "You never know!"

Since this was a case where a lawyer was suing a law firm, it was decided that Mark should also dress business-like. He was wearing a blue blazer, light grey slacks, white shirt and a striped red and blue tie. Typical dress for a young lawyer.

"Are you ready, Mr. Clark?" Judge Harpman asked.

With this Dillon rose slowing from his chair, looked over at Mark and said, "Yes, Your Honor. We're ready."

Dillon walked over to the speaker podium that sat between the two counsel tables and took a long thirty seconds looking at each juror. He leaned slightly forward toward the jury and in a voice that was low and soft, he said, "Ladies and gentleman, before we get into the details of this case, I would like to introduce my two clients. To my right is Mark Austin. Mark, would you please stand."

When Mark was standing, Dillon turned to the audience and said, "Suzzi, would you please stand." As she stood, he said, "This is Suzzi Austin, Mark's wife."

As he turned back facing the jury, Dillon continued. "The evidence in this case is fairly simple. You will hear Mark Austin and others tell you how the defendant law firm, Baukus & Johnson, wrongfully terminated Mark and, in doing so, breached that sacred obligation of any employer which is to act fairly and in good faith. You will hear that Mark excelled in his work and through his personal effort, he was responsible for the defendants gaining Floyd Gibbons and five of his companies as clients. A client, I might add, who has paid the defendants millions of dollars in legal fees. And for this great work, he was made a junior partner of the firm. And Wayne Bailey, a member of the Executive Committee, told him to write a memo requesting a bonus at year end because of his great work."

Dillon paused and again looked over at Mark. After a brief silence, he continued. "So far so good, right? Well, not really. Mark Austin was called up to meet with the Executive Committee of the law firm. He was excited and was thinking he was going to get a new terrific assignment. The day, incidentally, was December 22, three days before Christmas. But instead of a terrific new assignment or a pat on the back, he was fired!" These last words were said not in a soft low voice, but harshly.

Dillon took a deep breath and he now looked over at Harlan Cross, who was seated next to Jason Haverley at the counsel table. "Ladies and gentlemen, the evidence is clear that this shocking conduct was the result of one single memorandum from a partner, Alison Craft, who said she did not think Mark Austin was partner material. And worse yet, the Executive Committee didn't even bother to talk to Alison to find out if this fine young attorney could be salvaged. Judge Harpman will instruct you later on the law, and he will tell you that good faith means honesty of purpose without taking unfair advantage of an employee."

Jason Haverley stood and said, "I have to object, Your Honor. Mr. Clark is arguing the law in his opening statement."

Judge Harpman looked over at Dillon, but before he could say anything, Dillon said, "My apologies, Your Honor. Counsel is correct. We will get to the law in our final arguments on liability."

Directing his attention back to the jury, Dillon said, "After Mark was fired, you will hear Mark Austin tell you about his numerous efforts to find a position with another firm, and how no one ever called him back. But there is an explanation. You will hear from a few partners from the firms he applied to, and they will say that when they called the Baukus & Johnson firm for information, they spoke to Jerry Keller who told them that Mark was a trouble-maker and questioned his trustworthiness."

Dillon looked over at the entire jury panel and with a confident smile on his face concluded his opening statement by saying, "Ladies and gentlemen, this is not a complex case. We have one cause of action which alleges that the Baukus & Johnson law firm wrongfully terminated Mark Austin. And we have a second cause of action that alleges the firm intended to cause Mark severe emotional distress. Judge Harpman will later explain to you what constitutes a wrongful termination, so for now I will just say that the law forbids an employee from being fired if in doing so, the employer did not act fairly and in good faith. And in this case, the Baukus & Johnson law firm failed to act in good faith and that is wrongful termination. And by their conduct, they intended to cause Mark harm. Thank you."

Judge Harpman took a brief recess and when everyone returned, Jason Haverley gave his opening statement. As Dillon had predicted, Haverley told the jurors of Alison Craft's memo about Mark Austin not being partner material, and that it was her memo that caused the Executive Committee to ask Mark to leave. He denied that bad faith played any role. He put the issue as a pure business decision that was as much for Mark's benefit as the firm's.

As he sat listening to Haverley, Dillon glanced over at Mark. He was sitting as stiff as a statue, just staring at the back wall of the courtroom. "He must be going through hell right now," Dillon thought to himself." They had spent hours talking about the Craft memo and how the jury could easily decide, right or wrong, that it was a reasonable basis to ask Mark to leave.

As Dillon's mind was half-thinking about the jury, he heard Haverley pound away at why Mark was asked to leave. He carefully avoided using the word "fired."

Haverley said in his typically loud voice. "You will hear the partners at Baukus & Johnson explain why they asked Mr. Austin to leave. Harlan Cross, the firm's managing partner will explain that in addition to Ms. Craft's memo to the Executive Committee, Mr. Austin also insisted on doing the billings on the Boyd Gibbons's accounts and how dangerous that could be for the firm if Mark described things inaccurately. He will tell you that the normal procedure for an important client is for the chairman of the department to review any billings. The facts are that Mark Austin wanted to jump ahead of his peers and that, by definition, is someone who is not trustworthy. When Mr. Keller described him to future employers, he was just expressing a 'no confidence' attitude and that is perfectly permissible. This is a far cry from intending to inflict harm on Mark Austin. So in the end, we will be asking you to reject liability. The Baukus & Johnson firm had a good business reason for asking him to leave. Thank you for your time here today."

When the opening statements were over, Judge Harpman looked over toward Dillon and said, "Call your first witness, Mr. Clark."

Dillon stood and said, "I call Mark Austin as our first witness, Your Honor."

Notwithstanding all of the practice sessions, Dillon saw instantly that Mark was stiff and awkward as he rose and walked to the witness stand. It was also noticeable to all in the courtroom that his hands were slightly trembling as he took the oath. Dillon groaned a little internally but kept a relaxed confident look on his face. Rule one for trial lawyers is to never allow your disappointments to visually show to a jury or judge.

Dillon decided the best way to help Mark was to get him talking and fast. "Mr. Austin, the jury here knows this is a wrongful termination lawsuit, so why don't we just start from the beginning and let them know what happened."

Mark was hesitant at first, but visibly perked up some as he told his story. He explained his success in law school, how he was hired by Baukus & Johnson, how Boyd Gibbons liked his work and hired the firm for all of his companies, and then the sudden, still unbelievable, day he was fired.

"I still wake up in sweat thinking about that day," Mark explained with patent anger in his voice.

Dillon intentionally stood silent at the podium for a long fifteen seconds to let what Mark said sink in. He then looked up a Mark and asked, "Mark, after you were fired, did Wayne Bailey later say he would give you a letter of recommendation?"

"Yes, he did. And when I called and asked him for it to include in my resume, he told me the firm does not do recommendations and hung up."

Dillon then took Mark through his exhausting search for a job with another law firm and how he got no response and how he ended up working for a small firm doing family law.

"Mark, you later found out why you were not getting offers, correct?" Dillon asked.

"Yes sir. I was talking with one of my professors at Stanford to get a recommendation, and when I told him I was having no luck getting with another firm, he said he would call some of his former students who ran a few of the firms I applied to."

"Did he learn anything?" Dillon asked.

Mark at first said nothing. He then looked over at Harlan Cross with a cold stare and said, "He found out that someone from the law firm was saying I was a troublemaker and not trustworthy."

Dillon cleared his throat and said off-handedly, "Yes, we'll hear from a few of the managing partners of these firms and find out exactly what was said." Dillon knew that instead of objecting, Jason Haverley had just let Mark testify to things that he did not hear personally. This is hearsay and not permissible testimony, so he wanted to move on.

"Mark, did you ever do anything at Baukus & Johnson that would justify them calling you a troublemaker?" Dillon asked.

"Never," Mark replied as his hands began to shake.

"Did Alison Craft ever talk with you about your performance in the estate planning department?" Dillon asked.

"Never," Mark answered as he moved his head side to side in frustration.

"Did any member of the Executive Committee, and by this I mean Mr. Harlan Cross who is setting here at counsel table as well as Wayne Bailey and Derrick Warner, ever talk to you about your performance before the day they fired you?" Dillon asked in an unbelieving tone.

"Never," Mark replied.

"Did any partner at Baukus & Johnson ever talk to you about your performance, good or bad?" Dillon asked with firmness in his voice.

Mark now smiled for the first time and said, "Yes. Wayne Bailey talked to me about what a great job I was doing in getting the Gibbons's accounts and that he had recommended that the Executive Committee make me a junior partner."

"And were you made a junior partner?" Dillon asked inquiringly.

"Yes sir," Mark answered. "I was actually advanced six months ahead of the other new attorneys."

"Did you enjoy working at Baukus & Johnson?" Dillon asked.

"Of course I did," Mark replied. "With Mr. Gibbons and his companies giving us all of their work, I felt I would be a full partner in a few years."

Jason Haverley jumped to his feet objecting. "It is pure speculation whether Mr. Austin would have stayed with the firm or made a partner. This line of questioning is totally improper."

Dillon stood and started to explain but Judge Harpman held up his hand and said, "I'm going to allow the question for now. But this really gets to damages so I want you to move on to another area Mr. Clark."

Dillon turned back to Mark and asked, "Mark, the defendants have raised an issue about your status as an employee. When you were made a junior partner, were you still an employee?"

"Yes sir. As far as I know, my status never changed. I still got my monthly pay check with deductions and I know I never signed anything that said differently," Mark replied.

"One final question, Mark," Dillon said. "Who fired you when you met with the Executive Committee that morning on December 22?"

Mark looked over at Harlan Cross and said, "It was Mr. Cross."

"Did he give you any instructions?" Dillon asked.

"I, ah...." Mark started to answer but the words got caught in his throat.

Dillon knew this was rough territory for Mark. They had gone over this in practice, but next to what happened between Mark and his wife, this was the second deepest long-lasting wound.

"Take it slow, Mark," Dillon said with encouragement. "The jury will understand."

Jason Haverley wanted to object, but he knew this was the wrong time to put emphasis on bad facts so he sat silent.

Mark cleared his throat and said in a quivering voice, "He told me to go to my office and remove my personal things and to turn in my cell phone and key to the elevators. He said I was to leave the building."

"What else happened?" Dillon asked.

"By the time I got to my office, everyone knew I had been fired. The personnel lady was there with a couple of boxes and, ah, well..." Mark replied haltingly and stopped.

Dillon paused, waiting for Mark to finish. The courtroom was dead silent when Mark finally added, "It was the second most humiliating thing in my life to walk out of that building with someone carrying a box with my things in it for every secretary and attorney to see. I've never been able to put into words what that felt like. All I know is that I was numb when I got into my car to drive home."

"Mark, you said the 'second most humiliating.' What was the most humiliating thing in your life?" Dillon asked in a voice so soft that it was hard for all in the courtroom to hear. But it was loud enough for the jury to hear.

The uncomfortable silence in the courtroom grew as Mark's shoulders sagged and he stared down at the witness table in front of him as if he had not heard the question.

Dillon rarely got emotional in a trial, but now he found himself fighting back tears as he nudged Mark to answer. "Mark, I know this hurts, but you have to tell the jury what happened."

Mark's heart was pounding inside his chest and he found it hard to breath. It was like he was paralyzed even though he knew everyone in the courtroom was waiting for his answer. Finally he raised his head, looked out to the audience and got eye contact with Suzzi and quietly said, "Telling my wife I was fired!"

The consequences to Mark and his wife were a critical part of the evidence. Dillon also knew the time was now or never with Mark. The answer to one question had been practiced over and over because it covered the impact his firing had on their sex life. "Mark, did your relationship with your wife change after you told her you had been fired?"

Haverley couldn't wait any longer. "Objection," he shouted. "Whatever happened between Mr. Austin and his wife is not relevant to this case."

Judge Harpman peered down at counsel over the top of his glasses and said, "I'm going to allow this question as background. But keep it short, Mr. Clark. This is really testimony for damages if we get there."

Mark was still looking out at Suzzi. When he heard Dillon's question, he shook his head from side to side and felt a chill of absolute fear run through his body. A small drop of sweat on his cheek suddenly felt like a tidal wave as he just sat frozen in his chair.

"Mark, did you hear my question?" Dillon asked.

When Mark remained silent, Dillon knew that all of their hard work had not been enough. He was just not going to talk about what happened to his sex life in front of a jury. This was a critical part of the damages and Dillon had to make a snap decision to push on or depend just on their psychologist expert. Asking a witness more questions when they are terrified can be risky so Dillon stood and said, "Thank you Mark. No more questions, Your Honor."

Judge Harpman looked over at the jury and said, "We've been at this for about two hours now, so let's take a short twenty minute break.

As soon as the jurors left the courtroom, Dillon motioned for Kelly and Suzzi to join him and Mark at the counsel table. Turning to Mark, he said, "You did a good job, Mark. I know how difficult this is for you, and we can get the evidence we need from Dr. Knight and maybe a little from Suzzi."

"I'm really sorry, Mr. Clark," Mark replied apologetically. "I just freeze-up and I just can't will myself to get by it."

"OK," Dillon said as he rubbed his hands together in thought. After a moment of reflection, he added, "Haverley is faced with a difficult decision when he questions you, Mark. He can stay away from the sex questions to minimize damages, or he can question you himself."

"But what if Mark freezes again?" Kelly asked with more than a little apprehension creeping into her voice.

"What about it, Mark?" Dillon asked. "Do you think you can answer his questions?"

"I'll try," Mark answered with an obvious lack of conviction.

When the trial resumed after the break, Jason Haverley had his turn with Mark. He was a large man with a deep authoritative voice that could be heard anywhere in a courtroom even without a microphone. He stood, walked slowly over to the speaker stand. He took a moment to just look at Mark and then asked, "Mr. Austin, you understand that as a plaintiff, you have the burden of proof in this case, right?"

Mark nodded his head and said, "Yes."

"Good. So let's see what proof you have. Mr. Austin, if you were a partner in a law firm and knew another partner opposed making an associate a partner, would you honor that partner's request?" Haverley asked quickly.

"Objection, Your Honor," Dillon said. "This is totally irrelevant to the issues in this case. The issue here is whether, with what

Mr. Austin did for the firm, they acted in good faith by firing him. It is not a simple question of one partner being opposed."

"I disagree, Your Honor," Jason Haverley replied. "The Executive Committee received Alison Crafts's memo and relied on it. Whether that reliance was reasonable is the issue and I think the jury should hear what Mr. Austin thinks he would have done?

Judge Harpman thought about it for a moment and then said, "The facts are for the jury to decide, but I think it is relevant to know what the plaintiff would have done. I'm going to allow the question."

"Thank you, Your Honor," Haverley said. "Mr. Austin, would you have honored a partner's request and passed over the associate for partnership?"

Mark had been thinking as the attorneys argued the issue and replied, "The answer is yes and no. What a partner thinks should be considered, but I would have investigated why the partner was opposed. In my case, Alison got the idea that I was weak on taxes, and that is just not true. If the Executive Committee had looked at my work, they would have seen a number of sophisticated tax plans that I did."

"What if the partner just had no confidence that the associate could do more complex estate planning? Or just didn't like the associate's personality? Would you force the associate on that partner?" Haverley asked aggressively.

This was the core issue in the wrongful termination case. Mark hesitated and then replied, "If I was convinced the associate was an excellent lawyer, I would try to convince the partner to change her mind, and if that failed, yes I would still vote to make him a partner. In a large firm, no one single partner should be able to black-ball an associate."

"So if I understand correctly," Haverley continued, "you agree that the opinion of other partners should be a factor to consider, right?"

Mark realized his mistake and hesitated briefly before he answered. "Yes, I agree."

"You say you would still vote for the associate if in your judgment he was a top lawyer. But I presume you agree that the decision to make an associate a partner is an important business decision by any firm, right?" Haverley pressed.

Dillon had anticipated that Haverley would argue that the decision to ask Mark to leave was a business decision and he and Mark had discussed how this should be dealt with at trial.

Mark did not hesitate this time. "Yes sir, it is an important business decision. But it can't be made in bad faith. I mean, a decision on the future of someone should take into consideration all of the circumstances. In my case, I was doing great work and I was not weak in the tax area. But as far as I know, Mr. Cross or the other members of the Executive Committee did not even ask. They just saw Alison's memo and made the decision. That's not right."

"I know you're trying to argue your case here in front of the jury," Haverley said critically, "but let's be honest here. The Executive Committee is responsible to run the law firm and make sure things run smoothly. Are you saying it is automatically bad faith for an Executive Committee, which gets a memo from a partner saying an associate is not partner material, to decide it is best for the firm, and by the way for the associate as well, to let the associate know he should move on now rather than waste more years? Are you unwilling to concede that leaders of a law firm might just make that business decision in good faith for the firm and the associate?" Haverley urged aggressively.

Mark was rattled by the aggressive approach by Haverley and had somewhat of a bewildered expression on his face when he answered. "Yes, I suppose some could see that as a reasonable decision."

This was one of those moments when Dillon lost at least a few months off his life when he had to just sit and say nothing, yet knowing that Haverley had just extracted what could be a winning concession from Mark.

Haverley reached over to pick up another file which he opened and inspected the contents briefly. Finally, looking up at Mark, he said, "Thank you, Mr. Austin. I appreciate you honesty."

Again looking at his notes, Haverley continued. "On another subject, when Boyd Gibbons became a client, he asked that you do the billings, right?"

"Yes sir," Mark replied.

"And you did review the billings, right?" Haverley asked.

"Yes," Mark said.

"And you were aware, were you not Mr. Austin, that the chairmen of the different departments doing work for Gibbons, had to review what you did so no mistakes were made. Isn't that true?" Haverley snapped in anger.

"I, ah, I collected the bills from the lawyers, prepared the bills to be sent out and, yes, they were reviewed before they actually went out," Mark conceded.

"Did you think that made the department chairmen happy with that arrangement?" Haverley asked with growing intensity.

"No one ever told me that," Mark answered.

"Mark, did you persist on doing the billings so you could get advanced faster?" Haverley asked with his eyebrow raised inquiringly.

"No. Of course not," Mark replied.

"I see," Haverley said with an accusing smile. "And then we all know you wrote a memo asking for a bonus from the Tier Two pool, right?"

"I did that after Wayne Bailey suggested I do so because I had been made a junior partner," Mark said.

"Did you do anything at all to verify that you were entitled to seek a bonus from Tier Two which is for senior partners?" Haverley asked.

"No. I thought it was ok because it was Wayne's idea," Mark explained.

Haverley paused and looked back at the clock on the rear wall of the courtroom. It was 4:00 p.m. and close to when the court would recess for the day. He looked up at Mark with a sober, appraising look and said, "Mr. Austin, part of your claim for wrongful termination is a claim of emotional distress. Your counsel asked you a question earlier today that you never answered, so let me ask you again. Did your relationship with your wife change after you told her you had been fired?"

When he heard Haverley's question, Mark's head jerked quickly in Dillon's direction and he started to stand up when suddenly from the audience Suzzi Austin stood, and with tears streaming down her cheeks, she shouted, "No. You don't have to answer that. Leave him alone!"

Haverley's head turned to face the audience, but before he could say anything, Judge Harpman interjected, "It is late and I think this is an appropriate time to recess for the day. I'll see all of you here at 8:30 tomorrow."

As the jurors and the few on-lookers left the courtroom, Mark left the witness stand and walked over to where Suzzi was still standing in the audience. Suzzi grabbed Mark around his neck and just stood there holding him tight.

Dillon and Kelly stood and watched and they both heard Suzzi say to Mark, "I'm ok, honey. We can just withdraw any claim for damages to what happened to us. I don't want you hurt anymore."

As they were all leaving the courthouse and walking to their cars, Dillon and Kelly took Mark and Suzzi to one of the benches in the outside courtyard and discussed what Suzzi had in mind.

Dillon explained, "The judge allowed me to ask about the impact on the two of you. If Mark now refuses to testify on the impact his firing has had on the two of you, Haverley will have a field day with this. He'll argue we just tried to get this into evidence to prejudice the jury. You both need to understand that this could lead the jury to conclude he is right!"

But in the end, Suzzi would have none of it. She sat close to Mark and did all of the talking. "No matter what you say, Mr. Clark, I want no more questions about our private lives. Period. Do you understand that? Do whatever you have to do to stop any more of these questions."

When Mark and Suzzi got in their car and drove up the ramp to exit the parking garage, Kelly turned to Dillon and said, "Boy, she's been pretty much a silent player up until now! She's jumped in this thing like a lioness protecting a cub. And, you know what? I think she's right. And better yet, I'll bet their relationship will be ten times better for what she just did."

When Dillon got home that night, he threw his old beat up briefcase on the kitchen table and poured himself a large double sixteen year old Macallan single malt scotch. As he took a sip and walked over and sat down at the kitchen table, he noticed the briefcase. It had been a gift from his wife some twenty years ago. It had been at his side ever since in more than fifty major trials. When his wife bought the briefcase, she had the leather shop carve his name on top in large gold letters, but those had gradually worn aware from constant use.

Thinking back to how he would come home and talk over with his wife what had happened that day in trial, he longingly said to himself, "Well, honey, if you have any great ideas, now is the time for sharing."

Dillon sat at his kitchen table for a long time thinking about what he would have to say to Judge Harpman in the morning. "It's not the judge I'm worried about," he mused to himself as he sipped his scotch. "It's what the jury is going to think. Will they be good citizens and follow the judge's instructions and not consider the impact on Mark and his wife, or will they think we are now trying to hide something important from them?" He knew full well that if it was the latter, they were sunk.

After a few more scotches, Dillon took a hot shower, went to bed and had a terrible night.

CHAPTER 9

Trial – Day Two
(Tuesday, January 5)

When the trial resumed the next morning, Dillon asked to speak with Judge Harpman in his chambers before the jury was brought into the courtroom. When he and Jason Haverley were seated, Dillon explained to the judge the decision to waive any claim for emotional distress because of any adverse effects Mark's firing may have had on his relationship with his wife.

Judge Harpman was surprised and took a moment before he responded. "This is a big concession, Mr. Clark. If this jury happens to find liability, you could be throwing away a major portion of your damages. Do Mr. Austin and his wife both understand this?"

"Your Honor, I can assure you that I've spent hours going over the pros and cons. You could see for yourself how Mrs. Austin reacted when she saw the difficulty Mark was having answering questions in this area. They just want to bring a stop to any more questions. This is why our offer is conditioned on defense counsel not asking Mark any more questions on the issue. It is obvious he is embarrassed and finds it difficult to speak about his sex life," Dillon explained with emphasis.

Judge Harpman leaned forward in his chair and said, "Well, it is most unusual. But if that's what they want, I'll go along with it."

He turned to Haverley and asked, "I assume you have no problem with the offer?"

Jason Haverley was delighted to accept the offered agreement. He knew from painful experience how juries can get carried away with emotional damages. The law does not set any real measure for a jury to follow in assessing emotional distress damages and numbers can run from a few thousand to hundreds of thousands of dollars depending on how any specific jury reacts. "So stipulated, Your Honor," he said with a smile on his face that was hard to disguise.

Before the meeting in chambers ended, Judge Harpman discussed with Dillon and Haverley how and when the jury would be told of the agreement. Haverley wanted the judge to tell the jury immediately in the hope it would prejudice the jury.

"Your Honor," Haverley argued, "I was in the middle of asking questions about this exact issue and Mr. Austin would not answer. I think we should tell the jury now so they don't speculate."

"The issue is best explained when you instruct the jury on damages," Dillon replied. "You will have to instruct them then anyway, and to do it now would be putting too much emphasis on the issue."

Judge Harpman finally decided to wait until the damage phase of the trial. He explained, "This is turning out to be a close case and I don't at this point know what the jury might decide on liability. If they find for the defendant, then the issue is moot because the trial would be over. So I'm going to wait."

When they returned to the courtroom and the jury was again seated, Jason Haverley finished with his cross-examination of Mark. After seeing Suzzi stand up and yell the previous day, Dillon could tell the jury was curious. A number of jurors stole quick glances at

Suzzi sitting in the audience with Kelly. All Dillon could do was hope for the best.

Dillon knew, as does every trial lawyer, that the system of justice is not perfect. The winner is who the jury likes and how they perceive the facts. Justice, when it occurs, is often accidental. And this is exactly why trial lawyers try so hard to settle cases before a jury takes over their destiny.

When Haverley finished with Mark, Dillon called Harlan Cross as his next witness. Cross was dressed in a dark pin-striped suit, white shirt and a black bow tie. He looked every bit of a successful lawyer as he walked up to the witness box and took the oath.

Dillon quickly took Cross through the events leading up to Mark's termination. After establishing that Mark performed at a high level and was responsible for Boyd Gibbons's bringing all of his companies to Baukus & Johnson, Dillon asked, "Mr. Cross, as the law firm's Managing Partner and a member of the Executive Committee, you voted to make Mark a junior partner, before you fired him. Correct?"

"Yes, that is true," Cross replied, "but that was before we received the memorandum from Alison expressing concerns that Mark would not be senior partner material. As I have said many times, we just can't force an associate on partners. They are the ones who decide who is and who is not made a partner. The whole concept of a partnership is that we have to trust and rely on each other. If even one partner does not want to work with someone, that is the end of the discussion. It is then best for the firm, and I might add the associate as well, to part company."

"So it was Alison Craft's memo that you relied on in making the decision?" Dillon asked as he leaned in over the counsel table and engaged Cross with an incredulous stare.

"Yes, that is correct," Cross replied. "We were very happy with Mark up to that point. But you must understand, a firm just cannot..."

Before Cross could finish, Dillon said, "Yes, I've heard that speech before," Dillon said. "Mr. Cross, I have only one further question," Dillon added. "When you got the memo from Alison Craft, no one from the Executive Committee, and that includes you personally, made any effort to talk with Alison Craft to see if there was something that could be done to change her mind. Am I correct, sir?"

This was obviously a dent in the defense's position and Harlan Cross paused just briefly before he answered. He recalled how Jason Haverley had told him to answer. "Just say yes and move on. Don't comment. Get by the issue quickly."

"Yes, that is correct," Harlan Cross said in a crisp matter of fact tone.

"Thank you, I have no further questions." Dillon said.

Dillon knew that Alison Craft was going to be a key witness and he wanted to be the first one to ask her questions, so he had decided to call her as a witness himself rather than wait for Jason Haverley to call her.

"Your Honor, we have subpoenaed Alison Craft and I would like to call her as our next witness. She's outside the courtroom. May I have my associate bring her in?" Dillon asked of the judge.

"Yes, please do," Judge Harpman replied.

Kelly stood and walked out and brought in Alison Craft. Judge Harpman said, "Please take the witness stand."

Alison Craft looked nervous as she walked up to the witness stand and sat down. Charmaine Parker, the clerk, instructed her to raise her right hand to take the oath. "Do you swear to tell the truth and nothing but the truth in the matter now before the court?"

"I do," Alison Craft said as her hand shook ever so slightly but enough to be noticed by Dillon and Kelly.

Dillon had not seen Alison Craft since her deposition and the first thing he noticed was that she had put on a few pounds. She was wearing a tan two-piece business suit with a jacket, but it did nothing to conceal the tightness of her blouse underneath. And the extra pounds translated into ever more pressure on the precious threads keeping the buttons from flying across the courtroom. And this was all evident to everyone in the courtroom when she raised her right hand to take the oath.

As much as he tried to look elsewhere, Dillon could not help but let his eyes drop down a little to take a quick peek at the buttons as she raised her hand. He stepped over to the podium, cleared his head of any thoughts of Alison Craft's buttons, and asked, "Ms. Craft, I assume you are aware that the memorandum you wrote to the Executive Committee about Mark Austin resulted in his termination. You of course know that, right?"

Alison Craft by now had folded her arms tightly across her chest. "I am aware of that, Mr. Clark. That was really why I wrote the memo. I did not think Mark was sophisticated enough in the tax areas for the type of clients Baukus & Johnson serviced. So I thought it was best for Mark and the firm to make a decision."

Dillon sighed irritably and thought, "Boy, they got that line down pat!"

"If you don't mind, I would prefer you to just answer my questions," Dillon said firmly but politely.

"Did you ever sit down and talk with Mark Austin about his tax experience?" Dillon asked.

"No. I was a partner and reviewed a lot of his work, and I could tell he lacked experience in many key areas," Alison Craft answered.

"I'm certainly no tax expert, but what was it that Mark was lacking?" Dillon asked.'

Alison Craft threw a glance over at Harlan Cross and then said, "It was tax planning for wealthy clients. This involves forming family partnerships and corporations to own valuable assets, gifting limited partnership interests to family members so when they inherit they get a minority discount on the value of the assets, and that saves on taxes. Things like this. Mark had no experience doing work like this and we were far too busy to be a training ground."

"Wayne Bailey was the head of the estate planning department at Baukus & Johnson. Did you talk to him about Mr. Austin's short comings?" Dillon asked.

"Not really. But I gave him my memo so he knew how I felt," Alison Craft explained.

"Did it occur to you, Ms. Craft, to go to Wayne and say something like, 'Mark is a really good lawyer, but he is weak in some areas? Why don't we send him to a tax seminar so he can get current?' Anything like that?" Dillon asked.

Alison Craft felt she was in safe territory and sat upright in the witness chair, unfolded her arms and said confidently, "Baukus & Johnson was far too busy dealing with client matters to do training. We expected associates to know their area of the law and be able to do the work."

"Even if not doing so could result in a good lawyer being fired?" Dillon snapped with firmness in his voice.

Alison Craft was looking down at the desk in front of her when Dillon asked the last question. Her head bolted up and she engaged Dillon with a cold hard stare before she answered.

Dillon could tell that Alison Craft was irritated, but he had no way of knowing what was bothering her so he let the silence hang for a moment. Finally, she said, "I know it may be hard to understand, but Baukus & Johnson has thousands of clients and their work always comes first. It would have been nice to have the leisure to train attorneys, but that just was not possible. Whether you like it or not, I thought I was doing Mark a favor by writing the memo when I did. If he was not going to be a partner, he needed to know that."

Dillon let his voice drop to almost a whisper and, turning slightly toward the jury said, "Yes. I can see how you were doing him a favor!"

Whether all of this was going to be perceived as acting in good faith was up to the jury, so Dillon said, "I have nothing further Ms. Craft."

Judge Harpman took the morning's recess and when everyone returned, Jason Haverley stood and announced, "Your Honor, I really have no questions of Ms. Craft. She can be excused."

As Alison Craft left the witness stand and exited the courtroom, Kelly made eye contact with her and Craft immediately looked away. Call it a hunch, women's intuition or whatever, but Kelly felt uneasy and stood up and followed Craft out into the hallway. Craft did nothing out of the ordinary, but Kelly did see Jerry Keller walk up and greet her with a not too friendly look on his face. They were talking rapidly to each other, but they were moving towards the elevator and Kelly could not hear what was said.

With the issue of good or bad faith now up to the jury, Dillon turned to Mark's difficulty in securing another position. Dillon and his whole team had carefully considered calling Jerry Keller, but decided against it. Keller was very smart and articulate and would no doubt stick to the story he gave at the time of his deposition. He had acknowledged he had been a bit critical of Mark, but denied saying he was a "troublemaker."

So instead of Keller, Dillon called three of the partners at firms where Mark had applied for a position. Each said that Jerry Keller had used the words "troublemaker" and questioned his trustworthiness. One of the attorneys, Phil Atkinson, was particularly impressive. When Dillon asked him whether the comments by Jerry Keller made a difference in his firm hiring Mark, he said, "Most certainly. Mark had a first-rate resume and we would have had no reason to think anything critical of him. In fact, I'm sure we would have hired him if Mr. Keller had not called him a troublemaker."

Jason Haverley's cross examination of the attorney witnesses was the same for each one. "Sir, is it possible that Mr. Keller used words other than "troublemaker" when he talked about Mark Austin? I know he left you with a feeling that he was saying Mark was a troublemaker, but we need to be precise. So again, could he have used other words that you just don't now recall?"

None of the attorney witnesses were trial lawyers used to being cross examined, so they answered cautiously. When asked this question, Phil Atkinson said, "Yes, it is possible. But I clearly got the impression that Mark Austin was not to be trusted and that is why we didn't hire him. It has been over a year now, so I can't be sure of the exact words used."

This type of concession was enough to permit Haverley to argue that Keller was just expressing his opinion that Mark had showed immaturity when he accepted the task of doing the Gibbons' billings. Haverley's theory was that a disagreement over business practices is not a basis for a wrongful termination lawsuit.

When the trial stopped for lunch, Dillon took Mark, Suzzi and Kelly up to the top floor cafeteria for lunch. It is mediocre food, but convenient. When they were all seated with their meals, Kelly told Dillon that she saw Jerry Keller in the hallway greeting Alison Craft.

"He could have been there to give her support," Dillon said casually. "They are partners."

But before the conversation went any further, Suzzi set the fork that she was about to eat with down on the table with enough force to cause everyone to look her way, and said vehemently, "I know you all are the experts at this stuff, but every fiber in my body tells me she's lying. Not once during her testimony did she ever make eye contact with Mark. It's like, well, you know, if she really looked at him, he would know she was lying."

"I was not watching as close as Suzzi was," Kelly added, "but when I made eye contact with her as she was leaving the courtroom, she just looked away. I think that is why I followed her out."

"You might be right," Dillon replied. "But it could also be that Haverley had her well prepared and she stuck to the script."

Dillon leaned back in his chair and thought for a moment and then said, "I didn't ask her on the witness stand whether she and Keller talked about the firing of Mark. We covered that in her deposition and she denied any conversation except, I think, some casual conversation, and she no doubt would have to say the same thing here at trial."

"Mark, what do you think?" Dillon asked.

"I don't know, Dillon. We all sort of knew they had a thing going before they left the firm, so it's not unusual to see him meet her here at the courthouse," Mark replied. He then looked over at Suzzi and added, "She's got pretty good intuition. Can we get Alison back to ask her more questions?"

"We can try," Dillon answered with some hesitation. "That will be up to the judge. We both dismissed her and that usually means the witness does not have to return."

Kelly was now fidgeting in her chair and they had all lost any interest in lunch. With a grimace she anxiously said, "Dillon, the more I think about this the more it smells like a dead fish. Let's ask Judge Harpman to authorize us to subpoena her again if she won't voluntarily appear."

Dillon nodded his head in agreement and said, "Kelly, go call Alison on her cell. Ask her if she will voluntarily come back for more questioning. If you don't have the number, call Jeannie at the office. Her cell is on the on-call letter Craft signed."

When court resumed after lunch, Dillon notified Judge Harpman's clerk that they had a matter to take up with the judge before he brought back the jury. Charmaine Parker called Judge Harpman and explained Dillon's request.

A minute later, Judge Harpman came out of his chambers and took his seat behind the judge's bench. He looked over at Dillon and said, "I understand you have a matter that we should deal with before the jury comes in. Is that right Mr. Clark?"

"Yes, Your Honor," Dillon said. "I would like permission to recall Alison Craft for more questioning. She is obviously a critical witness since the defense is relying totally on her memo as a reason for firing Mr. Austin. My associate is calling her now."

Jason Haverley almost jumped out of his chair and in his loud voice said, "This is highly improper, Your Honor. Mr. Clark finished his questioning and I was satisfied and she was dismissed. If we start indulging Mr. Clark's indecision by letting him call back witnesses because he has thought of a few more questions, we're gonna be here for weeks!"

"Your Honor," Dillon started to say but Judge Harpman cut him off. "Gentlemen, the witness was excused and that normally precludes calling the witness back. But in this case, Ms. Craft's memorandum is certainly a pivotal piece of evidence."

"Your Honor, I really object. And I would like some time to have someone research the issue for the court. We certainly don't want any grounds for an appeal," Haverley said with his voice growing in intensity.

Haverley's comment was as close as an attorney can get to threaten a judge and the courtroom briefly went silent.

Judge Harpman looked at Haverley for a long moment and finally said in a stiff voice, "Mr. Haverley, I agree we want to be correct. I'll recess the trial until 9:00 a.m. tomorrow. If either counsel finds any law on this, email it to me tonight. You can get my email address from the clerk before you leave." With this statement, Judge Harpman stood and briskly walked out of the courtroom.

When Kelly returned to the courtroom, she noticed that everyone was leaving. She walked up to Dillon and asked, "What happened?"

"The judge gave Haverley time to research whether the court can order a witness back once they have been dismissed," Dillon explained.

"Did you reach Alison?" Dillon asked.

"Yes, and she's willing to return so I asked her to be here today at 2:30 p.m. I assumed that would be about the right time," Kelly said.

"Call her back," Dillon replied, "and tell her to be here at 9:00 a.m. tomorrow."

As soon as Jason Haverley could exit the courtroom and find a private spot, he called Alison Craft on her cell phone and she answered right away. "Alison, this is Jason. Clark wants you to come back for more questions."

"I know," Alison Craft replied. "His associate just spoke with me. He wants me there tomorrow morning."

Haverley had no idea of what Dillon had in mind, so he asked, "Alison, is there something that I don't know? Do you know what Dillon wants to ask you?"

"No idea at all," Alison Craft replied with confidence that was something less than one hundred percent. "You heard my testimony. My answers are going to be the same no matter how many times he asks."

When he finished talking with Craft, Haverley was more or less at ease. But there was that tingling in the back of his neck that trial lawyers often get that bothered him. He shook his head negatively and said somewhat reassuringly to himself, "Clark knows things aren't going well and is just groping for whatever he can find."

As Haverley walked out of the courthouse towards the garage to drive back to his office, he placed a call to Harlan Cross. When he answered, he said, "Harlan, get your guys on researching the authority of a judge to order a witness to return once they have been dismissed. Clark wants Craft back for more questions, and I think Judge Harpman is going to let him."

When the trial was recessed for the day, Harlan Cross had immediately driven back to his office to attend to other legal matters. After his conversation with Haverley, he sat at his desk for a long time thinking about Alison Craft. He then called Derrick Warner to get someone started on the research, but it was Craft that was bothering him. "What the hell did Clark think he can get from her?" he mumbled to himself irritably.

After pondering what Clark had in mind for a while, Harlan Cross reached over to the telephone on his desk and tried to reach Alison Craft or Jerry Keller. When he was told neither was in, he said gruffly, "Have them call me," and slammed his phone down.

Harlan Cross stood and walked over to the window and looked out at the city below. He was no trial lawyer, but in his gut he was feeling a growing concern. He didn't know why, but he knew the feeling. "God damn it, we should be able to get this thing stopped!" he said to himself in frustration.

Cross turned quickly and walked back to his desk and called his old partner and now the presiding judge of the Los Angeles Superior County Court. He had a direct line and when Judge Dale Bannerman answered, Harlan Cross wasted no time getting to the point. "Dale, things aren't going so good at the trial. Haverley just called and said Dillon Clark wants to recall Alison to the stand. He already dismissed her as a witness, but he thinks Harpman is going to let him call her back. What can we do here?"

Judge Dale Bannerman had been a partner and friend of Cross for over forty years and thought that his earlier conversation with Judge Harpman had been enough to cut short the plaintiff's case. "I'll see what I can do Harlan. These things can be touchy, as you know. I can't just walk down the hall and tell Harpman what to do."

"Damn it, Dale, I know that," Cross said angrily, "but can't you get him to at least play it conservative? I mean, both attorneys were finished with Alison, and now Clark wants to take a second crack at her. Harpman should just say no and move on."

Judge Bannerman was well aware of Harlan Cross's temper and just sat back in his chair. He took a deep breath and said slowly, "Harlan, you need to back off. I'll see what I can do, but we really have to be careful. Harpman is in charge of that trial and he has the final word."

"Well hell, Dale. You know I know that," Cross said in a more relaxed and friendly manner. "But this thing with Alison is making me nervous. We've built our whole defense on her memo to the Executive Committee. And I saw her testify. She did a great job sticking to her memo. It's just not right that Clark now has second thoughts and gets to cross examine her twice. Can't Harpman see that?"

"I agree with you, Harlan. As I said, I'll talk with him," Judge Bannerman replied.

"Harpman gave the lawyers until this evening to get him any law that might control his discretion, so he won't rule until tomorrow. I've got some folks doing research right now, but this gives you this afternoon to talk with Harpman," Cross almost pleaded.

"I'll walk down to his chambers right now," Judge Bannerman replied somewhat sharply. Even old friends can take umbrage at being lectured to.

Rather than go down to Judge Harpman's chambers, which was three floors below his, Judge Bannerman called and asked him if he had time for coffee in the judge's lounge. Judge Harpman was free for the afternoon since he had recessed the trial until the following morning and agreed.

When both judges were seated in a corner table with a degree of privacy, Judge Bannerman asked, "How's the Austin trial going?"

Judge Harpman smiled and said, "Getting a bit testy, but its moving along. It makes a real difference when you have two fine trial lawyers involved. Most of the time, one side is dramatically better than the other. But Clark and Haverley are pretty evenly matched."

Judge Bannerman took a sip of coffee and then said, "Jerry, I got a call from Harlan Cross earlier today. He can't understand why you're giving Clark a second bite at Alison Craft." He had already decided on how to approach the subject, so he added, "Aren't you favoring the plaintiff here?"

Judge Harpman expected that his invitation for coffee with the presiding judge was not purely social. He smiled and said matter-of-factly, "Nothing like that, Dale. I'm pretty sure the law will say that I have the discretion to bring back a witness for more questions if I think the witness is critical to the issues. And you have to agree, Dale, the Baukus firm has made her the star witness in the case. If the jury believes her, the firm wins. If they don't, the firm in all like-lihood will lose. So I think it is fair to give either attorney a second chance. It just so happens to be Clark that is asking."

"Well, it's your decision," Judge Bannerman said with an in-quiringly look, "but I'd be careful. We don't want to favor either side. It might be best to just let the lawyers do their thing with the witnesses, but only once. No one can be critical of that approach."

When Dillon got home that night, he felt exhausted and was worried about losing Mark's case. He knew how much was at stake for Mark and his wife. Being fired is one thing, but to also lose his only chance at resurrecting his career could prove far more fa-tal. He had parked in the garage and entered the house through the door from the garage to the kitchen. He flipped on the light switch, dropped his briefcase on the kitchen floor, took off his coat and threw it on top of the briefcase and immediately walked over to the liquor cabinet. After he fixed himself a healthy portion of Macallan scotch, he walked out into the family room and sat down in his favorite leather chair and turned on the television. He flipped the channels until he found a basketball game, took a healthy sip of scotch and tried to relax.

But relaxing was not to be. Dillon's mind wandered back to the trial. He knew that the case might have been fatally crippled when

Mark agreed with Haverley that partners cannot be forced to make an associate a partner. "This is the whole defense and it's a good one," he ruminated to himself. "And all because of that Goddamn memo!"

Dillon thought of his wife. He usually talked things over with her when he got in a tight spot and she many times came up with a saving idea. "Well kiddo," Dillon said out loud as if she were in the room, "I've been on a pretty good roll for the last few years, but this one just may be my Waterloo."

CHAPTER 10

Trial – Day Three
(Wednesday, January 6)
(Alison Craft Recalled)

When Dillon reached Judge Harpman's court room the next morning, Kelly was already there. She had faxed to his home the research memo that she and Laurel Kennedy had prepared and emailed to Judge Harpman. They had found no case that dealt with the issue of recalling a dismissed witness, but the law was plentiful that a trial judge has broad discretion in running a trial. And Haverley came to the same conclusion in his brief.

"What do you think Harpman is going to do?" Kelly asked a bit anxiously.

"The decision is his," Dillon replied. "It sounded like he was going our way yesterday. And Haverley found nothing more than we did."

As the courtroom began to fill, Mark and the Suzzi walked in and came to the table where Dillon and Kelly were standing. "What's the verdict?" Mark asked.

"We'll know shortly. Whatever the judge does will be final," Dillon replied.

Kelly noticed that Mark and Suzzi both looked exhausted and she said to Suzzi, "Are you both OK?"

Suzzi nodded her head but it was Mark who answered. "This whole trial thing is getting to both of us. I think we've probably only slept an hour or so last night."

Dillon was ruffling through his papers, but he overheard what Mark said and he slowly set his papers down on the counsel table. Turning to Mark and Suzzi he said, "Mark, we've talked about this before, and I know it is easy for me to say and not so easy for you two to follow. But what you're feeling is what almost every client feels when their future is in the hands of a jury. Trials are a little like a tug of war contest. One side scores and you feel depressed. Then your side scores and you feel elated. It goes back and forth until the jury makes up its mind."

It was obvious that Mark and Suzzi were not up to a pep talk so Dillon reached out and squeezed Mark's shoulder and said encouragingly, "Just sit back and watch. I've learned years ago not to draw conclusions on how a case is going by just one or two days of testimony. Let the thing play out. We've still got a good case."

It was almost 10:00 a.m. when Judge Harpman finally came out. As he walked up and took his seat at the judge's bench, Suzzi and Kelly walked back and took their seats in the front row of the audience section. Dillon and Mark remained standing until the judge spoke.

As soon as he was seated, Judge Harpman looked out at counsel and the parties, cleared his throat and said, "Gentlemen, I've read over the research memos you both sent. As I see it, a trial judge could, under the right circumstances, permit a witness to be called back for more questioning even if the witness had been dismissed by both counsels, as was the case here with Ms. Craft. The guideline which is discussed in the cases is to ensure a fair trial to both sides."

Judge Harpman paused a moment and looked down at his notes. Dillon could see that something was troubling him. "Good God, is he thinking of denying our request" Dillon thought as he felt a bolt of adrenalin shoot up his spine.

When Judge Harpman continued, he said, "What bothers me in this case is that both counsel had a fair chance to ask all the questions they wanted, and then dismissed Ms. Craft. So when I think about it, I have to ask myself, is there an area that counsel could not have asked when they had the chance. And the answer is no. I placed no times limits on either one of you."

As Dillon sat listening, he now saw that the judge had cut right to the heart of the issue. He could have asked whatever he wanted.

Judge Harpman leaned forward in his chair and looked over at Dillon and said, "Mr. Clark, you have offered no reason to question Ms. Craft again. You understand, I'm sure, that it's a bit unusual to let counsel call a witness twice. I have to also ask myself whether it would be a waste of the jury's time to recall her."

Dillon knew he was losing the issue and he was momentarily stunned. And apparently everyone in the courtroom was stunned as well because there was dead silence and all eyes were on Dillon, including Haverley who was looking over in his direction.

Dillon stood, sucked in his breath and started to object. But Judge Harpman raised his hand and said, "But in this case her memo seems to be the critical piece of evidence. And, of course, her reasons for writing it. So I'm going to let you recall her but I'm going to limit your questions to the memo and why she wrote it. Any questions?"

Haverley knew when to stop pushing so he just nodded his head and said, "Understood."

Dillon still did not know what they were going to get from Craft. Their decision to recall her was based on Suzzi and Kelly's instincts that said she was lying. He looked up at Judge Harpman and said, "Thank you, Your Honor. Ms. Craft is waiting outside the courtroom."

Dillon looked back to where Kelly was sitting and motioned for her to get Craft. By the time Judge Harpman brought the jurors into the courtroom, Craft had been seated at the witness stand looking anything but pleased to be back in court.

It was obvious that the jurors were curious why Alison Craft was back on the witness stand. Dillon noticed that they were all looking at her so he hesitated a moment to let their curiosity linger.

After a very long thirty seconds, Dillon stood and looked up at Alison Craft. And this time he managed to ignore her buttons. "Ms. Craft, I want to thank you for returning. I won't take long in my questions. From what you said yesterday, you had concerns about Mark's experience and decided you could not support him becoming a partner. Is that correct?"

"Yes. As I explained, Mark did not have the experience in certain aspects of estate planning that we needed."

"Ok, we got that part. Your concern about Mark then led you to write the memo to the Executive Committee. Am I still correct?" Dillon asked.

"Yes. The memo says just that," Craft replied testily.

Craft could see that Dillon was plowing the same ground he covered with her before and she sat up straight in her chair in a confident manner. "If I stay with what I said before, he can't touch me," she thought to herself as she waited for Dillon's next question.

"OK. I think we got that all straight," Dillon said. He paused and asked "When did you reach the decision to write the memo? I mean, did you think about it for months?"

Craft hesitated a second and a frown formed on her forehead as if she was thinking back to what happened before she answered.

She suddenly knew that Dillon was after something new but she had no idea what it was and she just sat and stared at Dillon.

Up to this point, Dillon had been talking in a low key voice. But now he raised his voice and asked her in a tone of accusation, "Ms. Craft, the question is not difficult. When did you first think about writing it? Give me a day, week or month."

Craft stiffened slightly and she said, "I honestly don't know. I think it was in the later part of the year. You have the memo. It was dated November 15 and I had been thinking about it for some time."

Dillon sensed that Craft was now embellishing her story from what she said at trial. He walked over to the podium between the two counsel tables and suddenly switched topics. He asked rather sharply, "Did you talk to any of your partners, including Jerry Keller, about Mark and his performance before you wrote the memo?"

Craft quickly looked over at Haverley and was now unsure of how to answer. She had not been asked this exact question before. Her breathing was becoming heavy and she had a bewildered expression on her face.

Before she could reply, Dillon, still standing, slammed his fist down on the podium and almost yelled, "Are you telling this jury that you did not speak to a single partner before you wrote a memo that you knew would destroy Mark Austin's career at Baukus & Johnson? You knew, didn't you, that it would cause him to be fired?"

At this point Haverley jumped to his feet and said, "Objection, Your Honor. Mr. Clark is not letting the witness answer before he asks another question. Which one does he want her to answer?"

Without waiting for the judge to rule, Dillon said, "OK, Ms. Clark. Here is a simple question. Did you know your memo would result in Mark being terminated? Yes or no."

Craft again glanced quickly at Haverley before she answered. She then said, "Yes. I knew that. If a partner objects, no associate would be advanced."

"OK. We now have that straight too. You wrote the memo knowing that Mark would be terminated," Dillon said firmly.

"Objection, Your, Honor," Haverley said. "Does Mr. Clark have a question or is he trying to testify himself?"

Judge Harpman looked down at Dillon and said, "Just ask your questions, Mr. Clark."

Dillon looked up at Judge Harpman and said, "Sorry, Your Honor. Mr. Haverley is correct."

Turning his head back toward Craft, Dillon fixed her with an intense stare and asked heatedly, "Ms. Craft, here is my next simple question. And I do hope you see it as simple. Before you wrote your fateful memo, did you talk to a single one of your partners, and by that I include Jerry Keller, Wayne Bailey or anyone else, about your concerns over Mark's performance?"

Everyone in the courtroom could see that Craft was having trouble breathing. Her chest was heaving in and out, much to the distress of the buttons, and she seemed like a deer caught in a head light. Her eyes darted back and forth between Judge Harpman and Haverley.

Judge Harpman was watching the whole episode but did nothing to come to Craft's defense.

Dillon pressed further. Again raising his voice he demanded, "Ms. Craft, do you not understand my question? Did you or did you not talk to anyone?"

Dillon now walked over to the counsel table. As he did so, he said, "Ms. Craft, you have five seconds to answer my question. If you don't, I'm going to ask Judge Harpman to hold you in contempt of court. Do you understand?"

Haverley was puzzled by Craft's reluctance to answer, but he thought he should give her some time to think. He stood and said, "Objection," Your Honor, the witness is obviously distressed. Can we have a short recess so she can collect herself and be able to answer the questions?"

Judge Harpman looked at Craft and said, "We'll take a ten minute break."

When the jurors had left the courtroom, Haverley walked up to Craft, who was still seated at the witness stand, and tried to talk with her. But she refused. In fact, she never left the witness stand during the break. Dillon could see that she had pulled her cell phone out of her purse and was trying to call somebody, but the distressed look on her face suggested that whoever she was calling was not answering.

During the break, Dillon remained seated at the counsel table with Mark. He turned to Mark and asked, "What do you think, Mark. Is she lying?"

Mark was not a trial lawyer and he just shrugged his shoulders. "Ask Suzzi or Kelly. They both have a better take on Alison than I do."

Dillon turned around and motioned for Suzzi and Kelly to join him at the counsel table. When they were all together, he asked them in general, "What do you think? Something is wrong, but I just don't see it."

Suzzi was the first to reply. She said hurriedly, "She's just lying! I know she is."

"I agree with Suzzi," Kelly added. "Push her hard, Dillon."

When the jurors were again all seated, Dillon stood and was about to start his questioning again when he noticed that Craft was slumped down in her seat and for the first time during the trial, was looking at Mark Austin.

Dillon took a sip from the bottle of water sitting on the counsel table and asked, "Ms. Craft, you are aware that Mark Austin was fired because of your memo. So again, I am asking you, did you write the memo without talking to a single partner?" This time there was clear disgust in his voice.

Craft tried to get control of her anxiety, but her hands began shaking and she said in almost a stutter, "I didn't talk to anyone. I have said this dozens of times. I, well, Jerry said...But what I said was true. Mark really didn't have the experience we needed."

Dillon stopped and stood looking at Craft for a full ten seconds. He then leaned over the counsel table as if trying to hear more carefully and asked, "You just said Jerry. Were you referring to Jerry Keller?"

Craft's whole body now stiffened like a stone monument. Her chest again started bulging in and out as she tried to get air. Finally her shoulders slumped and tears began to roll down each of her cheeks. Looking right at Mark she said in a markedly subdued voice, "I'm so sorry. Jerry asked me to write the memo."

As she said this, the entire courtroom was gripped by a stunned silence.

Notwithstanding Perry Mason's dramatic successes, attorneys rarely get a live confession from a witness during a trial. But when you do, you never want to give the witness time to explain it away. Dillon let the silent drama play out for a very long minute and then said, "Ms. Craft, we all heard what you just said. But for clarification, am I correct that the whole idea of writing a critical memo about Mark Austin was Jerry Keller's idea. Is this correct?"

Craft was looking down at the table in front of her and was holding her hands together to keep them still. Without looking up, she said, "Yes. He asked me to write the memo and to send it to the Executive Committee."

"Thank you, Ms. Craft. Nothing further," Dillon said as he sat down.

Judge Harpman looked over at Haverley and asked, "Do you have any questions, Mr. Haverley?"

Haverley had been thinking that in all of the years he had been trying civil cases, he had never seen such a turn-around in the testimony of a key witness. He also knew what Craft said could be fatal.

Haverley slowly stood and said, "I do Your Honor. But I will keep them brief."

Haverley stood and was looking down at the papers on the counsel table in from of him. He reached down and picked up one of the papers, looked up at Craft and said, "Ms. Craft, in the memo you wrote, the one I have here in my hand, you expressed concerns about Mr. Austin's experience in sophisticated estate planning, especially in the tax area that often governs the type of estate planning for wealthy client. Is that correct?"

Craft was now sitting up straight again and knew she was being asked questions by a friendly attorney. She said matter-of-factly, "That is correct. Mark didn't have the experience we needed."

"So you personally felt that he should not become a partner. Is that also correct?"

"Yes. As I have said before, we had no time to do training," Craft replied.

"So am I correct that you felt that Mark Austin would not be a partner and that he would be better off leaving the firm so he would not be wasting his time?"

"Absolutely," Craft answered.

"Nothing further," Haverley said.

Judge Harpman looked over at Dillon and asked, "Mr. Clark, anything more?"

"Briefly, Your Honor," Dillon replied.

"Ms. Craft, you said Jerry Keller asked you to write the memo and to send it to the Executive Committee before the end of the year. Correct?"

"Yes," Craft answered but now in a voice that was leery of what Dillon was going to ask next.

"Did Mr. Keller tell you why he wanted you to write the memo?" Dillon asked.

Dillon could see that Craft's hands were now shaking again and she was holding them together in a vice-grip on the table in front of her. She knew what she was about to say would affect the case greatly. Almost in a whisper, she said, "He didn't like him asking for merit compensation and felt he showed immaturity when he agreed to do all of the billings on the Gibbons's matters. He, well, he just didn't want him as a partner."

"One last question," Dillon said. "Would you have written the memo if Mr. Keller had not asked you to?"

"I don't know, Mr. Clark," Craft replied almost in a whisper. "I probably would not have voted him to be a partner, but I just don't know if I would have made an issue before that."

"Thank you. I have no further questions," Dillon said.

Judge Harpman looked over at Haverley and asked, "Anything further counsel?"

"Just briefly, Your Honor," Haverley replied.

Turning to Alison Craft, Haverley asked, "Ms. Craft, apart from Mr. Keller asking you to write the memo, what you said was all correct. You were expressing your own conclusions about Mark Austin's work. Is this correct?"

"Yes. That is right," Craft answered.

"Nothing further, Your Honor. The witness may be excused," Haverley said.

Turning to Dillon, Judge Harpman asked, "Mr. Clark, anything more? I don't want this witness back for a third time."

"Nothing more," Dillon replied.

Judge Harpman looked over at the jury and said, "Ladies and gentlemen, I know it is still early, but I need to talk with counsel in chambers. So I'm going to let you go early. Please be back here at 8:30 a.m. tomorrow."

As the jurors were exciting the courtroom, Judge Harpman said, "Counsel, would you both please join me in chambers."

When they were all seated in his chambers, Judge Harpman took off his robe and walked over and hung it up in a small closet. As he turned around and walked back to his desk he looked right at Haverley and said with a frown, "Jason, I think it is time to settle this case. You now have your key witness saying she wrote the memo at the request of Jerry Keller and doesn't really know if she would have written one if he had not asked. This contradicts her prior testimony that she wrote it herself. Her whole credibility is at stake. I wish Harlan Cross was here. I would tell him the same thing."

Haverley looked surprised at what Judge Harpman had said. After a brief pause, he said, "Your Honor, I will of course talk with my client. But you must understand that Alison Craft also reaffirmed that what she said was true and she would have voted against him as a partner. It really does not change things. The Executive Committee based their decision on what was said in the memo, not on who thought of writing it."

Dillon knew enough to stay out of any discussion a judge was having with the other counsel when it was helpful, so he just sat silent.

"You can argue that to the jury," Judge Harpman replied, "but if the jury thinks Craft is lying, you can be in real trouble. Go talk with Harlan and tell him what I said. I expect an answer before we start tomorrow."

As soon as Haverley left the courtroom, he pulled out his cell phone and called Harlan Cross. "Harlan, we've got a problem. When Craft was called back, she said Jerry Keller asked her to write the damn memo. She doesn't even know if she would have written one if Keller had not asked."

"What the hell is she doing?" Cross yelled into the telephone.

"Dillon got very aggressive with her and she just lost control and blurted out Keller's name. Dillon jumped on it and the next thing she's crying and saying it was his idea," Haverley explained.

By now Cross was fuming. "God damn Keller. What was he thinking?"

"I have no idea," Haverley replied. "Can you talk to Keller and find out what he has to say?"

Cross was silent for a few seconds and then said, "We don't get along much since he up and left with the Gibbons work, but I'll give it a try."

"This is not all, Harlan," Haverley added with a sigh. "Judge Harpman called us into his chambers and suggested in somewhat strong language, that we should settle the case in light of Alison's testimony. He wants an answer tomorrow morning."

"Get on over here. I'll get Derrick and we can talk then," Cross replied.

When Haverley arrived at the Baukus & Johnson firm, the receptionist told him to go straight up to Harlan Cross's office. When he entered, he saw that Derrick Warner was sitting at the conference table along with Wayne Bailey. Harlan Cross was sitting behind his large antique desk.

"Come on in," Cross said as he motioned for Haverley to have a seat.

"Harlan has told us about Craft's surprising testimony," Derrick Warner said. "We've been talking about whether there is a legal basis to sue Jerry Keller for getting us into this mess. Boy, he is one self-centered son-of-a-bitch. He thinks of nothing but what is good for Jerry Keller."

"Do you think Alison's testimony is damaging?" Harlan Cross asked.

Haverley took off his coat and threw it on an empty chair as he sat down with an audible release of breath. "I've been thinking about this as I drove over here from court. It is definitely a problem if the jury thinks Alison is lying when she says what she wrote was actually true. She has changed her testimony and, well, hell, a jury could do anything with that!"

Haverley absently took a sip of water from a bottle of water that had been placed on the conference table. "But the real issue is damages. If we can get the jury to see that if Austin would not have been made a partner, then he would have been asked to leave anyway in at most a year later when he would have come up for consideration as a senior partner. If they accept this, his damages would be one year's income as a junior partner, less of course what he had made at his new firm. His whole damage could be less than $50,000."

Wayne Bailey shook his head negatively and said, "Jason, I hear what you say, and you know I'm not a trial lawyer, but what about Jerry Keller bad mouthing Mark? Won't a jury get upset with this?"

"Yes and no," Haverley replied. "The key to this whole case is to frame the decision to let Austin go as a normal business decision.

This means the Executive Committee made a proper decision when they got Craft's memo and decided to let Austin go. If there was no wrongful termination, and this is the key, then there can be no damages. Remember, the judge bifurcated the trial so the jury has to decide the issue of liability first. If they don't find liability, then the case stops. We never get to damages and Keller's conduct."

Harlan Cross sat quiet listening to the debate. Finally he looked over at Derrick Warner and asked, "Derrick, you're the trial lawyer. What do you think?"

Derrick Warner leaned forward in his chair, pondered the question for a second and said, "Haverley is right in his analysis. The jury won't get to damages if there is no liability. But we have no control over what the jury may be thinking when they go into that jury room and decide on liability. The gamble, I guess, is whether they believe Alison when she says what she wrote was true or just made up because Keller asked her to write the damn thing. For this reason, I think a settlement should be offered."

Harlan Cross got up and leisurely walked over to the window and stared out. The others remained silent. After a few minutes, he turned and said, "I agree a settlement offer is needed, especially since Judge Harpman thinks so. The question is how much. And before you answer, I want you to know that I also think we did the correct thing in letting Austin go. He would not have been made a partner and he should just get on with his life."

Haverley tapped his pen on the conference room table as he thought about his answer. "Harlan, I really think we can win the liability issue, but there are no guarantees in litigation. So I suggest we offer Austin $250,000."

Harlan Cross was known as a hard ass negotiator in the bankruptcy area and that reputation now reared its head. "I have a better idea. Dillon Clark must have taken Austin's case on a contingency.

Why don't we put the screws to their relationship? Offer to pay Austin $50,000 and to pay Clark's fees to date at his regular hourly rate but put a cap on it of $150,000. This takes the risk of losing away from Clark and his firm and puts money in Mark's pocket."

There was a period of brief silence before everyone in the room saw the strategy and they all began laughing. Derrick Warner slapped the table and said with glee, "A brilliant idea, Harlan. This puts the screws to Dillon Clark. He settles and gets $150,000 or risks getting nothing!"

"I sure wouldn't want to sit across from you in a poker game, Harlan," Haverley said. "But to be safe, give me authority to go up to $100,000 for Mark if it looks like we are close."

"OK. You got it," Harlan Cross replied.

After Haverley left the meeting, Harlan Cross, Derrick Warner and Wayne Bailey stayed and talked about what they could do with Jerry Keller.

"That bastard has come close to ruining this firm," Harlan Cross said with considerable irritation in his voice. "I did a count, and between the business lawyers and trial lawyers he took with him when he split, we lost twenty-four attorneys, and four of them were partners."

"Are we going to replace them?" Wayne Bailey asked.

"We have to," Harlan Cross replied. "If we don't we're going to be stuck on our lease for another five years. Hell, we leased too much to begin with thinking we would grow into the space. We're sitting on over 20,000 square feet right now of empty office space. That's costing us a bundle every damn month. And you know what? We may lose more partners once they hear about what Jerry and Alison did?"

The three said nothing for a few minutes thinking of the potential for a grim future for the law firm. Harlan Cross broke the silence and, looking at Derrick Warner, said, "Derrick, I know we decided not to sue Jerry for soliciting the firm's clients, but things are different now. I want you to have someone do an extensive research memo on Jerry's potential liability. We all know there is a fiduciary duty between partners and the partnership agreement prohibits soliciting firm clients when a partner leaves voluntarily. And get our employment guys to do the same research. Let's see if we can sue the bastard!"

As quickly as Alison Craft could get out of the courthouse, she pulled out her cell phone and called Jerry Keller. It was Keller she had been trying to reach on her cell phone during the break.

Jerry Keller could see it was Craft on his cell phone and he answered. "How did it go today?" he casually asked.

"Not good, Jerry. I tried calling you but you didn't answer," Craft said nervously.

"I was in a meeting, Alison. Just calm down. Tell me what happened," Keller replied.

Keller could audibly hear Craft take in several deep breaths before she answered. "Clark kept pushing and pushing and, well, I... Well, I'm sorry Jerry. He got me to say that you asked me to write the memo!" Craft explained.

"What the hell, Alison. How did he do that? All you had to do was stick to your story," Keller said in exasperation.

"I don't know. At one point I used your name and he just kept asking me 'Did I mean you' and, well, he just wouldn't let it go. So I said you asked me to write the memo and send it to the Executive Committee."

Keller had his cell phone in a vice-grip as he thought over what could now happen. He, Alison and the others had been allowed to leave the Baukus & Johnson firm with no fuss, but he knew this could change things dramatically. In a suddenly subdued voice he said, "Alison, come on back to the office and we can talk this over."

"But I did say that what I wrote was true, and that seemed to make Mr. Haverley happy," Craft added.

"Shit," is all Keller said in reply.

"Jerry, I'm so sorry. What happens now?" Craft asked pleadingly.

Keller did not immediately answer. He thought over what had happened and was concerned about Harlan Cross, who was not someone you wanted as your enemy. But he also knew he had to get Alison out of the courthouse and back to the office, so he said, "Alison, we're ok on this. Haverley is right. What you said was true and that's why Austin was let go."

"But what about Harlan? He's going to be furious when he hears what I did," Craft asked anxiously.

"Frankly, I don't give a damn what Harlan thinks. Get on back to the office," Keller said angrily as he switched off his cell phone.

After the meeting in chambers with Judge Harpman, Dillon told Mark and the others that he wanted a meeting back at his office to discuss what had happened and the idea of a settlement. Mark and Suzzi were emotionally exhausted and wanted to go straight home. Dillon understood and said, "You both go on home. But call me if you have any ideas on settlement. I'll give you a ring later tonight."

Kelly called ahead and Laurel Kennedy was already in the conference room when she and Dillon arrived back at the office.

When Dillon entered the conference room, he threw his suit coat on top of the table and walked over to the bar and poured himself a generous portion of Macallan scotch. As he gently placed one ice cube in the glass he said, "Well, quite a day!"

They sat around the conference table discussing Alison Craft's testimony and what Judge Harpman had said in chambers and what the jury was thinking. "We have to just wait and see if the firm makes a settlement offer," Dillon explained. "The judge is right in his concern that a jury might think Alison is not being truthful, but we still have Mark's concession that even a vote by one partner is enough to deny Mark a partnership. This could kill any chance of getting meaningful damages for wage loss."

Dillon swiveled his chair around and plopped his feet up on the conference room table, and asked, "Is there anything that we are missing?"

Kelly had been thinking of the issues as they drove back to the office. She replied, "Dillon, remember the computer expert we used in the Shannon case? We hired him to see if the computer that was used still had other drafts of the key documents. I still have his card. So why don't we ask the judge for an order requiring the firm to produce whatever computer Craft would have been using? We can have the expert look it over to see if she did other drafts. If she did, maybe they contradict what she sent to the Executive Committee."

Dillon smiled and said, "OK. I like it. Craft went out of her way to say what she said was the truth even if it was Keller's idea. Good job Kelly. Prepare a subpoena for the computer and bring it to court tomorrow. If the judge goes along, we can serve Cross if he shows up. If not, I suspect Haverley will accept service. He won't want us sending a process server over to the law firm."

Changing subjects, Dillon asked, "Any thoughts on settlement?"

Kelly spoke first. "With everything Mark and Suzzi have been through, I can't see settling for less than six or seven hundred thousand. Mark may still not be able to get into another large firm."

Dillon threw a glance over towards Laurel Kennedy and asked, "Laurel, what's your take?"

Laurel Kennedy smiled and said, "I have to be with Kelly on this one. Mark and Suzzi have gone through hell all because Jerry Keller did not like Mark. If I were on the jury, I'd hit them with at least a million."

"You're both missing something important," Dillon replied. "If the jury doesn't find liability, we never even get to the issue of damages. The case just stops at that point and Austin goes home with nothing!"

Kelly and Laurel looked at each other and Laurel finally asked, "So what do you suggest?"

"If we can get two or three hundred thousand into Mark's pocket, I would take it. I'd even cut our fees to maybe fifty thousand just to see them recover something. But right now, we just have to wait and see what Baukus & Johnson offers tomorrow morning."

Before leaving for the day, Dillon told Kelly to call Jerry Keller. In light of Alison Craft's testimony, he now for sure wanted to ask him some questions. And he called Mark at home and explained what they had in mind on settlement.

CHAPTER 11

Trial – Day Four
(Thursday, January 7)
(Efforts to Settle Fail)

The weather in Los Angeles was unusually hot and muggy for January and Dillon was sweating by the time he walked the hundred yards or so from the parking garage under the Music Center to the entrance of the Los Angeles County Superior Court building.

As he passed through the security x-ray system, Dillon felt the same anxiety he felt when he first awoke that morning. "We now know that Alison Craft had been lying, but so what? How is the jury going to view that when she also said her criticism of Mark's performance was true?" he thought to himself as he walked over to the elevators to go up to Judge Harpman's courtroom.

When he entered the courtroom, Dillon saw that Haverley and Harlan Cross were already seated at the counsel table and that Mark and Kelly were standing to the side talking. When he approached, Kelly said, "I've got the subpoena ready if the judge agrees."

When the clerk saw that all counsel were present, she said, "Judge Harpman would like to talk with counsel before court starts."

The clerk, Charmaine Parker, added, "You know the way, gentlemen. He'll see you in his chambers.

As they entered Judge Harpman's chambers and sat down in the chairs in front of his desk, he said, "The clerk tells me that

Harlan Cross is in court today. Have you considered my comments on settlement?"

"We have, Your Honor," Haverley replied. "We all know there is no certainty with a jury, but my clients believe they acted properly. This case is not complex. Alison Craft said she would not have voted to make Mark Austin a partner. This right there ends the case for the plaintiffs."

Judge Harpman raised his eyebrow inquiringly but said nothing.

Haverley shifted slightly in his chair and then added, "But the firm does want to settle if possible. We will offer to pay Austin and his wife fifty thousand dollars cash and will pay Dillon Clark's fees at his regular rate but with a cap of one hundred and fifty thousand. We think we can win the liability issue, but this guarantees that Austin and his wife will get money in their pocket. We pay the fees."

Judge Harpman looked over at Dillon and asked, "What do you think, Mr. Clark? At bit unusual, but it sure beats rolling the dice with the jury."

Dillon by now was more than a little angry. He had seen attorneys try to put a wedge between an attorney and client before by trying to essentially bribe the lawyer into taking a crappy settlement. The lawyer gets paid but the client gets next to nothing."

"Your Honor, this is clearly an improper settlement offer. I'm actually stunned to think that a firm like Baukus & Johnson would consider trying to entice me to settle by paying my fees."

It was now Judge Harpman's turn to get angry. "Mr. Clark, you have an ethical obligation to go out there and inform your clients of the offer. Do it now! And if they say no, then just remember, I warned you about what a jury could do in this case. If they don't like the offer, come back with one of your own. We'll start the trial in ten minutes if I don't hear back. Just tell the clerk that the case is going to settle or not," Judge Harpman said testily.

It took Dillon only a few minutes to explain the settlement offer and why it was improper. "They're just playing games," he told Mark and Suzzi. "If you want, I'll tell Haverley that you will settle for three hundred and I'll cut our fees to fifty. That will put two fifty into your bank account."

Mark looked over at Suzzi and then back to Dillon. "We'll do whatever you recommend."

Dillon walked over to the defense table and asked Haverley and Cross to join him out in the hallway. When they reached the hallway outside of the courtroom, they walked down the hallway where they had some privacy. Dillon spoke first. "Gentlemen, following the judge's direction, we are prepared to make a settlement offer. What you offered is not only unacceptable, but probably unethical. You know as well as I do, what you were doing is trying to bribe me into settling so I get paid." Dillon shook his head and added, "I'm surprised you didn't learn more about me, Mr. Haverley. If you had checked, you'd know I don't need the money. And even if I did, I wouldn't accept such a sleazy offer!"

Haverley started to speak, but Harlan Cross raised his hand to stop him and said, "Mr. Clark, you're playing with Mark Austin's life. He's going to lose this case, or if he wins his damages will be minimal. I think our offer was more than fair."

"Mr. Cross, I don't want to argue the point with you. Mark and I are more than happy to let the jury decide. But again, following the judge's direction, Mark will settle for three hundred thousand. You can leave what fee I get up to me."

Harlan Cross didn't wait for Haverley to reply to Dillon's offer. Instead, he said, "Mr. Clark, this is the biggest mistake you've ever made. If we win liability, you and your client get nothing." As he said this, Cross turned and walked back into the courtroom.

Dillon looked at Haverley and said with a smile, "I guess that was a no!"

When he walked back into the courtroom, Dillon told Mark and Suzzi what happened and then walked over and told the clerk, Charmaine Parker, that there was no settlement.

When Judge Harpman entered the courtroom and took his seat at the bench, Dillon stood and said, "Your Honor, in light of the rather surprising testimony by Alison Craft yesterday, we are asking for an order directing the Baukus & Johnson firm to permit our computer expert to examine whatever computer Alison Craft was using when she wrote the memo to the Executive Committee. I know Mr. Haverley will say we could have done this before, and that is true. But this would not waste any court or jury time. The whole task is on our nickel. But there may have been drafts of her memo that might contradict what she wrote, and this would go to her credibility. As you said before, Your Honor, Ms. Craft's memo is a pivotal piece of evidence and any inconsistencies could raise real questions about whether her testimony should be accepted by the jury."

While he was waiting on word of the settlement, Judge Harpman had reflected on the offer made by Baukus & Johnson and decided it really was a game. He actually got irritated at himself for even insisting that Dillon pass the offer on to his clients. So he was sympathetic as he sat listening to Dillon's argument. He remembered his conversation with Judge Bannerman and his comment about being conservative. He heard Haverley stressing in his argument that discovery was over and it is far too late to open it up now mid-trial. But he too was surprised by what Alison Craft had admitted to when she said that Jerry Keller asked her to write the memo.

When counsel finished arguing the issue, Judge Harpman made his ruling. "Gentlemen, my goal is to ensure a fair trial. I think we were all surprised with what Ms. Craft said yesterday. The law firm can run their own tests, if they haven't already, so I see no harm in letting Mr. Clark have the same right. So I will order that the firm produce the computer to Mr. Clark's designated expert by noon tomorrow. The expert is to focus only on communications written by Alison Craft that involve Mark Austin. We'll resume the trial at 1:30."

Harlan Cross was visibly upset with Judge Harpman's ruling. As he exited the courtroom with Haverley, he looked nervous and the muscles in his neck were slightly bulging as he tried to control his feelings. "God damn, Jason. What the hell does he think he's doing?" Cross snapped in anger. "Have you examined Craft's computer? Do we even know what's on it?"

"Are you saying there's something there we should be concerned about?" Haverley asked somewhat anxiously.

"Hell, who knows," Cross answered.

"I think you should talk with Alison asap and see what she says. It's her memo that created this mess. She should know if anything is wrong," Haverley replied.

Cross reached into his inner coat pocket and pulled out his cell phone and dialed Craft's number as they were taking the elevator down to the first floor. It rang several times and then went to voice mail. "She's not answering. I'll get her when I get to the office," Cross told Haverley.

When Cross got back to his office, he called Alison Craft again and she answered on the first ring. Cross explained Judge Harpman's ruling and asked, "Alison, did you use your laptop or desk top to type your memo?

"I used my desk top," Craft explained.

"Is there anything on that computer that we should worry about?" Cross asked. "Did you do any drafts of your memo on Austin before you gave it to Wayne Bailey?"

There was a brief pause before Craft answered. She thought back to her memo and her conversations with Jerry Keller. "Stupid of me to let him talk me into doing it!" she thought to herself. "Harlan, I only did one memo on Austin and that's the one I gave to Wayne. There's nothing else about Mark on the computer."

Satisfied with Craft's answers, Cross called Haverley as soon as he hung up. "She says the computer is clean. She wrote only one memo and no other drafts."

Jason Haverley heard what Cross just said, but as a trial lawyer, he wanted no unknowns. After reflecting for a second, he said, "Harlan, I hate surprises. Have your IT man take a look at the computer. Go back to the first of the year. No. Better yet, go back to when Mark first started with the firm. Do a search for anything Craft ever wrote about Mark Austin for the whole time. Right up to when she and Keller left the firm."

As Cross was about to hang up, Haverley added, "To be super safe, have your man also search for anything Craft may have received from others dealing with Austin as well. I want it all."

While Haverley and Cross were talking about Alison Craft and her computer, Dillon was meeting with Mark, Suzzi and Kelly in the cafeteria discussing what they wanted from the computer expert.

"Mark, are you familiar with what an expert can do with a computer?" Dillon asked.

"No way," Mark said quickly. "I can type and use the email system, but that pretty much exhausts my knowledge."

Dillon looked over to Kelly and said, "You probably know more than any of us. You worked closely with Jeff. I can't think of his last name."

"Jeff Hunt," Kelly said.

"Yes. Thank you," Dillon added. "What should we have him do with the Craft computer?"

Kelly turned toward where Mark and Suzzi were seated and said, "Jeff specializes in helping lawyers in litigation matters like this. He's testified in hundreds of cases."

"But how can he help in my case?" Mark asked.

Kelly clapped her hands together in excitement and said, "What most people don't know is that it is almost impossible to erase documents from a computer's hard drive. When you draft a letter, email or anything, and then change your mind and hit erase, you might think you are safe and no one would ever know what you said. Like the things we all write at times in anger but then tear-up and never send. Anyway, you'd be wrong."

"But now days the computer will ask you if you want to permanently delete an item. Are you saying that if I said yes, it would still be there?" Mark asked.

"That is exactly what I'm saying," Kelly replied. "A skilled expert can, in most cases, reconstruct the material. So in your case Mark, we want to see if Alison ever wrote other draft memos before she did the final one that went to the Executive Committee. If she did, who knows? She might have said things that will let us impeach her story, like a memo to another partner saying how great you were."

As Dillon sat listening to Kelly explain, he thought to himself, "Boy, we really are fishing in the dark here!" But with Mark's concession to Haverley on cross examination, he also knew they needed something to keep the jury from concluding that is was reasonable for the law firm to rely on Alison's memo, even if Keller put her up to it.

When Kelly finished explaining the process to Mark and his wife, Dillon said, "Kelly, give Jeff a call. Find out where he wants the computer delivered."

As they all stood to leave, Dillon paused and turned back to Kelly and added, "Kelly, tell Jeff to watch carefully for any recent deletions. I'll bet Craft has somebody looking at that computer right now as we speak. And Kelly, make sure Jerry Keller is here when court starts."

"Mark, I'm going to skip lunch today. I want to spend time reviewing my notes for Keller and reviewing his deposition before he testifies," Dillon said as he grabbed his old beat-up briefcase and went down to the attorney room next to Judge Harpman's courtroom to work.

As soon as Dillon left, Kelly pulled out her cell phone and called Jeff Hunt. Jeff answered right away and recalled his prior work with Kelly and Dillon. After they chatted for a few minutes about their last case, Kelly told Jeff about Mark's lawsuit and the significance of Alison Craft's memo and the hope he could find some prior drafts. She concluded by saying, "And Dillon asked that you specifically look for any recent deletions on the computer. He doesn't trust those running the law firm and thinks they might just delete anything there if it is harmful to them."

"OK. Got it," Jeff Hunt said. "Have the computer delivered to my LA office. I'll run a mirror image and see what we can find. And fax me a copy of the memo so I know what it looks like."

When Kelly hung up, she said, "He can get right on it. If we get him the computer by tomorrow, which is Friday, he might have something to us by the afternoon. But that could be pushing it. It could be over the weekend. It takes time. They first do an image of the hard drive to see what is there and then they start looking for other drafts that might have been done and then deleted."

When the trial resumed, Jerry Keller was sitting at the defense table with Haverley. Harlan Cross did not return.

Jerry Keller was wearing an immaculate light grey suit that evidenced the highly successful lawyer that he was. He had been the highest paid partner at Baukus & Johnson and a member of the Executive Committee before he and Alison Craft bolted to form their own law firm. He looked successful and very confident.

While it was subtle, Dillon also noticed that Keller was talking softly with Haverley. He assumed that when Kelly called Jerry Keller to attend the afternoon session, Keller had called Haverley to find out what was happening and was now getting an update.

After Keller was sworn by the clerk, Dillon began his questioning. "Alison Craft has testified that you asked her to prepare and send her memo to the Executive Committee saying that Mark Austin was, shall we say, not future partner material. Was she correct?"

"Yes, she was," Keller answered as he looked over at Mark sitting at the counsel table. He turned back to face Dillon and added, "I had concerns about Mark from the time he agreed to do all of the billings for the Gibbons companies. It showed a distinct lack of maturity. Once he prepared the bills, the department heads had to review them and Mark knew that. No bill would ever go out to a client as important as Gibbons without a senior partner making sure things were correct."

"When you asked Alison to prepare her memo, was it your intention to have Mark Austin fired?" Dillon aggressively asked.

"Absolutely not," Keller shot back with firmness in his voice. "Alison and I talked about Mark and she expressed her own concerns about his experience on tax problems. I told her that she should then share her concerns with the Executive Committee. Nothing more."

"Mr. Keller, you had served on the Executive Committee. Surely you knew that if a partner said Mark was not partner material, this would end his career at Baukus & Johnson?" Dillon asked.

"Part of what you say is true, Mr. Clark. We all know as partners that if any partner objects, the firm would never make an associate a partner. To do otherwise would fly in the face of what a partnership is all about. Partners have a fiduciary duty to each other. You just can't force them to accept a new partner."

This was the line of defense that Haverley got Mark to concede on cross examination and Dillon's gut tightened slightly. This was a brilliant defense and deadly if the jury bought into it. And the Baukus & Johnson partners had the script down pat.

Dillon paused, locked his eyes with Keller and with impatience asked, "Mr. Keller, when did you first talk with Alison Craft about writing a memo? It was dated November 15."

Keller thought for a moment and replied, "I can't be positive, but it had to be in late October or early November. Alison is the one who brought up the subject. We were in her office, as I recall. I don't know why the issue came up, but I presume she made her comment because she knew I was not happy with Mark"

"Mr. Keller, you later got upset with Mark Austin when he sent a request for a bonus because he brought in the Gibbons's accounts. Isn't that right?"

Keller stiffened as he sat in the witness chair and said irritably, "That is correct. Mark's memo asked for the origination credit, but that is part of the Tier Two compensation that goes only to senior partners. And the partnership agreement says it goes to whoever first did work for the client. I had done work for one of the Gibbons's companies a few years back, so I was the one who first worked Gibbons."

Keller hesitated a second and then added, "I'm aware that Wayne Bailey told Mark to make the request, but Bailey was wrong. Once we realized there was some ambiguity, we amended the language so it applied only to senior partners. This is how we had always interpreted it so we were only making a clarification."

"Yes, I understand that," Dillon replied. "But what I want to know is whether Mark's request and your belief that you should get the origination credit had anything to do with you telling Alison to write her memo?"

"No, that had nothing to do with it. I think Mark's request had not even been sent to the Executive Committee when Alison and I were talking about him," Keller answered.

Dillon now looked up to Judge Harpman and asked, "Your Honor, may I approach the witness and show him an exhibit?"

Judge Harpman waived his hand in consent and Dillon picked up an exhibit and walked up to the witness stand and handed it to Keller. "Mr. Keller, do you recognize this as the memo that Alison Craft wrote to the Executive Committee?" he asked.

Keller took a quick glance at the exhibit and said, "Yes. This is the memo."

"Please note the date of November 15. Did she show you this memo before she sent it?" Dillon asked.

"Of course she did," Keller replied.

"Did you tell her what to write?" Dillon asked with equal irritation.

"Mr. Clark, I told you already. Alison expressed her concerns and I just told her to go ahead and do a memo to the Executive Committee. Nothing more," Keller said with growing indignation.

Since he was getting nowhere with Keller, Dillon switched to when Mark was fired. "You were at the meeting when the firm decided to fire Mark. Right?"

Keller glanced over at Harlan Cross who had decided it might be best to return and attend the trial while Keller was testifying, and then said, "Yes. That is correct. Harlan asked me to attend because Derrick Warner was out of town.'

"Did you vote as part of the Committee to fire Mark?" Dillon asked.

"No. Only the Executive Committee can fire an associate," Keller replied. "I sat in and listened and when Harlan and Wayne made the decision, I stayed while they informed Mark."

"So the decision to fire Mark was made the day he was informed?" Dillon asked.

"Yes. We met early that morning," Keller replied.

"That was December 22. Correct?" Dillon asked.

"I think that is right," Keller answered.

"OK. After Mark was fired, did the three of you talk about…" Dillon started to ask. But before he finished, Haverley objected.

"Your Honor, this question clearly violates …" Haverley started to argue, but Judge Harpman raised his hand to stop him and turning to the jury he said, "We're going to take a recess now and give you all a few minutes to relax."

When the jurors had all excited the courtroom, Judge Harpman said, "I don't want arguments like this in front of the jury." Turning to Haverley, he asked, "What is your objection?"

"The Executive Committee runs the law firm, Your Honor. What they say to each other is protected by the attorney-client privilege and privacy rules," Haverley asserted.

"This issue is expressly covered in the pretrial order," Dillon replied. "The attorney client privilege does not come into play until the lawsuit was filed. What the Executive Committee said and did relating to firing of Mark Austin before and up the time he was fired, is highly relevant and is not protected."

"I have to agree with Mr. Clark," Judge Harpman replied. "I think any member of the Executive Committee or anyone they spoke to can be questioned leading up to the lawsuit. If I don't allow this, the appellate court would reverse me."

After the recess, Dillon took a more aggressive approach with Jerry Keller.

"Mr. Keller, do you remember the question? I asked you to tell the jury what everyone said to each other at the Executive Committee meeting the day Mark was fired."

Keller sat stiff in the witness chair and it was plain to see he was not pleased with the judge's ruling. He locked his eyes with Dillon's and said, "I don't recall the exact words, but we discussed Alison Craft's memo and how the firm cannot force an associate on a partner who doesn't want to work with the associate. There was some discussion about Mark's memo requesting a Tier Two bonus and it was agreed that only partners were entitled to participate."

"Anything else?" Dillon asked skeptically.

"Not that I recall," Keller replied.

"You said that only partners were entitled to Tier Two compensation. Please explain to the jury what Tier Two means" Dillon asked.

"The law firm's profits are divided into two parts. The Executive Committee sets an amount for each partner to receive monthly. This is called Tier One. The balance of the firm's profits goes into another pool that is called Tier Two. This pool is divided at the end of each year based on merit. The idea is to compensate each partner according to what they have contributed to the firm during that year," Keller explained.

"Was Mark's request for a bonus a factor in firing him?" Dillon asked.

"Not to my knowledge," Keller answered. "The decision was Alison's memo. You just don't want to string an associate along if a partner feels that the candidate is not partner material."

"You were upset with the whole idea that Mark asked for a bonus because you felt you were the originating attorney. Isn't that correct?" Dillon demanded.

"Upset is not the right word. He was not entitled to a bonus from Tier Two," Keller replied.

Dillon was becoming frustrated. He could sense that something was not right but it just would not come into focus so he again changed subjects. "Mr. Keller, when Mark was fired, you instructed the personnel folks at Baukus & Johnson to pass any calls from other law firms making inquiries about Mark to you. Am I right?"

"Yes, I did," Keller answered.

"But you were not Mark's boss at the firm. He worked in estate planning under Wayne Bailey. So why did you get involved?" Dillon asked skeptically.

"I was asked by Harlan Cross to attend the meeting. I had been a member of the Executive Committee in prior years and Mark worked in my department for a while, so I just volunteered. It would have been either me or Wayne and to be honest, there were only a half dozen or so calls and I thought nothing of it," Keller explained.

"But you took that role seriously, right?" Dillon asked.

"Of course," Keller replied.

"Taking your role seriously, did you tell any of the attorneys who called asking about Mark Austin that he was a troublemaker?" Dillon asked in a stiff angry voice.

Jerry Keller knew that Dillon had asked these same questions in his deposition which he had read over quickly once he got the call to testify. So he cautiously said, "I don't recall using those exact words. I did say that Mark showed a lack of maturity for asking for origination credit for bringing in a large client."

"Mr. Keller, the jury here has heard from several managing partners of firms that Mark Austin applied to and who called you. They have said you questioned his trustworthiness. That is a serious allegation. Did you question his trustworthiness?" Dillon now demanded.

"No. I was upset when Mark insisted on being the billing attorney for the Gibbons accounts. Gibbons wanted him to do the billings, but he should have thought of the firm above all else and politely declined. Because he didn't, we had to have the department heads review all of the billings before they were mailed out. I did then, and still do, think that Austin's conduct did put into question his trustworthiness. I don't think I used that word, but I may have given that impression. Mark was not using good judgment," Keller explained.

"So if I understand you correctly, you are telling this jury that you were upset with Mark and may have given the 'impression' he was not trustworthy because of the way he handled the billings. Is that correct?" Dillon asked incredulously.

"Mark was just not using common sense when he insisted on doing the billings. This to me was a sign of immaturity and that relates to whether he is trustworthy. They are all one and the same."

"Mr. Keller, as the saying goes, it's time to cut to the chase on this issue. If you were asked today, point blank, was Mark Austin trustworthy, you would say no. Am I right?" Dillon asked now with firmness in his voice.

"Yes, you are correct," Keller replied with a scowl on his face. "You have to understand that whether someone is trustworthy is somewhat subjective. In my book, when an associate has an opportunity to do what is best for the law firm, but instead acts to promote himself, as Mark did, he puts his own character in question. That to me is not being trustworthy."

Dillon took a long hard look at Keller before he continued. It was obvious that he had prepared himself for his testimony, so he decided to end on a high note. "Mr. Keller, I have just one more question." As he said this, he glanced over at the jury and saw them watching intently. "Knowing that Alison Craft's memo would result in Mark Austin being fired, you advised Alison to nevertheless send the memo to the Executive Committee. Is this correct sir?" Dillon asked with obvious scorn.

Keller took a long ten seconds before he answered. "Yes," he finally replied.

Judge Harpman recessed the trial for the day after Haverley asked Keller a few clarifying questions. As they were leaving the courtroom, Dillon saw that Harlan Cross waited for Jerry Keller to step down from the witness stand. They were each visibly upset and pointing a finger at each other. It was not hard to guess the topic.

Dillon and Kelly walked with Mark and his wife to the parking garage under the Music Center where they had all parked their cars. As they reached their cars, Dillon said, "We've now seen the defense in all its glory. Haverley is clever. He has positioned the firm as making a business decision. How many times have we heard so far that a firm can't make a lawyer a partner if even one partner objects?" Dillon mused. "Haverley has them well coached. They've read the jury instructions on wrongful termination and know we have to show bad faith. They'll argue that once Alison objected to Mark being a partner, they had no choice. It was just a reasonable business decision!"

Kelly was the first to reply. "For sure that is the defense. But I've been watching the jury and they seem concerned. Maybe they think the firm acted hastily without giving Mark a chance to prove himself?"

"Don't you think that Craft was just blindly doing whatever Keller wanted?" Suzzi asked. "She did cover up the fact that he asked her to write the damn thing!"

Dillon reached out and touched Suzzi's arm and said, "I know you don't like her, but even if Keller asked her to write the memo, she still said her objections to Mark were the truth. So we still get down to whether it is a valid business decision."

Mark had not said a word since they left the courtroom. He now stopped walking and looked at Dillon. His voice cracked slightly as he asked, "Do we still have a chance?"

"Of course we do," Dillon replied. "Go home and get some rest. We should hear something from the computer expert tomorrow. Maybe he'll find some other drafts. Who knows?" Dillon said with an encouraging smile.

CHAPTER 12

The Trial – Day Five
(Friday, January 8)
(Alison's Computer)

After Jerry Keller finished his testimony and the trial recessed for the day, Haverley and Cross went back to the Baukus & Johnson firm's conference room for a strategy discussion. Cross had phoned ahead and Derrick Warner joined them.

After they each fixed themselves a drink from the bar, Harlan Cross took off his coat, loosened his tie and said to Haverley as he plopped himself down in one of the leather conference room chairs, "Well, for what it's worth, I think we had a pretty good day despite that idiot Keller. You've set up the defense brilliantly."

Derrick Warner shook his head and asked, "Jason, is there anything more we can add to the liability issue? I'm asking because if the jury has all of the defense evidence, maybe we should consider asking the judge to cancel the bifurcation order? If we stick with it, and the jury is just asked whether what happened constitutes a wrongful termination, they might feel sorry for Austin and vote liability."

"I've thought about this option," Haverley said with a hesitant look. "But what concerns me is that Austin has been unable to get another job with a major law firm. If we go ahead and let Clark put on damage evidence now, this could back-fire on us if the jury is sympathetic and votes yes on liability."

Cross thought for a moment and asked, "Derrick, what has our IT department come up with on Alison's computer? Anything damaging?"

"The thing is clean," Derrick Warner replied. "No prior drafts. Just her normal work stuff. We sent it to Clark's expert earlier today. He should have it by now."

"Anything at all on it about Austin?" Haverley asked.

"There are some work memos from her to Mark, but those just deal with some assignments she gave him. There's absolutely nothing that Clark could use to get at her testimony," Derrick Warner answered.

"Incidentally," Cross said, "I got a call from Dale Bannerman. As you know, he did some employment law before he went on the bench. Anyway, he came up with a good suggestion. He thinks that on the issue of liability, we should argue that Mark, as a junior partner, was not an employee and therefore not covered by the wrongful termination rules. His idea is to ask Judge Harpman to grant a motion for judgment in favor of the defendants at the close of the plaintiff's case."

Haverley liked the idea immediately. "Hot damn," he said. "I like it. I'll get the motion prepared so we are ready when the plaintiffs rest.

"It may not be so easy," Derrick Warner interjected. "I think we give junior partners a normal 1040 just like any employee. They don't get a K-1 like the partners."

Cross pondered the matter for a second and said, "Do it anyway. I think Dale has mentioned this to Harpman so he just might go our way."

Cross looked over at Haverley and smiled. He raised his glass and said, "May the great principles of justice continue to flow in our favor!"

After Dillon and Kelly said goodbye to Mark and his wife when the trial recessed for the day, they, too, drove back to their offices. Laurel Kennedy had been checking on the progress of Jeff's examination of Craft's computer and she met them in Dillon's office.

"Has he found anything?" Dillon asked as he was pouring himself a healthy splash of Macallan scotch.

"Nothing yet," Laurel replied. "He's imaged the whole hard drive and it is clean."

"What about other memos or deletions about Austin? Anything?" Dillon pressed.

Laurel sighed audibly and said, "I'm sorry, Dillon. He's found nothing but work assignments."

Dillon began rolling his pencil between his fingers in agitation. "Damn it all. I wish the jury could hear what this whole mess has caused Mark and his wife. It might make a difference."

What bothered Dillon the most was the uncertainty. He knew from years of trials that the winner is often who the jury likes the most and not justice. Justice, if at all, was often accidental. And this is what scares trial lawyers. They never know what might appeal to a jury; or what might be that one single tiny piece of evidence that turns a jury against one side or the other.

After discussing the evidence for a while, Dillon decided that they had to put Mark back on the witness stand to explain again that it was Bailey who suggested he ask for a bonus. Bailey was a member of the Executive Committee and surely the jury would not find fault with Mark following his suggestion. Or at least this was the theory.

Dillon reached down and pulled out his cell phone and dialed Mark's number. He answered on the second ring. "Sorry, Mark, but Jeff found nothing helpful on Alison's computer. But I've been kicking around the evidence so far on liability with Laurel and

Kelly, and we have decided we need to put you back on the stand to clarify again exactly why you wrote the memo to the Executive Committee. I know the defense is resting on Alison's memo, and we can't do anything about that. But Jerry Keller did say they discussed your bonus memo when the Executive Committee met the morning they decided to fire you, and we need to remind the jury that it was Wayne Bailey who suggested you write it. But I want to take no chance on the jury forgetting that it was Bailey who told you to write it."

Mark did not respond at first and Dillon finally asked, "Mark, are you there?"

"I'm still here," Mark said so softly that Dillon could hardly hear what he said.

"Mark, there's nothing to worry about. My questions will be short. Just tell the jury it was your boss, Wayne Bailey, who suggested you write the memo," Dillon explained.

After he finished talking with Mark, Dillon had Laurel check on the status of the computer examination. She called Jeff Hunt and passed on his comments to Dillon. "Still nothing. But he's still working on it."

When Dillon got home that night he felt unusually pessimistic. He desperately needed something to take away the sting of Mark's admission. And that something, if it existed, was buried somewhere beyond his mental reach.

After several healthy pours of Macallan along with warmed up Chinese food that was probably a week old, Dillon changed clothes and put on a warm-up suit and tennis shoes and went for a long walk. He lived in the hills above Santa Monica, so even a short two mile walk was good exercise and usually cleared his head. But not tonight. His head felt like it was in a vice and he could not shake the uneasiness that he felt thinking about what would happen to Mark and his wife if he lost the case. By the time he got back to his house, he was sweating but could almost feel a chill of fear.

CHAPTER 13

Trial – Day Six
(Monday, January 11)
(Law Firm's Motion for Defense Judgment)

After working with Mark and Suzzi on their testimony over the weekend, Dillon met them at the courthouse cafeteria before the trial started on Monday. He went over the questions he planned on asking Mark. Mark seemed relaxed and knew he was on safe ground because even Wayne Bailey agreed he told him to write the bonus memo.

As they took the elevator down to Judge Harpman's floor, Dillon could see the tension increase in Mark. He began walking stiffly and his head hung down and he had a stony-look on his face.

The hallway outside the courtroom was packed. There were about twenty courtrooms on Judge Harpman's floor and easily a hundred or more lawyers and their clients were walking in every direction and talking all at the same time. As they approached Judge Harpman's courtroom, Dillon lightly touched Mark's shoulder and said, "Just tell the jury your conversation with Wayne Bailey and how he suggested you write the memo asking for the bonus. No big deal, OK?"

Mark just shrugged his shoulders. When they entered the courtroom, he walked up to the counsel table and sat down. Suzzi took her seat in the audience section and looked equally distressed.

When Judge Harpman took the bench, he looked down at Dillon and asked, "Are you ready to proceed, Mr. Clark?"

Dillon looked over at Mark and saw him nod his head in approval. "I would like to recall Mark Austin for a few clarifying questions in light of the testimony by Alison Craft and Jerry Keller."

As he said this, Mark stood and walked up to the witness stand. He was clearly nervous and every one of the jurors watched his every step. When he sat down, Mark started to raise his hand but Judge Harpman stopped him by saying, "There is no need to be sworn again, Mr. Austin."

Dillon had been watching the jury and today they looked passive and he could not detect what they were thinking. After a second, he turned toward Mark and asked, "Mr. Austin, you heard the testimony from Mr. Keller that he thought you showed a lack of maturity when you wrote a memo to the Executive Committee seeking a bonus for being the attorney who brought in the Gibbons's accounts. You heard this, I presume?"

"I did," mark answered with a stiff voice.

"I know you explained this before, but to clarify, please tell the jury why you wrote that memo," Dillon said.

Mark grimaced as he looked over at the jury and in an obviously strained voice said, "Honestly, it never occurred to me to seek a bonus. It was Wayne Bailey who walked into my office and told me that as a junior partner, I was entitled to the origination credit for the work Mr. Gibbons brought to the firm. He told me to write the memo. I, well . . ." He took a deep breath, looked out to where Suzzi was sitting with Laurel and added. "I would never have done it if Wayne had not told me to. I loved my job." He swallowed hard and added, "And, well, that's it."

Dillon took a quick glance at the jury and saw that they were watching Mark and said, "I have nothing further, Your Honor," Dillon said in an equally quiet voice.

Judge Harpman now looked over at Haverley and asked, "Any questions, Mr. Haverley?"

Haverley, Cross and Derrick Warner had discussed for hours whether to question Mark further on the Alison Craft memo. It was the key to the law firm's defense. Consequently, they made the decision last night to call Mark themselves. They wanted to remind the jury that the Executive Committee based their entire decision to ask Mark to leave before the end of the year on that memo. If he was gone before the year ended, even as a senior partner, he would not be entitled to origination credit or any bonus.

Haverley hesitated for a moment as he thought back to the decision to recall Mark for further testimony. He knew that Mark's admission that the objection of even one partner was enough to kill any chance an associate had of becoming a partner should result in a defense verdict. And he didn't want to give Mark another shot at explaining away his admission. But the decision was made, so he slowly stood and replied to Judge Harpman's question. "I have just a few questions."

Haverley walked over to the clerk's desk and retrieved Craft's memo and set in down on the witness table in front of Mark and walked back to the defense table. "Mr. Austin, the exhibit I just handed you is the memo Alison Craft wrote to the Executive Committee. You've seen this memo before, right?"

"I have," Mark replied.

"You heard her explain that, while it was Mr. Keller's idea, what she said was nevertheless accurate about your performance?"

"I heard what she said," Mark said but now with a cold stare.

"Now, just so we have no misunderstanding, you agreed with me earlier in this trial that if even one partner does not want an associate to be a partner, the partnership cannot force that associate on the partner by going against his or her wishes. You did say that, right?"

Mark stared at Haverley for a long moment. He finally swallowed hard, looked over at Dillon and said, "I did. Yes."

"Thank you, Mr. Austin. I have no further questions," Haverley said with a wry smile as he watched a number of jurors nod in agreement."

There are times in almost every trial where the trial lawyer knows a potential mortal blow has landed on his case, and this was one of those times. Dillon tried his best to act as if nothing important had happened, but inside he was angry with himself for exposing Mark to a second cross examination by Haverley, and he could feel that old familiar ache forming deep inside his stomach.

Among the many so-called rules of litigation that every trial lawyer is taught from day one, is that you must never end your case on a negative. And Haverley's cross examination of Mark, reminding the jury of his concession, was a negative. Phase one of the trial on liability was now over. Dillon had now put all of his evidence before the jury and he now had no choice but to inform Judge Harpman that he had concluded his case and was ready to argue liability.

Dillon saw that Judge Harpman was looking at him, so he stood and said, "Your Honor, this concludes the plaintiff's case on liability."

Judge Harpman turned to Haverley and asked, "Counselor, do you have anything further?"

"No, Your Honor. We rest on the liability issue as well," Haverley replied.

Judge Harpman looked up at the clock and saw that it was getting close to noon. Looking over at the jury he said, "Ladies and gentlemen, as I explained at the start of this case, the issues have been bifurcated. The first phase of the trial, the one you have been hearing, has been on liability. The attorneys will now summarize the evidence and argue their respective positions and I will then instruct you on the law you are to follow. You will then be taken by the bailiff to the jury room where you will deliberate until you reach a verdict. If you find no liability, the case will be over. If you find that the defendants are liable for wrongful termination or intentional emotional distress, we will then proceed to the next stage and you will hear testimony on the issue of damages. When that phase is over, you will then deliberate until you reach a verdict on damages. But for now, I am going to excuse you until 1:30."

As the jurors were exciting the courtroom, Judge Haverley said, "Counsel, would you please join me in chambers for a moment."

When they were seated in the leather chairs in front of his desk, Judge Harpman said, "I just want to be clear on the jury instructions. Most of them are standard instructions, but I want you both to be absolutely clear on the key ones covering wrongful termination. The key one is the breach of the covenant of good faith, and I've had Charmaine type out the version I intend to give." As he said this, he handed a copy of the instruction to both Dillon and Haverley.

After reading over the instruction, Dillon and Haverley both agreed it is correct.

"Your Honor," Haverley said, "we have another issue before we argue the liability issue. We are asking for a judgment for the defense because Mark Austin was not an employee at the time he was terminated. He was a junior partner, and that is the only evidence that is before the court. If he was not an employee, the wrongful termination issues, including the covenant of good faith, do not apply. In fact, I have a formal motion to file." And he handed a copy to Judge Harpman and Dillon.

"This is absurd," Dillon replied angrily. "Austin's personnel file is in evidence and all he ever received was a 1040 which is what every employee receives. And let's remember, it has been the defendants who have said repeatedly that Mark was not a partner and therefore not entitled to share in the origination credit. They can't talk out of both sides of their mouth!"

This was a new issue for Judge Harpman. He leaned back in his chair and thought for a moment. "This is an entirely new issue, so I'm going to allow Mr. Clark until tomorrow morning to file a reply brief. This will put off until tomorrow your arguments and the instructions to the jury. Let's deal with this on Tuesday at 8:30."

When Dillon, Kelly, Mark and Suzzi left the courtroom and were standing in the hallway, Dillon explained the motion that Haverley had filed. He handed it to Kelly and said, "Take a look at the law, but I suspect you will find nothing. They are trying to say Mark was in some kind of special category as a junior partner. They don't want him to be a partner, but now they also don't want him to be an employee. The whole thing is crazy."

The frustration on Mark's face was overpowering. With great anxiety he said, "But they are right! I wasn't an employee after I became a junior partner."

"Mark, take it easy," Dillon replied. "The name junior partner does not mean you weren't an employee. It is a title only. You stay an employee until you become a senior partner entitled to all of the benefits. You become a part owner."

"I'm not so sure," Mark replied. "Harlan Cross is one smart guy and he wouldn't let Haverley file a frivolous motion. They must think there is merit."

"Mark, we'll research this, but they have denied you were a partner so I don't see how they can get around that inconsistency," Dillon replied in an attempt to allay Mark's concerns.

Later that afternoon, Kelly walked into Dillon's office with a research memo in her hand and laid it on his desk. "You were right. There is really no law covering a junior partner. The court just applies the same standards as for any employee. Haverley is correct that partners are not subject to the same covenant of good faith protections. If Mark were a partner, he would have to allege a breach of fiduciary duty or a violation of some provision in the partnership agreement. The trouble though, is that the jury instruction has as one element of the cause of action that the plaintiff must prove an 'employment relationship.' So it turns out to be a question of fact for the jury to decide."

"Boy, I sure wonder what the jury is thinking," Kelly asked in frustration. "

"Kelly, we have no idea what the jury is thinking at this point. If we're lucky and they think that Alison made up her criticism of Mark to please Keller, they just might find that she knew what she said was a lie. And if they do, the instruction that the law firm is responsible for the acts of any of its partners comes into play. This is the old 'Respondeat Superior' doctrine you learned in law school. The only difference is we have a partnership and they are all responsible for the conduct of each partner," Dillon explained with a big smile."

"Do you think the judge will give that instruction?" Kelly asked skeptically.

"He pretty much has to," Dillon replied. "The partnership can only act through the partners. And Craft and Keller were both partners."

"Kelly was shaking her head and said almost in a whisper, "You know, if I was on the jury, I think I would favor the law firm. The Executive Committee based the decision on Craft's memo!"

Who knows," Dillon answered. "But they are trying to play games with the employee issue and Harpman just might let the whole thing go to the jury. I've said all along, if they believe Alison Craft, we have lost."

After Kelly left his office, Dillon sat at his desk for the good part of an hour thinking. He began to question his own logic. "Sure, we don't know what the jury is thinking, but I have to be honest. It is a huge stretch to think they will find that Alison was lying. And without that, there is no basis to find an intent to harm Mark," he mused to himself with more than a little doubt.

"Hell, we don't even know if they will find any liability. Haverley is going to argue like crazy that the firm relied on Craft's memo and that is the end of the ball game," Dillon said out loud in frustration.

Dillon reached down and picked up the instruction that Judge Harpman said he was going to read to the jury. He read it quietly to himself. It said:

> "Mark Austin claims that the Baukus & Johnson law partnership violated the duty to act fairly and in good faith when they decided to terminate him. To establish this claim, Mark Austin must prove all of following:
>
> 1. That Mark Austin and the Baukus & Johnson partnership entered into an employment relationship;
>
> 2. That Mark Austin substantially performed his job duties;

3. That the Baukus & Johnson partnership terminated his employment;

4. That the Baukus & Johnson partnership's conduct in terminating Mark Austin was a failure to act fairly and in good faith; and

5. That Mark Austin was harmed by the conduct of the Baukus & Johnson partnership.

Both parties to an employment relationship have a duty not to do anything that prevents the other party from receiving the benefits of their agreement. Good faith means honesty of purpose without any intention to mislead or to take advantage of another. Generally speaking, it means being faithful to one's duty or obligation.

If you find that the Baukus & Johnson partnership violated the duty to act fairly, we will move to the second phase on damages and I will give you additional instructions at that time.

Dillon also read the instruction for intentional infliction of emotional distress. Kelly and Laurel had convinced him to add this second cause of action, but he was never convinced it applied. The instruction required the jury to find that the conduct was "outrageous" and that the defendant either intended to cause emotional distress or "acted with reckless disregard" to the probability that severe harm would result.

"Well, it sounds good on paper," Dillon thought to himself as he tossed the instruction aside. "But only the jury knows whether any of this applies to Mark."

By the time Dillon got home, serious apprehension crept into his thoughts. He could not get out of his mind Haverley's strong defense. He has placed the firm's decision to fire Mark squarely on the memo from Alison Craft. He kept thinking, "This is a simple thing for the jury to understand. If they believe Alison, we've lost. And she never wavered in her story that what she said was the truth even though Jerry Keller asked her to write the memo."

Dillon thought of going for another walk, but he knew it would do no good. Instead, he helped himself to some Macallan scotch and walked into his study and sat down at his large leather bound desk. He took a sip of his drink and reached over and moved a photo that was on the corner of the desk up close. It was a photo of his late wife. He stared at it for a long time. As a tear began running down his left cheek, he said, "Hell, honey. You don't have to say anything. I'm drinking too damn much and too old to fool around with trials like this that eat at your gut."

CHAPTER 14

Trial – Day Seven
(Tuesday, January 12)
(Surprise Evidence)

Dillon arrived at the courthouse early the next morning and had breakfast in the cafeteria on the building's top floor. He was about done when Kelly joined him and a few minutes later, Mark and Suzzi arrived.

Dillon was wearing his dark blue trial suit, white shirt and a light blue tie. And of course he had his lucky suspenders. He never went to trial without them. Other attorneys would kid him about his superstition, but his answer was always the same. "You never know!"

They had all talked about what Mark and Suzzi should wear. Mark was wearing a blue blazer with grey slacks, white shirt and a yellow tie with red stripes. And for the first time since the trial started, he looked relaxed. His task was over, at least for now. They just hoped it was not over permanently.

Even though they had dismissed her as a plaintiff following the stipulation, they all knew the jury was watching Suzzi closely. So they decided to keep her looking like the teacher she was. She had on a white blouse tucked into a tan skirt, dark low-heel black shoes that matched her purse.

These are all part of the silly things trial lawyers think about. All because they never really know what a jury may like or dislike.

Oh yes, there have been many studies on how and what a jury thinks. But none give much satisfaction. Some jurors are turned off by flashy clothes, some by scruffy shoes, some because a witness or party never smiles, some because a party does smile, and some just because. This is why every person facing litigation should try to settle without a trial. And it can be just as unpredictable even if a judge alone is deciding the case.

Dillon looked at his watch and said, "OK folks. Time to see what our wonderful jurors think of our case."

They were all seated at the counsel table waiting for Judge Harpman to take the bench. Dillon had given him their brief replying to Haverley's motion to dismiss on the employee issue and a copy of the new jury instruction that Kelly had prepared.

When Judge Harpman finally took the bench it was evident to everyone in the courtroom that he was not happy. He looked out at counsel and said in an agitated tone, "The issue of whether Mark Austin was an employee is a valid defense, although a bit late in the game. But I'm going to let the jury decide. As part of the breach of the covenant of good faith is the requirement that the plaintiff prove an employment relationship."

Dillon started to stand to object, but Judge Harpman raised his hand and said, "I understand your objection, Mr. Clark. It is late in the game and you were not aware that the defense was raising the issue and therefore had no chance to produce evidence or call witnesses. So I'm going to reopen the trial to let you introduce further evidence."

Judge Harpman turned to Haverley and said, tersely "Mr. Haverley, it was your decision to raise the employment issue, so I assume you have no objections?"

Haverley knew he could not change the judge's mind so he just shook his head.

"OK," Judge Harpman added. "I have already alerted the jury that there may be nothing further. Will you be ready by tomorrow, Mr. Clark?"

"Your Honor," Dillon said as he rose. "If I may have a moment to discuss this with Mr. Austin, we may be able to proceed. His personnel record is already in evidence and all of us in this courtroom are fully aware that the Baukus & Johnson firm has said more than once in this trial that Mark was never a partner." He then looked over at Mark and added, "Of course we know why. They didn't want to pay him part of the bonus money!"

There was a ripple of laughter from the audience. Dillon paused to let the courtroom quit down and said, "It may be, Your Honor, that I have only one or two questions for Mr. Austin and we can then argue the liability issues."

Judge Harpman sat silent for a moment and then said, "OK, gentlemen. We'll take a fifteen minute recess." He turned to the bailiff and said, "Tell the jury we may be starting after all."

Dillon and Mark remained seated at the counsel table. As soon as everyone was out of earshot, Dillon said, "Mark, we have the option of calling the human resource person from Baukus & Johnson to testify that the file shows you as an employee, or even call Harlan Cross back. But this jury will never buy their argument and I think we should proceed. I'll put you back on the stand and ask two questions. Were you every made an actual partner of the partnership? All you have to say is no. The second question is whether you were paid a salary and year-end bonus? The answer is yes."

Mark understood, but reflecting on the last time he testified and went through an unpleasant cross examination by Haverley, he asked, "Can Haverley go beyond those two questions?'

"No. The judge is going to keep this tight. I don't think he will let him stray into old areas again."

As they sat waiting for the judge to again take the bench, Dillon saw Laurel Kennedy breathlessly fly into the courtroom. She first went to Kelly who was sitting next to Suzzi and said something that Dillon couldn't hear as she handed her an envelope.

Kelly opened the envelope and quickly read a short note that was inside. Her heart began pounding in her chest as she got up and walked with Laurel over to where Dillon and Mark were seated. "You can say thanks to your lucky Irish ancestors today. Guess what?"

"Too early to start guessing."

Laurel Kennedy had worked with Dillon at his old law firm, and when he and Phil Burnam left to start a new firm, she took the gamble and came with him. After a dozen trials together, she knew his moods. She smiled and explained, "Finally some good news," she said.

After letting the suspense play out a bit, Laurel handed Dillon the note. It was a note from Jeff Hunt that said, "I was just playing around with the image we took of Craft's hard drive and saw something that might be important. Still no drafts or the things you were looking for, but Craft's memo was actually created on December 10 even though she dated it November 15. She must've put November 15 on it by mistake or to make it look like she did it earlier!"

"Hot damn," Dillon said as he slammed his hand down on the counsel table with such force that it startled those still in the courtroom.

"What happened?" Mark asked with some alarm as Dillon handed him the note.

As Mark read Jeff's comments, Dillon could see Mark's body tighten like a fist and the muscles began to bulge in his neck. "What the hell is going on?" he finally blurted out. "How does this help us?"

"Mark, without asking Craft, we won't know why she did that. We can, of course, call her back. I'm sure the judge will allow it because this puts her credibility into question. Or we could call Keller back. But I think we should just call Jeff to testify. This is one of those dumbfounded things that could piss off the jury and turn them our way," Dillon explained.

"I still don't get it, Mr. Clark," Suzzi said with a puzzled look. "Why is the date significant?"

Dillon thought for a second and then explained, " Suzzi, if we can question the credibility of Craft and Keller, then maybe the whole story she gave the jury about really questioning Mark's ability to do sophisticated tax planning was not the truth. Right now, unless Haverley calls either of them back to testify, the date change leaves the door open for me to argue that the memo was really written in a hurry so the Executive Committee would get it before year end. Remember, it was Jerry Keller who was upset that Mark had sent in a request for a portion of the Tier Two bonus money. He knew the memo would cause the Committee to fire Mark, and that got him what he wanted. Only he would get credit for landing Gibbons as a new client."

They all sat in silence for a minute as they thought about the meaning of the date change. It was Laurel who finally interrupted the silence and said, "Mark, this could really turn this jury. As Dillon has told you, juries can go crazy when they are faced with judging credibility. And when the chips are down, they need something to hang their hat on. I know this is scary, but here we have something solid. Let them try to explain why the date was... well, I guess faked is the right word."

"Laurel is right," Dillon added. "What are they going to say? The jury will know the date was, as Laurel put it, faked. I suspect the jury won't believe anything they say now."

No one spoke for the longest time. Finally, Laurel cleared her throat and said softly, "Dillon, we know this whole thing is going to come down to who the jury believes in the end. Mark's admission doesn't help, but we can now show that not only did Keller ask Craft to write the damn memo, she did so and back dated it."

Looking a little flustered, Laurel continued. "Damn it, Dillon. They conspired to set Mark up to get him fired so Keller would get the whole origination bonus. This whole thing stinks!"

Mark and Suzzi were still unsure of what was happening and they just sat and said nothing. Dillon smiled and said to Laurel, "Get Jeff to the courthouse with his stuff as soon as you can. I want him to testify today if possible."

When Judge Harpman resumed the trial, Dillon stood and said, "Your Honor, we've had a rather astounding discovery. I just heard from our computer expert, Jeff Hunt, and he informs me that the memo that Alison Craft sent to the Executive Committee, the one they used to fire Mark Austin, was back dated to November 15. It was actually created on December 10. As you well know, the defendants have said many times that the decision to fire Mr. Austin was based solely on Alison Craft's memo. We respectively ask that the court allow us to call Mr. Hunt so he can explain to the jury what he discovered and how."

Haverley was literally sputtering as he jumped to his feet and said with patent anger, "Objection, Your Honor. Mr. Clark rested his case on liability. This will just prolong this trial unnecessarily."

"Your Honor," Dillon retorted, "it was Mr. Haverley who interjected an entirely new issue, and one of some major importance I must say, when he requested a dismissal because Mr. Austin was not an employee. He did this after he rested his case. You allowed him to proceed and fair is fair. You should allow us the same flexibility, especially when it touches on the single most critical piece of evidence in this entire case."

Judge Harpman had a bemused smile on his face as he looked over at Haverley and said, "Mr. Clark has a point. You did reopen matters with your motion. I'm going to allow Mr. Clark to call his expert. You of course may call your own expert if you disagree."

Judge Harpman looked over at Dillon and added, "By the way, do you have evidence you want to provide on the employment issue?"

"We do, Your Honor, but only two questions for Mr. Austin. We can cover that now if you prefer."

It was now almost noon and Judge Harpman said, "We will take his testimony at 1:30. Since it will be short, is there any possibility we can move things along and get your expert here as well?"

"I have a call into him now. I think we can have him here. Thank you, Your Honor," Dillon replied.

Harlan Cross was not in court today so when the noon break occurred, Haverley rushed out into the hallway and called Cross on his cell phone. "Jesus Christ, Harlan, I thought Craft's computer was clean!" he said in a rush of urgency.

"What are you talking about," Cross replied quickly. "What's happened?"

"Clark got the judge to reopen the trial to allow his computer expert to testify. He says Craft's memo was backdated to November but was actually created by her on December 10. This has the potential of a disaster," Haverley explained with a heavy sigh.

"How the hell does he know that?" Cross asked demandingly.

"It's the damn hard drive," Haverley explained. "It shows when every document is actually created. We never asked your guy to look at the hard drive because Craft said her computer was clean."

"When is he testifying?" Cross asked.

"Probably this afternoon," Haverley replied.

"I'm coming right over," Cross said as he slammed his cell phone shut.

Jeff Hunt was in his late forties, wore glasses with thick black frames that made his eyes look larger than normal. Because he spent so much time with computers, his skin was pale for lack of exposure to sun. When he arrived at the courthouse, he was wearing grey slacks and a black sport coat that looked like it had not seen a cleaners or an iron for a decade. But none of this mattered. Dillon knew he was an expert on taking computers apart and seeing what was on the hard drive.

Jeff Hunt met Dillon, Laurel and the others in the cafeteria. Dillon looked at Laurel and asked, "Are you ready?"

Laurel and Dillon had decided early on that if Jeff Hunt found anything good on Alison Craft's computer, that she would be the one to question him. She had done this in prior trials and she had a way of making technical things seem simple and clear.

Laurel smiled and replied, "You bet. Jeff has given me a list of questions that will let him show the jury what he found."

"Are you still ok with Laurel asking the questions?" Dillon asked Mark.

"This is your area, not mine," Mark answered. "You two do what you think is best."

Dillon looked at his watch and said, "OK. Time to have some fun!"

When Dillon and the others returned to the courtroom after lunch, Haverley was already seated at the counsel table along with Harlan Cross. He also saw that Derrick Warner had joined the defense group.

"I wonder what he's doing here," Dillon mused to himself.

When Judge Harpman entered the courtroom and seated himself at the judge's bench, he directed the bailiff to bring in the jury. When the jury was all seated, he turned to Dillon and asked, "Mr. Clark, are you ready to proceed?"

"We are," Dillon replied.

Judge Harpman said, "Proceed, Mr. Clark."

Dillon called Mark and asked him the two questions. For once Mark seemed relaxed and answered the questions as they had discussed. No, he was never a partner. And yes, he was paid a salary and year-end bonus.

When Dillon was through, Haverley was also brief but razor sharp. "Mr. Austin, did you consider yourself a partner of any sorts? By this I mean, you were promoted to a junior partner, correct?"

"Yes, I was promoted to junior partner," Mark answered.

"So in that sense, you were a partner. Isn't that right?"

Mark hesitated and replied, "Yes, in that sense I was a partner. But it was a title. I was never a real senior partner."

"Yes, I understand you are trying to make that distinction," Haverley said with a skeptical look. "But you do agree you were a type of partner. Isn't that right?"

"Yes, I had the title of 'Junior Partner'. But that's all."

"Thank you Mr. Austin. Nothing more, Your Honor," Haverley said as he sat down.

As Haverley was sitting down, Laurel Kennedy rose and walked over to the speaker's podium and said, "We call Jeff Hunt as an expert witness on the contents of Alison Craft's computer."

Jeff Hunt was seated in the audience. He stood and walked up to the witness stand and raised his right hand and took the standard oath to tell the truth.

"Mr. Hunt, please explain to the jury what you do for a living and how many times you have testified in court as an expert witness on computers," Laurel Kennedy asked with confidence.

"I am what you call an expert on the internal workings of a computer. My company, Science for the Law, has ten computer engineers who work with me to assist lawyers and the courts in understanding and examining computer hard drives. I have qualified as an expert in hundreds of civil and criminal cases in both state and federal courts here in California and elsewhere in the United States. Those who employ us are usually attorneys, but at times I have served as an expert appointed by the court itself to help the judge understand what other experts are saying."

"Mr. Hunt, were you asked by our firm to analyze the computer used by Alison Craft when she was still with the Baukus & Johnson law firm?" Laurel asked.

"Yes. I was told that the court had entered an order giving me the right to examine her computer. It was delivered to my office by the Baukus & Johnson firm," Jeff explained.

"What did we ask you to do?" Laurel asked.

"The writing in question, which was a memo to the firm's Executive Committee, was dated November 15. You asked if there were other drafts or versions of that memo," Jeff Hunt replied.

"Explain to the jury, Mr. Hunt, what you did to determine if there were other drafts," Laurel asked.

"The first thing we do is to make an image of the entire computer hard drive. And when I say the entire hard drive, I mean we try to find and image even documents that have been erased. This is why we call it imaging. We can see all of the work done on the computer," Jeff Hunt explained.

"And did you find other drafts that had been deleted?' Laurel asked.

"No. We found many memos, even hundreds, but they all related to work assignments given to Mark Austin or to others, and many draft wills and trusts that Ms. Craft had prepared. But no other version of the November 15 memo. And no versions that had been deleted," Jeff Hunt replied.

"If a computer user drafts a document and then deletes and permanently erases it, can you still find it on the hard drive and read it?" Laurel asked.

"Yes indeed," Jeff Hunt answered with a big smile. "This is usually what we are hired to find. But in this case, I saw no deleted prior draft. There were deletions of many documents, presumably drafts, but none related to the memo about Mark Austin."

Laurel walked over to the counsel table and picked up a document and walked back to the speaker's podium. "Mr. Hunt, after you reported to us that you found nothing, did you continue with your analysis of Ms. Craft's computer?"

"Well, yes. I knew we had not found what you were looking for, so I sort of just prowled around that night. And I did find something peculiar," Jeff Hunt replied.

Dillon had been listening and watching the jury as Laurel questioned Jeff Hunt, and he thought they were bored. He could actually see several jurors drawing pictures on their note pads. But now several sat up straighter in their chairs and were obviously listening.

"And what did you find?" Laurel asked.

"Well, when you create a document, the hard drive registers the date. I hadn't looked at the registry before because we were looking for other drafts and deletions. But when I took a look at the registry, I saw that it was created on December 10. This caught my attention because all along we were basing our search on the memo from Craft dated November 15," Jeff Hunt explained.

"Mr. Hunt, did you copy or in some way make a photo of this register that shows when Ms. Craft's memo was created?" Laurel asked.

"Yes. You can actually print out the registry. It shows the name of the document, or title, and the date it was created. And you can print out a copy of the document so I printed it out. And it was the Craft memo dated November 15. I also printed a copy of the registry," Jeff Hunt replied.

Laurel walked over to the counsel table and picked up an exhibit that she had given to Charmaine Parker to mark before the trial resumed. "Your Honor, may I approach the witness and give him an exhibit to identify?"

"Yes. Of course," Judge Harpman replied.

Laurel walked over to the counsel table where Haverley and Cross were seated and showed the exhibit to Haverley. He looked at it quickly and nodded his consent. She then approached Jeff Hunt and handed him the exhibit and asked, "Is this exhibit the copy you made of the registry showing the date the memo was created?"

"Yes, it is," Jeff Hunt replied.

"Mr. Hunt, in your experience as a computer expert, did you draw any conclusion as to why Ms. Craft dated the memo

November 15 when it was really created on December 10?" Laurel quickly asked.

"It is obvious she intended to…" Jeff Hunt started to say but he was interrupted by Haverley. "Objection, Your Honor. What may or may not have been on Ms. Craft's mind is beyond this witness's expertise."

"Objection sustained," Judge Harpman ruled. "What reason Ms. Craft had for dating the memo is pure speculation. Move on counsel."

"Your Honor, I move into evidence plaintiff's exhibit 12," Laurel said to Judge Harpman.

Haverley was facing his own moment of truth. The testimony of Jeff Hunt and the exhibit was, to put it mildly, highly dangerous to the core of the defense strategy which was to have the Executive Committee rely on Craft's memo. It hurt like hell, but the last thing he wanted to do now was to highlight its importance by objecting.

"No objection," Haverley said with an air or confidence he did not feel inside.

"The exhibit is accepted," Judge Harpman said with a slightly raised eyebrow that only the attorneys noticed.

"Thank you, Your Honor. I have no further questions," Laurel announced.

Judge Harpman turned to Haverley and asked, "Any questions, counselor?"

There are times in every trial when the lawyers must make instant decisions without time to reflect and strategize. And this was one of those times for Haverley. He saw no hope in turning Jeff Hunt's testimony and decided to stay with their core defense, which was the truth of what Alison Craft put in her memo regardless of Keller asking her to write it and regardless of the date when she created it. If the jury believed Craft, they would win.

As he was making his decision, Haverley slowly stood to give him more time to think. He knew the judge would prod him to move along if he waited any longer, so he said, "I have no questions for Mr. Hunt, Your Honor. I am familiar with his reputation in the computer industry and am satisfied with what he said."

Judge Harpman looked in the direction of Dillon and said, "Mr. Clark, can we now proceed to final arguments? Any more evidence?" he asked with the same slightly raised eyebrow that he revealed to Haverley's decision to leave the expert alone without questions.

"Yes, Your Honor," Dillon replied.

Judge Harpman looked up at the clock. They had used most of the afternoon session with testimony and there was no way to complete final arguments so he said, "Counsel, and ladies and gentlemen of the jury, we will now proceed to hear the arguments of counsel on the liability phase. But we can't finish them today, so I am letting you go a bit early and we will start again at 8:30 a.m. tomorrow."

As soon as Judge Harpman excused them, Haverley, Cross and Derrick Warner hustled back to the firm's conference room. This time they skipped the drinks.

Cross was angry with Derrick Warner for not making sure that Craft's computer was really clean. "God damn it, Derrick, this is a fucking mess right now. What the hell is the jury going to think? You all know as well as I do what happened and so will the jury. Craft back-dated the damn memo. This makes it look more like the whole thing was just to get the EC to fire Austin."

"Hold your horses a second Harlan," Haverley interjected. "I'm not saying this Hunt stuff is good for us, but we still have Craft confirming that what she wrote was true. Don't forget. This is the key to our defense. If the jury pays attention, it doesn't matter what date she put on the memo."

Cross was about to reply when his cell phone rang. He looked down and knew the number by heart. It was his old partner and now Presiding Judge of the Los Angeles Superior Court. "Hello Dale. What can I do for you?"

"It's not what you can do for me," Judge Bannerman replied. "It's what I can do for you. Don't be stubborn on the Austin case. Judge Harpman told me what happened today. For God's sake Harlan, settle the damn thing before the firm really gets hurt."

"Jerry, we tried. Dillon Clark refused," Cross replied as he switched his cell phone to speaker so the others could hear.

"Nonsense," Judge Bannerman said. "Your offer was too low. You could get hit really hard if this jury thinks Alison and Jerry conspired to get Austin fired. And, by the way, that is how Harpman sees the evidence right now."

There was a long silence before Cross replied. Finally he said, "Thanks Dale. I appreciate the heads-up. Tell your lovely wife hi for me and I'll see you both at the club on Sunday."

Cross looked over at Haverley and asked, "What do you think now?

"I still think this is a defensible case," Haverley replied cautiously. "Remember, Austin agreed he would not be a partner if even one partner voted no. And the emotional distress damages as to the wife are out. So even if the jury finds liability, the damages are not going to be large. He has at best missed two years of salary and it would be pure speculation for the jury to think in terms of what he might have made as a partner. So you maybe have distress damages to Mark of at best a hundred thousand or so."

"Shit," Cross said as he now stood and walked over to the bar and poured himself a large whisky and soda. With his back still turned, he added, "Derrick, are we going to lose any more partners over this?"

What Cross was referring to was the run-for-the-door by ten partners once they heard that Keller had asked Craft to write the now infamous memo. It was not just Craft's admission. When Jerry Keller and Alison Craft left, the firm's income sharply declined, mostly due to other clients going with the departing partners. If any more partners left, the firm would be in real jeopardy of closing the doors.

When Cross was again seated at the conference table, his shoulders sagged and he said longingly, "It used to be that there was a deep sense of loyalty between law partners. Most partners stayed together for their entire legal careers. Some went off to be judges or to do government work. But not just run off and start their own damn law firm. It's just all for the money now. Too bad."

The others just sat without saying anything, deep in their own thoughts. Cross finally cleared his throat and said to Haverley, "Offer them one million. Get this settled."

Dillon, Laurel and Kelly also high-tailed it back to the firm when Judge Harpman recessed for the day. Mark and Suzzi went home to relax since Mark would not have to worry about testifying again, at least not until the damage phase if they got that far.

When they were all seated at the conference room table, Dillon asked Kelly, "Kelly, have your secretary take Jeff's printout of the registry down to the photo shop. I want a three-by-four foot blow-up with the name of the document and date boxed in yellow. I want to use it in argument."

When Kelly left, Dillon turned to Laurel and said, "Good job today. The jury was finally paying attention. I think they see that she back-dated the memo. I just hope they do what the judge would forbid and speculate on why she did it!"

CHAPTER 15

Trial – Day Eight
(Final Arguments on Liability)
(Wednesday, January 13)

Giving a final argument seems to bring out the best in every trial attorney. When Dillon awoke the next morning, he was feeling rested and ready. He dressed in his trial lawyer's blue suit, white shirt, blue and maroon stripped tie and, of course, his ever present favorite pair of straps. He was not really superstitious. But then again, he never tried an important case without his straps.

As Dillon entered Judge Harpman's courtroom, he saw Haverley sitting at the counsel table. Cross and Derrick Warner were absent. Laurel Kennedy and Kelly stayed back at the firm and Mark and Suzzi had not yet arrived.

As Dillon set his briefcase down on the counsel table, Haverley walked over and said, "Dillon, we'd like to get this case settled if we can."

Haverley was a skilled litigator and experienced in settlement negotiations. He knew to get a good settlement, you had to let the other side pry it out of you and not be eager and generous upfront.

"What is it going to take?" Haverley asked.

Dillon stood and motioned to Haverley with his hand to walk out into the hallway. When they were alone, he said, "A lot more than you offered before. We have a good opening now with Craft. If the jury doesn't believe her, your whole defense could go down."

"I'm not here to argue the issues," Haverley said a little testily.

"Make an offer and I'll take it to Mark," Dillon replied politely but firmly.

Haverley stared at Dillon for a long moment before he replied. He knew this could be the last time a settlement would be possible and he decided to jump right to the bottom line. "The firm will pay one million. That's a whole lot of money on a case Austin could lose."

"OK. I'll tell Mark as soon as he arrives," Dillon responded and the two walked back into the courtroom.

When Mark and Suzzi arrived, Dillon explained the offer and there was no surprise to Mark's answer. "We'll do whatever you think is fair, Mr. Clark. You know by now I'm not a litigator. And right now I have no idea who is going to win!

"It's a lot of money," Dillon said. "Go talk with Suzzi. If you take it, tell her I will cut my fee to fifty thousand."

"But what is your recommendation?" Mark asked pleadingly.

Dillon hated this question because there is never a good answer. They could easily win more from the jury; and they could easily lose the whole thing. While it didn't happen often, the worst times in his whole career as a trial lawyer were when he had to explain to a client that they had lost. His mind swirled with images of how clients reacted. Some broke out in tears; some got angry; but they all, sooner or later, asked why with the inevitable comment "But you said..."

Dillon took a deep breath and finally said, "Mark, I think with Jeff's finding on back dating, the jury is likely to get angry at Keller and Craft. If they do, and if they follow the instruction that the firm is responsible for their actions, we should win liability. It is then just an issue of how much the jury awards on damages. But there are no guarantees. The jury could believe Craft and we could lose. I would make a counter offer at $1.5m and see what happens."

Mark walked over to where Suzzi was sitting in the front row and told her what Dillon had said. She looked at Mark and said, "Honey, settle if you want. But I'm ok if you decide to let the jury decide. They seem like good folks and you will at least know what they think is right."

Mark squeezed Suzzi's hand and went back to the counsel table where Dillon was sitting and said, "I'd like the jury to decide."

"Are you sure you don't want to make a counter offer?" Dillon asked.

"No. We're going to be ok with whatever happens. I really want to see what the jury is going to do, especially with what Keller and Craft did" Mark said with firmness in his voice that Dillon had not detected before.

Dillon passed on Mark's decision to Haverley who only shrugged as if they had just made the most foolish decision possible.

As he took his seat at the counsel table, Dillon felt his gut tighten like a fist. "Maybe Haverley is right," he thought to himself.

Judge Harpman took the bench right at 8:30 a.m. and the jurors were all in their seats by 8:45a.m. Looking over at the jury, he said, "Ladies and gentlemen, as I explained before, we are now finishing the liability phase of this case. I will read to you the jury instructions you must follow in deciding the issues and the attorneys will then give their final arguments."

As he sat listening to Judge Harpman read the instructions to the jury, Dillon's mind wandered to what would happen if the jury ruled in favor of the Baukus & Johnson firm. He visualized Mark working in a small law firm earning a meager income compared to the millions that Jerry Keller and Alison Craft were no doubt now pulling in with their new firm. He looked back to where Suzzi and now Kelly were seated in the audience section and a tingling sensation shot through his spine. The kind of shot you get when you are suddenly in danger. Although he was about to give his own closing argument on liability, all he could think about was Mark's concession under cross examination that no associate would ever be made a partner if even one partner said no. "So if the jury buys Craft's testimony that what she wrote was true and she would not have voted for Mark's advancement, the Baukus & Johnson law firm will walk out of the courthouse at the end of the day the victor," he ruminated to himself irritably.

When Judge Harpman finished reading the instruction on the covenant of good faith and the instruction on intentional infliction of emotional distress, Dillon perked up and began watching the jury. He and Haverley had argued with the judge over what instruction would come next. Dillon wanted an instruction that told the jury that the law firm was responsible for the actions of Keller and Craft as well as the Executive Committee. Haverley fought hard to keep it out but Judge Harpman finally agreed with Dillon.

They had agreed that the instruction would follow the covenant of good faith instruction and Judge Harpman now read it to the jury:

> "A partnership like the defendant Baukus & Johnson law firm, and each of its partners, are responsible for the wrongful conduct of a partner acting within the scope of his or her authority.
>
> The Baukus & Johnson partnership is responsible for the decisions of the Executive Committee. But you must also decide whether the partnership is responsible for the actions of either or both Jerry Keller and

Alison Craft if you find their conduct to be wrongful as it relates to the plaintiff Mark Austin. To reach this conclusion you must find that they were acting within the scope of his or her authority as partners."

When Judge Harpman finished with the instructions, he looked at Dillon and said, "Mr. Clark, are you ready to give your closing argument?"

Dillon stood and slowly walked over to the speaker's podium and addressed the jury. He took a moment to look at each juror and said, "On behalf of my client, Mark Austin, I want to first thank each of you for your patience and the time you have spent on this case. As Judge Harpman explained, your task at this point is to decide if the Baukus & Johnson firm wrongfully fired Mark Austin. While there have been some interesting surprises in the evidence, this is not a complicated issue so I won't take up much of your time with my arguments."

Dillon paused and looked at each juror for a brief second before he continued. "You know, of course, that we believe Mark was wrongfully fired. He was a star at the firm. He not only did excellent legal work, but he also was the key to bringing in Boyd Gibbons and his many companies to the firm. They liked him so much they advanced him over many other associates and made him a junior partner. And his boss, Wayne Bailey, thought so highly of him that he suggested he put in a request for a bonus from what the firm calls the Tier Two pool."

Holding his hands out with the palms up in a plaintive manner, Dillon asked, "So what went wrong? I think you already know the answer. Mark irritated Jerry Keller, a senior partner, when he asked for the bonus. And Mr. Keller got Alison Craft, another senior partner, to write her memo to the Executive Committee, knowing full well that it would cause the Committee to fire Mark."

Dillon reached over to the counsel table and picked up the memo that had been marked as an exhibit. He waived the memo in the air and continued. "This memo right here in my hand. The one that Jeff Hunt said was prepared on December 10 but which Ms. Craft back-dated to November 15. Why would she back date it? Faking the date, and that is exactly what she did, may not seem important to you right now, but I think you will change your mind when you realize why she did it."

Dillon now walked over and stood next to Mark. "You will recall that the Tier Two pool is given out after the year closes. You heard Harlan Cross, the firm's managing partner; explain that a big portion of the pool is given to partners who originate new business, like Boyd Gibbons. The credit goes to the one who first brings in the client and Jerry Keller believed he and he alone should get the credit and bonus for Gibbons moving his companies to the firm. So now you need to pay attention to the chronology. We know the memo was written on December 10, a date after, and I emphasize after, the Executive Committee got Mark's own memo asking for a share of the bonus for brining Gibbons and his companies to the firm. We now have a clash at this point. Keller sees Mark's memo and gets furious. The year is about to end and Keller, who had served on the Executive Committee, knew he needed to get rid of Mark before the year ended. Why? So if there was any ambiguity in the partnership agreement about junior partners being entitled to a bonus, he would still get the bonus himself because Mark would be gone without working the full year! So he goes to Alison Craft and asks her to write her memo, and she complies. It was December 10, and on December 22, Keller gets his wish and Mark is fired."

Dillon now leaned over the speaker's podium and said almost in a whisper, "This, ladies and gentlemen, violates the duty that the Baukus & Johnson firm had to act fairly and in good faith. You heard Judge Harpman tell you about this good faith rule. It requires that the Baukus firm have an 'honesty of purpose' when they fired Mark. The Executive Committee no doubt thought they were acting in good faith when they got Alison Craft's memo, but what they didn't know was that Keller and Craft conspired to get Mark fired. And they succeeded. The law firm, as Judge Harpman explained, is responsible for the actions of both Keller and Craft. They were both acting within the scope of their functions as senior partners of the law firm. Craft was evaluating Mark, not because she didn't like his performance, as she tried to get you to believe, but because Jerry Keller asked her to."

Dillon took a sip of water, looked at the jury and said, "You know, as well as I, that Alison Craft lied to you when she first testified. It was only by chance that our expert, Jeff Hunt, caught her in the lie. She said she prepared her memo on November 15 when in fact she prepared it on December 10. Why the change? She wanted it to look like she had been thinking about it so no one would think it had anything to do with year-end numbers and Mark's request for an origination bonus. She and Keller wanted it far removed from any issue over who gets origination credit. This is not a decision made with the requisite honesty of purpose."

Dillon's tone had been matter-of-fact up to this point. Now he picked up the Craft memo and gradually turned it so every juror could see it straight on. He fixed the jury with a steady gaze and, holding the exhibit out in front of him, he said sternly, "You are the ones who decide what is true and not true in this case. But I respectfully suggest that this memo not only has a fake date, but it also shows that you can't believe Alison Craft or Jerry Keller. You heard Harlan Cross say over and over that they based their decision to fire Mark on the Craft memo. And I'm sure you'll hear their very able counsel argue that these changes mean nothing because what

Craft said about Mark was true. But this all depends on whether you believe Alison Craft. I suggest she is a liar and you should hold the law firm liable for wrongfully firing Mark Austin. And you should find that the firm is responsible for the actions of Jerry Keller and Alison Craft, who, I respectfully submit, acted with the intent to cause severe harm to Mark Austin. Thank you."

The courtroom was intensely silent when Dillon finished with his closing argument. He had been speaking for only thirty minutes and it was like everyone expected him to say more. Judge Harpman finally rustled his papers and said, "We'll take our mid-morning break now. Mr. Haverley, be ready with your arguments when we return. I want the jury to start deliberations right after lunch if possible."

Mark, Suzzi and Kelly were all delighted with Dillon's argument. "How can they possibly believe Craft after this?" Kelly asked excitedly.

"It's not over until the jury decides," Dillon cautioned. "Remember, even if we win on liability, Haverley will argue that Mark would never have been made a partner. So even if the jury is sympathetic at this point, the damages could be very minimal. If the jury buys the argument that Mark would have been asked to leave anyway, his wage loss could even be zero and we would have only the emotional distress that Mark may have suffered unrelated to any difficulties he and Suzzi had."

The ups and downs of a trial can have a calamitous effect on the litigants. When Dillon concluded his argument, everyone was happy and confident. But now Mark and Suzzi were enveloped in gloom thinking the whole trial was a waste of time. It was Kelly that jumped in and said, "Look folks, everything still depends on whether the jury believes Alison. I wouldn't believe her if she sat on a stack of Bibles and I bet the jury won't either."

No one wanted to leave the courtroom, so after a few more comments, the group just sat and waited for the trial to start again.

Haverley had been a trial lawyer for some forty years and he knew it was risky to ever think you know what a jury might be thinking. He watched each juror as they returned from the recess and took their seat in the jury box. A number of the jurors looked over at him with a friendly smile and that usually means they are thinking favorably towards the defense.

When Haverley rose to give his argument, he, too, thanked the jurors for their time and attention and promised to be brief. Then he proceeded over the next hour to pound away at the weakest part of Dillon's case, which was the concession, or as Haverley put it, the "confession" by Mark that no one can force an associate on any partner. In reality, a single no vote can deny any advancement decision.

"Folks, I feel sorry for Mark Austin, but that is not what this trial is all about. It is about his claim that he was wrongfully terminated. But you heard Harlan Cross explain that it was nothing more than a business decision. Once they got the memo from Alison Craft, they had no choice. And, as he explained, they were actually doing Mark a favor by letting him go when they did so that he could find another law firm."

Dillon noticed that several jurors were taking notes as Haverley presented his arguments.

"Much has been made by Mr. Clark in his argument about Jerry Keller asking Alison to write her memo and the back-dating," Haverley said by way of summarizing. "But this is really not relevant. It is a lot of smoke to throw you off."

Haverley paused for a long five seconds, raised the level of his voice and said sternly, "What is relevant is her testimony that what she said was true! You heard her testimony. She never wavered once in her statement that what she said in her memo was true and she would not have voted to make Mark a senior partner. The end result was always going to be the same. No one at Baukus & Johnson violated any duty to act fairly with Mark Austin. And no one at Baukus & Johnson acted to intentionally harm Mark Austin. This means, when you are deliberating in the jury room and you are handed a verdict form that asks you to say yes or no to liability on each of the plaintiff's causes of action, you should say no and no. Thank you."

Judge Harpman gave the jury their final instructions on how to select a foreman and sent them off to begin their deliberations after the lunch break. Dillon told the judge's clerk, Charmaine Parker, that he could be reached on his cell phone and they were going to the cafeteria.

Waiting for a jury can be the most agonizing experience for a trial lawyer. As they wait, the lawyers can think of a thousand things they should have done or said; and the fear of losing is an ever present cloud hanging around ready to ruin the day.

In Mark's case, Dillon expected a fairly short deliberation. The issues were not complex and juries are usually quick in deciding who to believe. No one wanted to eat, so they all sat around talking about anything but the trial. When 3:00 p.m. came with no verdict, Suzzi could not conceal her emotions any longer. Tears began dripping down her cheek and she said in anguish, "What's taking them so long? I can't just sit here any longer and do nothing. What if they can't decide?"

Mark quickly put his arm around his wife's shoulders and said quietly, "We agreed to let the jury decide. They're just doing their job. It takes time."

Dillon added quickly, "Suzzi, it's only been a couple of hours. I don't think there is anything to be worried about. I bet they come back before the day is over."

Kelly said nothing. She, too, was getting concerned.

So it was disappointing and an alarming surprise when Charmaine Parker called Dillon on his cell phone at 4:30 p.m. "Sorry, Mr. Clark. The judge sent the jury a note asking if they could finish today and the foreman sent a note back saying they needed more time. So he let them go home for the day. They'll be back at 8:30 tomorrow morning."

After Dillon explained what Charmaine Parker told him, Mark's shoulders noticeably sagged. He threw a glance at his wife and quietly asked, "I assume this is not good? What do you think went wrong?"

"No way to know," Dillon answered. "They hopefully are just doing their job and discussing things slowly. You and Suzzi go home and get some rest. I'll see you here in the morning."

When Mark and Suzzi got home, they said almost nothing to each other. Suzzi's mother had taken their daughter, Cheryl, to her house until the trial was over so they were alone in the apartment. They ate some leftovers out of the refrigerator and, after dumping the dishes into the dishwasher, Mark walked out into the living room and flicked on the television. Suzzi opened a bottle of some kind of cheap red wine, poured out two glasses and came in and sat down next to Mark on the coach and handed him a glass. Keeping her voice low, she said in a sad and almost defeated manner, "I'm so sorry I talked you into this trial. I know it's eating at you. I can see it in your face."

"No, it's ok," Mark replied. "Dillon knows what he's doing."

"Honey, when we were sitting in the cafeteria today, I kept thinking. What is going to happen to you if we lose? And I guess

I saw for the first time that you'll think of yourself as a loser who couldn't make it in a big firm. And that's when the tears came. I'm the one who forced you to stand up and fight," Suzzi said with nervous frustration.

Mark had his own doubts about what would happen, but trying to be tough and resolute, he said, "Honey, you don't have to feel that way. I'll be just fine --- whatever happens."

Suzzi didn't believe Mark, but she said nothing. They sat and sipped their wine and went to bed.

When the jurors went home for the night, Haverley drove over to the Baukus & Johnson firm and met with Harlan, Derrick Warner and Wayne Bailey.

"What's going on?" Harlan asked critically.

"I'll be damned if I know why they haven't decided by now," Haverley replied. "I watched the jurors during Dillon's argument and they just sat there without reacting. But several took lots of notes during my argument. But who knows! I've learned a long time ago not to try to second guess what they're thinking."

Wayne Bailey was drawing circles on his legal pad. Without looking up he asked, "Do you think they're hung up on Alison's back-dating of her memo?"

"No, I don't," Haverley answered confidently. "She made it clear that what she said was true. If the jury believes that, Mark would have always been terminated."

"What do you think is going to be the hook for this jury?" Derrick Warner asked.

Trial lawyers use the term "hook" to refer to the key factor that usually turns a case to one side or the other. It typically means a critical piece of evidence.

Haverley had given this considerable thought when he was preparing his final argument. "Good question," he replied. "I think the hook is going to be Austin's confession that if only one partner disagrees with making an associate a partner, then the associate will not be advanced. Mark agreed with this twice on cross examination."

"But how does this help on liability?" Derrick Warner asked.

"Two ways," Haverley replied. "It tells the jury that this whole case is worthless. Even if they were to find liability, the damages would be minor. Probably the difference between what he would have made here at the Baukus firm and what he actually earned. If they see this, they'll turn against Austin."

"So what you're saying is that even if they find liability, we still win because the damages will be insignificant?" Harlan asked.

"Exactly," Haverley said.

Harlan smiled and said, "OK. Time for a little cheer!"

CHAPTER 16

When Dillon arrived at court the next morning, he was still feeling perplexed over why the jury had not reached a decision. He checked in with Charmaine Parker and went up to the cafeteria to wait. When Mark and Suzzi joined him in the cafeteria, he could tell they were also worried.

"I know this waiting is a killer, but for now the jury is the boss. They work and we wait," he said jovially to make them feel better.

As they waited, Dillon and Mark talked about the damage phase of the case if the jury found liability. Dillon intended on calling a psychologist to describe the emotional distress suffered by Mark from being fired. It was going to be a fine line because they had to stay away from the most damaging aspect which was the affect it had on their sex life.

They were deep in conversation when Dillon's cell phone rang. It was Charmaine Parker who said, "The jury has a verdict. Come on down."

They all hurried down to Judge Harpman's courtroom and took their seats. Haverley was already sitting at his table. When Judge Harpman entered and took his seat, the bailiff brought in the jury.

When the jurors were all seated, Judge Harpman asked, "Have you reached a verdict on liability?"

The foreman stood and said, "We have, Your Honor."

"Please hand your verdict to the bailiff." Judge Harpman directed.

The bailiff took the verdict form and handed it to Judge Harpman. He read it over and handed it back to the bailiff who gave it to Charmaine Parker.

"Please read the verdict," Judge Harpman directed Charmaine Parker.

Charmaine Parker glanced at the verdict form and read it out loud. **"On the first cause of action, do you find that the Baukus & Johnson law partnership wrongfully terminated the plaintiff Mark Austin? Answer: Yes."**

Charmaine Parker paused and then continued. **"On the second cause of action, do you find that the Baukus & Johnson law partnership intentionally inflicted emotional distress on plaintiff Mark Austin? Answer: Yes."**

Judge Harpman looked over at Haverley and asked, "Do you wish to poll the jury, Mr. Haverley?"

"Yes, please, Your Honor," Haverley replied. He was clearly upset and had a big frown on his face as he spoke.

Judge Harpman turned to Charmaine Parker and said, "Please poll the jurors."

The polling of a jury means each individual juror is asked if the verdict, as read, was truly their verdict. In a civil case, the jurors must have a majority of nine out of the twelve jurors to reach a verdict. And surprisingly, many verdicts are thrown out because not enough of the jurors voted the way the verdict form read. If, for example, only eight voted for liability, it would be a faulty verdict and they would have to go back and deliberate further.

It took several minutes for Charmaine Parker to ask each individual juror. And, in fact, it turned out that the verdict was not unanimous. One juror, an elderly gentleman, was even angry. When asked if it was his verdict, he said in a loud grumpy voice, "Absolutely not. I am opposed to the verdict that the foreman gave you."

As it turned out, two other jurors said they disagreed with the verdict. But nine did agree, so Judge Harpman accepted the verdict. He said, "Ladies and gentlemen, this now concludes the liability phase of this case. As I explained when we started this trial, the attorneys will now go forward with the damage evidence. When they conclude, you will go back into the jury room and deliberate again on how much, if any, damages should be awarded."

Judge Harpman looked at the clock and added, "I'm going to let you go home for now and we will start again at 8:30 a.m. tomorrow morning."

A split verdict is always a bad sign, especially when you are only half through a trial and Dillon was worried. He watched the panel as they left the courtroom and they all marched out without looking at either attorney and he knew this was equally bad. Jurors who favor a side usually appear at least a little friendly. "What the hell is going on?" he asked himself with more than a little alarm.

Mark and Suzzi were of course happy with the verdict. In their mind, Mark was vindicated and the Baukus & Johnson firm had wrongfully fired him. As they walked out into the hallway, Mark said with a huge smile on his face, "This is great, Dillon. I can't thank you enough."

When Dillon didn't reply and just kept walking, Mark asked, "Is there something wrong? We won, didn't we?"

Dillon stopped and turned around to face Mark and his wife and said in a terse rigid manner. "Look, Mark. There's something wrong with the jury. The split you saw was not friendly and the jurors who voted no were seriously upset with the others. This could be a disaster if they're upset with each other when they consider damages. All those three need is to get one more juror on their side and we lose big time."

"I don't understand," Suzzi said with hesitation. "They did find that the firm wrongfully fired Mark, didn't they?"

"Yes, Suzzi, they did. But they're obviously in disagreement. But we just have to wait now until they decide damages. You two run on home. I need to get back to the office and think about how to play tomorrow."

What Dillon didn't say was what he was thinking. "Haverley and the crew at Baukus must love this. They lose yet win!"

Dillon called his office and informed Laurel and Kelly what had happened. They were as surprised as he was with the jury infighting. Kelly had sat through most of the trial and had no explanation. "I've been watching them now for days and they all seemed attentive and friendly. I can't imagine what went wrong!"

"All I can think of is the three think Mark's case is worthless and didn't want to sit through any more. Maybe they bought Craft's testimony. Maybe they just don't think people should sue when they are fired. Maybe… Hell, guys, I don't know. It makes no sense. I can see a split vote, but not the vehement protests by the three that disagreed."

"What are you gonna do?" Kelly asked anxiously. She had become close with Mark and Suzzi and Dillon could literally hear the concern in her voice.

"Well, for one thing, I want you to call our witnesses and have them at the courthouse by nine. And call the Baukus administrator and go over and pick up the financial records they refused to give us earlier. I want you to study them tonight to see if there is anything useful," Dillon replied.

"Do you need anything tonight?" Kelly asked.

"No. I'm going home and enjoy a little Macallan. And then I'm going to watch a little TV and then go to bed. Remember guys, in a trial there's always another tomorrow."

He could be nonchalant with Mark and Suzzi, and to an extent even with Laurel and Kelly, but Dillon could not kid himself. By the time he got home after the jury verdict, he was worried sick about what could be an out of control jury, and it was all he could do to control his anger at Jerry Keller and Alison Craft for what they had done to Mark and his wife simply because Keller was greedy and wanted more money.

As he sat sipping scotch, he thought back to when he and his friend and partner, Phil Burnam, first started their old law firm and reflected on how much they enjoyed being lawyers. As the firm grew, they made sure that they hired attorneys who really wanted to be a lawyer and help others. Attorneys who liked each other, and who were loyal to the firm, and to each other. Sure, they all wanted to make money, but that was never the driving force. They thought a partnership was something special and not just a legal entity. It was a feeling – a happiness to be together and to support each other.

But eventually things started to change. Partners began arguing between themselves about who should make more and it just became a business – a business about making money. This is why Dillon and Phil broke off and decided to start a new firm. "And this is exactly what has happened to the Baukus & Johnson firm. And Jerry Keller is the leader of the money means everything pack," he thought to himself.

Dillon got up from his chair in his living room and walked back into the kitchen to fix himself another little bit of Macallan. As he slowly poured the scotch into his glass, he suddenly slammed his hand down on the counter with such force that some of the precious scotch spilled onto the counter. "God damn!" he said out loud. "Why not add the son-of-a-bitch to the lawsuit."

What was going thru Dillon's mind was the jury instruction which says that every partner and the partnership are responsible for the wrongful acts of a partner. And he was aiming at Jerry Keller and Alison Craft.

"No harm in trying," he added.

While Haverley had been hoping the jury would not find any liability, the verdict was truthfully no surprise. As he was driving over to the Baukus & Johnson firm, he reflected back to the surprising testimony by Alison Craft. He shook his head and said to himself, "All she had to do was stick to her story and none of this would have happened!"

By the time Haverley got to Harlan Cross's office, Derrick Warner and Wayne Bailey were there to greet him. "What the hell happened?" Cross asked in a less than friendly manner.

"This should be no surprise," Haverley answered. "Once Alison changed her story, I think the jury, if they liked her before, changed their minds." He paused and glanced at each of the highly paid attorneys sitting in the room and added, "Look guys. It should seem obvious to all of you by now that Jerry Keller set up Mark Austin to be fired. Oh, I know no one has actually said that, but I suspect the jury is thinking that."

"So how do we defend the damage claim?" Derrick Warner asked.

"We stay with the same defense. The one thing that has never changed, is Craft's testimony that what she said in her memo was the truth. She had concerns and would not have voted to make him a partner. The jury has no evidence to contradict that testimony, and that means Austin would have left the firm with or without Keller asking her to write the memo. And that means his damages are at the worst one hundred thousand dollars, or something close to that."

Harlan Cross didn't like the idea of the jury finding wrongful termination, but he saw the logic in what Haverley said. "Well, I wish the verdict had been different, but I see your point. And just think, we actually offered him one million dollars!"

CHAPTER 17

Trial – Day Ten
(Friday, January 15)
(Damages Phase)

When Dillon arrived at Judge Harpman's courtroom the next morning, he told Charmaine Parker that he wanted a brief conference with the judge before the trial resumed. She advised Judge Harpman and when Haverley arrived, she told them both to go back to the judge's chambers.

As they entered his chambers, Judge Harpman said, "Charmaine tells me you wanted a brief conference, Mr. Clark. What can I do for you?"

"Well, Your Honor, in light of the evidence about Jerry Keller's role in bringing about the memo that Alison Craft wrote to the Executive Committee, I am making an oral motion requesting you to allow me to amend the complaint and add both Keller and Craft as defendants. This way the jury has a clear open door to decide who was the real culprit in getting Mark Austin fired," Dillon replied heatedly.

The motion at first startled Haverley, but he recovered quickly. "Nonsense, Your Honor. This trial is now half over. We never had a chance to defend either Keller or Craft and it would violate their rights to drag them in at this point. It is, well...I've never heard of such a motion in all the years that I've been a trial lawyer."

"Your Honor, except for the testimony of Jeff Hunt on the back-dated memo, the evidence has primarily all come from Alison Craft herself. And Jerry Keller admitted his role. Certainly no surprises here to either one of them," Dillon replied forcefully.

"Your, Honor, I must protest," Haverley replied with a stiff voice.

"Easy, gentlemen," Judge Harpman said. Looking at Dillon he added, "I think it would probably violate their due process rights if I added them at this late date. So your motion is denied. Do you want me to bring in a court reporter to so you can make your motion as part of the record?"

"Yes, Your Honor," Dillon answered. "I understand your position, but I fail to see any prejudice to either Keller or Craft."

Judge Harpman brought in the court reporter and after Dillon recited his motion, Judge Harpman reaffirmed his denial. "Ok, gentlemen, let's go out and get started with the damage phase of this case."

By the time Dillon and Haverley excited Judge Harpman's chambers, Mark, Suzzi and Kelly were in the courtroom. He quickly explained his motion and the denial but there was no time to discuss matters. Even though he lost his motion, he was still pleased because it had shaken, albeit briefly, Haverley's standard posture of confidence.

"Is the firm administrator here?" Dillon asked Kelly.

"She is and she has the financial records we requested," Kelly answered. "I went over and got a copy late yesterday after we talked. Pretty usual stuff. I did note that Gibbons actually paid very little the year he hired the Baukus firm, but then made a huge payment, over one million, in January. She also has the partner compensation records. The average total compensation to the partners was $1.5

million. And no surprise here, Jerry Keller got the top money at $3.2 million. Not bad for a complainer!"

"Good. I'll call her first," Dillon said. "And give my apology to Sam Archer for causing him to wait. Let him know I'll be with him shortly."

The firm administrator of Baukus & Johnson, Evelyn Marker, was in her mid-fifties with gray hair and a much-ridged demeanor that made her almost look mean when you added the permanently starched black suit she was wearing. Dillon had asked her to bring the billing and payment records for the Gibbons accounts and what each partner received as income and bonuses for the year when Mark was fired. She identified the records and Dillon let her go.

Dillon's next witness was Sam Archer, the legal affairs officer of the Gibbons's operations. When he had seated himself in the witness chair and took the oath, Dillon asked, "Mr. Archer, I know you work for Boyd Gibbons. Please tell the jury what you do for his companies?"

Archer smiled and said, "Well, I really do whatever Mr. Gibbons asks me to do." The jury as well as Judge Harpman chuckled at his answer.

"But my title is Executive Vice-President of Operations. And in this role, I hire and supervise the law firms we use here in California and in Washington DC," Archer added.

"What role did you play in bringing the Gibbons accounts to the Baukus & Johnson law firm?" Dillon asked.

"Boyd Gibbons had been impressed with Mark Austin. We were without labor law counsel at one point and I called the firm and Mark took the call. This was not his area, but he jumped right on it and gave me an answer, and that saved us a big confrontation with the union. Anyway, when Boyd remarried and wanted to amend his trust, I recalled that Mark did estate planning, so I recommend him to Boyd. Again, Mark jumped right on it and had the whole thing done in two days' time. So when we decided to change law firms, Boyd asked me to interview Mark's firm. I met with Harlan Cross and the others, and I liked what I saw so we switched firms."

"Did you ask that Mark play any particular role with the legal work done for your companies?" Dillon asked.

Archer laughed and said, "Yes, indeed. Mr. Gibbons wanted to help Mark so he insisted that he do all of the billings for the legal work. He has been involved with dozens of law firms over the years, and he knew that whoever was the billing attorney was usually looked at as sort of being in charge. He wanted to reward Mark so he insisted that he do the billings."

"Did you, as the legal affairs executive, form an opinion on Mark Austin's legal work?" Dillon asked.

"He was and is an outstanding attorney. Mr. Gibbons is a hard man to please, so when he goes out of his way to help someone, you can be confident he is top quality," Archer answered.

"Mr. Archer, I'd like to switch topics for a moment," Dillon said. "Jerry Keller was in charge of the corporate legal work. Is that correct?"

"Yes, sir. Jerry is a fine lawyer and he was our main man at Baukus & Johnson," Archer replied.

"When Jerry Keller left Baukus & Johnson to start his own firm, you moved all of the Gibbons accounts over to his new law firm. Am I correct?" Dillon asked.

"Yes we did. We had hundreds of matters and several major lawsuits and we just could not afford to switch counsel again. If we had stayed at the Baukus firm, a new lawyer would have had to take Jerry's place," Archer explained.

"I understand," Dillon replied. "But then you also transferred all of the litigation matters as well. You could have just left those at Baukus & Johnson?" Dillon asked.

"Well, yes that is true," Archer replied. "But when Jerry called me and said he was leaving the firm, he said he was taking the trial lawyers who were handling our case with him, so we had no choice. It would have been like starting from scratch all over again."

What Archer had said almost slipped by Dillon, but the light bulb went on before he proceeded with another question. "Mr. Archer, you just said that Jerry Keller called you and said he was leaving the firm. Did I hear you correctly?"

"You did. Jerry and I were actually talking about one of our matters, and when we were done, he said he was leaving to start his own firm," Archer replied.

"Did he ask if you would follow him to the new firm?" Dillon now asked with a raised eyebrow.

"Yes he did. That's when he said he was also taking the trial lawyers," Archer explained.

"So if I understand things correctly," Dillon said, as he threw a glance in Haverley's direction, "you felt you had no choice but to follow Mr. Keller because he was taking all of the attorneys who worked on the Gibbons's matters with him. Is this right?"

"Yes, that is true. We really had no choice at that point," Archer answered.

This line of questioning really had nothing to do with Mark's case, but Dillon knew that Haverley would report back to Harlan Cross what Keller had done. And Cross was going to be furious. It is a sacred rule that when a lawyer leaves a law firm, he can make an announcement to all of the clients about leaving, but he can never solicit the clients. And Jerry Keller broke this rule big time.

"Mr. Archer, I appreciate the time this has taken you away from your office, so I have only a few more questions," Dillon said. "I have here the financial records of the Baukus & Johnson firm relating to the Gibbons account. You started working with that firm in March of the year in which Mark Austin was fired. That comes to about nine months of work. Yet their record shows you only paid the firm a little over $600,000.00. Surely the billings were far greater than that?"

Archer looked over to Haverley as if he might have an objection, but when none came, he said, "You are correct. We usually make large payments toward the year end for tax reasons. But Jerry Keller called me sometime in November or early December and asked me to pay the balance in January. So I'm sure their records show a large payment at that time."

"Isn't this a bit unusual?" Dillon asked.

"Well, not really," Archer replied. "I've dealt with hundreds of law firms and they all run differently. Some firms manipulate the books to help on taxes by deferring income into the next year. Some defer expenses so the profit is higher. Some hold open their books and take into income what they actually receive in January but record it for the prior year to increase the profits for the prior year. All I can tell you is that Jerry called and asked us not to pay any more bills until January.

While Sam Archer may not have known why Jerry Keller asked him to pay later, it was bloody obvious to Dillon. "He knew that if Mark got any bonus for origination, it would be limited to a percentage of what Gibbons paid that year. So he made sure Mark was gone and he alone would get the full bonus," he thought to himself with disgust. "He'll do anything for money!"

Dillon got what he wanted from San Archer and said, "Thank you, Mr. Archer. I have no more questions."

Haverley had a dilemma. It was obvious to him too why Jerry Keller asked for payments to be delayed, but he decided he could only make it worse if he asked any questions that could back-fire. So he asked a few questions about Jerry Keller's reputation and the quality of his work. Sam Archer gave Jerry Keller high marks and he let him leave.

After the lunch break, Dillon called his economist to testify. This was pretty dry testimony but it is an essential part of any damage claim. The expert was a female economics professor at UCLA. Her name was Sarah Connery and she had testified in hundreds of lawsuits. Haverley knew her personally and stipulated to her credentials as an expert.

When Professor Connery was seated and gave the oath, Dillon asked, "Professor Connery, did you, at my request, do an analysis of what Mark Austin could have earned at Baukus & Johnson if he had been made a partner?"

"Yes, sir, I did," Professor Connery replied. As she did so, she stood and walked over to an easel that had been covered. Dillon had Kelly bring the easel to court several days ago so it would be ready if needed for the damage phase.

"Did you prepare a chart illustrating your conclusions?" Dillon asked.

"Yes," Professor Connery said as she took the protective cover off the easel so the jury could see her chart. "I took the total income of new partners over a ten year period, averaged the number and came to the conclusion Mr. Austin could have earned $550,000.00 the first two years; then $780,000.00 a year for the next three years; and then $1.3 million for the remaining five years." She pointed to the columns on her chart as she testified and then concluded, "The total over the ten years is $9,940,000.00."

"Did you calculate what Mark Austin has earned since he was fired and how much he will earn with his current firm over the same ten years?" Dillon asked.

"Yes," Professor Connery answered. Again she pointed to the second column on her chart and added, "As you can see, he would earn a total $1,500,000.00. I used a number of $150,000.000 a year for a small firm lawyer in southern California. The difference in what he could have earned at the Baukus & Johnson firm and his smaller firm is $8,440,000.00."

"Thank you, Professor. I have no further questions," Dillon concluded.

Haverley could not argue with Professor Connery's numbers, so he attacked her assumptions. An expert opinion is only as good as the facts are on which she relies. If the expert uses bad facts, his conclusion will be equally bad.

"Professor Connery," Haverley asked with a small grim smile of satisfaction, "Your conclusions on damages for Mark Austin would be totally wrong if in fact he had never been made a partner. Isn't that correct?"

"Of course," Professor Connery replied. "If he had never been made a partner, he would have earned only a salary as an associate. He would no doubt have left the firm and so his earnings would be what they are now. There would be no damages."

Haverley lowered his voice, took a quick glance at the jury and said, "Thank you for your candor, Professor Connery. I have no more questions."

"Nice job," Dillon thought to himself. "He's staying with his position that Mark would never have been made a partner if Alison Craft voted no. A clean and simple issue for the jury to grab onto. And it's like a javelin pointed right at our jugular."

As Dillon was about to call his next witness, the psychologist on emotional distress damages, when juror number eight, Mr. Jordanson, raised his hand and asked, "Your Honor, are we entitled to ask questions?"

Judge Harpman looked sternly at the juror. He knew as well as Dillon and Haverley, that the juror was one of the three who objected to the verdict on liability. He finally said, "No. If you have a question, write it down and give it to the bailiff. I'll take a look and decide if it can be answered."

"OK judge," the juror said, "I have a question already written down." He took it out of his pocket and handed it to the bailiff. The bailiff walked over and gave it to Judge Harpman who quickly read it. He looked over at the juror, gave him a stony stare and said, "This is something I think counsel needs to see. We'll take a fifteen-minute break." Looking at counsel he added, "Please see me in chambers."

When Dillon and Haverley were seated, Judge Harpman handed the note first to Dillon to read. It was short and Dillon handed it to Haverley. The note read: "Judge Harpman. This trial is wasting everybody's time. Can't you just stop it and let us decide. I think we've heard all the evidence we need."

Judge Harpman leaned back in his leather swivel chair, scratched his head and asked somewhat exasperated, "What do I say to him?"

Dillon was the first to react. This was what he feared all along. The minority jurors were unhappy and probably thought Mark should never have sued the law firm. Even one bad juror like this man can taint the rest. His tongue felt like the bitter taste of cold steel. He had to think quickly but from his years of experience in a courtroom, he knew what had to be done. He didn't know if Mark could take another trial, but he sucked in his breath and said, "Your Honor, I move for a mistrial. We obviously have a juror whose mind is made up and won't listen to the evidence or the arguments of counsel."

"Not so fast," Haverley replied. "This juror is just impatient. That note does not say or imply he won't listen to the evidence. We're almost finished with the evidence and, well, judge, Mr. Clark's client won the first part. You'd think he would be happy."

"Your Honor," Dillon said in desperation, "you saw how the three dissenters acted when they were asked about the verdict on liability. They were not shy. They said they didn't like it. And now they're angry that the trial is still going on. I think...."

Before Dillon could finish, Judge Harpman leaned forward as if he was uncertain of what to do. He hesitated and then slowly said, "This is obviously a critical issue. I'd like to think about it. So why don't you two fine lawyers do some research and email it over to me tonight. I'll pick it up on my home computer. We can then decide tomorrow morning. Tell Charmaine I said to give you my email address."

Judge Harpman walked out into the courtroom with Dillon and Haverley, stepped up to his bench and sat down. The jurors were already all seated. He said, "Ladies and gentlemen, the question asked by Mr. Jordanson is important and I've asked counsel to do some research for me. I'm going to send you all home for the day and we'll get this resolved in the morning."

Dillon and Haverley stood and each watched the jurors leave. Not one looked over at either counsel. They were not a happy group.

When the jurors had all left the courtroom, Kelly and Suzzi quickly walked up to where Dillon and Mark were standing and Kelly asked in a gush of excitement, "What the hell happened?"

Dillon looked over at Mark and initially said nothing. He felt angry and just generally pissed off. After a second he said, "Mark, we've got a bad situation with the jury. Jordanson, the one with the question, says he's heard enough and just wants the trial to be over. Remember, he's one of the three who made it very clear that they didn't like the verdict on liability. I asked the judge for a mistrial and that is what he wants us to research."

It took a minute before the dire situation was grasped by Mark and Suzzi. Mark tried to say something, but shock paralyzed his mind. Suzzi just grabbed Mark's arm and held on tight.

"Dillon, this is crazy," Kelly blurted out. "Do you really want a new trial?"

"We have no choice," Dillon replied. "Those three were adamant and with one of those now saying he doesn't even want to hear the rest of the evidence, we just can't take the chance. All they have to do is convince one of the other jurors to join with them, and we lose the whole thing."

Mark finally got ahold of himself and as he was negatively shaking his head back and forth, he said, "I can't do it again. No way. Suzzi and I are done. We're going home."

"I know this is disappointing," Dillon said trying to ease Mark's frustration. "Let us take a look at this now that we have some time to think it out. Why don't you and Suzzi go on home. It's still early and you can drive over to the beach. Do something that will take your mind off the trial until tomorrow."

Dillon saw the pain on Mark's face as he and Suzzi turned to leave the courtroom. He didn't say anything and Dillon didn't blame him.

The ride back to his office was like being in a dream for Dillon. "How can a couple of jurors wreck a case so completely?" he kept asking himself over and over.

Kelly obviously phoned ahead and told Laurel what had happened because Laurel and his secretary, Jeannie Davis, were waiting for him as he got off the elevator.

"I'm so sorry," Laurel said. "Kelley said you're asking for a mistrial."

"We have no choice," Dillon replied. "That damn juror has his mind made up and we already know which way. He's one of the three who spoke out against the liability verdict."

They walked down to the conference room and Dillon took off his coat and threw it the whole distance of the conference room table. Laurel and Jeannie just stared.

As Kelly entered the conference room, Dillon was walking over to the bar cabinet. He grabbed a glass and put in a few ice cubes and was starting to pour himself some Macallan scotch when he stopped and slammed his glass down on the counter, turned and said irritably, "Hell, I don't even want a drink!"

Jeannie Davis slowly walked backwards towards the door and gave a little waive to Laurel and Kelly as she departed. Laurel and Kelly just looked at each other questioning whether they should say anything. Finally Laurel, who had known Dillon the longest, said, "Dillon, let me do some research on this. You have an alternate juror. Maybe you can convince the judge to replace Jordanson with the alternate. That way you have a chance of calming things down in the jury room and you at least get rid of one troublemaker."

By now Dillon was sitting slumped down in one of the conference room chairs. He grimaced and said, "OK. See what you can find. I don't think there is any real law on this. But, well, see what you find."

"If Judge Harpman agrees to replace the juror, what then?" Kelly asked. "Will you go forward and finish the trial?"

Kelly had just asked the million-dollar question. Do you roll the dice with a new juror, knowing that at least two of the other disgruntled jurors are still on the panel, or do you still seek a new trial?

Haverley had already alerted Harlan Cross to the outrageous conduct of Keller in soliciting clients and Cross had immediately asked Derrick Warner to have someone research whether the firm could sue Keller for his actions. So when Haverley called Cross a second time and explained what was going on with the jury, Cross was more than concerned. They had lost the liability issue and he saw this as just further bad news until Haverley explained what it all meant.

"The plaintiff is screwed either way. If he gets a new trial, we will be prepared. We already know what Keller and Craft did and there will be no surprises this time around. If the judge denies the mistrial request, we know we have at least three angry jurors who are fed up with the whole case. They will either win over some allies and, hell, who knows. Maybe they'll just give Austin $1 dollar in damages. I've seen this happen when a jury gets mad at the plaintiffs. They'll do their job, but then get even with the damages."

Once Cross understood the predicament that Austin was in, he laughed and said, "Do me a favor. Tell Dillon our offer to settle is withdrawn."

When Cross concluded his conversation with Haverley, he asked Derrick Warner and Wayne Henry, the other members of the Executive Committee, to join him. He explained what Haverley had said and they were all happy as far as the Austin trial was concerned, but the adverse effect of Jerry Keller leaving with so many clients was having a serious impact on the firm's finances. The firm's income had dropped by almost forty percent, and this was serious because the firm's monthly lease payments remained the same. A few other partners had left and the firm's six floors of office space now had thirty-five vacant offices plus dozens of empty secretarial stations. This is what was behind Cross's decision to see if they could sue Jerry Keller and even Alison Craft.

"You know," Derrick Warner said, "what really gets me is how Jerry was cooking the books so he alone would get bonus money from the Gibbons's accounts. Do you really think he actually got Alison to write the memo so we'd fire Mark so he would not be at the firm by year end?"

"I do now," Cross replied. "It otherwise makes no sense. By shoving money into the next year meant he would get less compensation. So it only makes sense if he thought he would get the full origination credit. Remember, he was very upset when we told him that Mark was the real originator and did not reward him for Gibbons out of the Tier Two pool. When he deferred the income, he had no idea we would not give him the credit!"

"Have you had any luck talking to other firms about merging with us?" Wayne Bailey asked.

"Not so far," Cross answered. "Everyone in town knows about the lawsuit and they aren't going to buy into a liability. I think we won't have any success until the case is over."

"I'm frankly worried," Wayne Bailey said. "If we don't cut expenses or add a lot more attorneys and the work with them, there may not even be a Tier Two pool by the end of this year. If that happens, the remaining partners will really run for cover."

"I understand. I feel the same way," Cross replied. "But Austin's case is just about over. When he gets a low recovery, the risk to other firms joining with us will be gone. We'll be OK. We just have to wait."

Not wanting to take any chances, when Derrick Warner and Wayne Bailey left his office, Cross picked up his cell phone and dialed his old partner, the Honorable Dale Bannerman, the current Presiding Judge of the Los Angeles County Superior Court.

"Well, well," Judge Bannerman said when he saw who was calling. He had already been told about the jury fuss in an email from Judge Harpman earlier in the day. When he answered, Cross said, "Dale, we could be in a little trouble if we don't get this Austin case over with soon. Is there anything you can do to make sure that Judge Harpman does not grant a mistrial?"

"Harlan, I told you before I can't interfere," Judge Bannerman said.

"God damn it, Dale, this is serious. If we don't merge soon with another firm and fill up our space, we could be out of business!" Cross snapped with irritation.

Judge Bannerman slowly sucked in his breath for a moment and held on to it, afraid he would lose his temper. When he finally spoke, he said, "Look Harlan, I'll talk to Harpman. He's kept me informed and knows I'm following the case. But you have to remember, it is his decision. Not mine. "

Laurel called Dillon at home that night. As he suspected, there was no controlling law on substituting a juror with an alternate. This usually happens when a juror gets ill or for some reason can't continue with the trial. In this case, Mr. Jordanson was just unhappy and whether that constitutes grounds for a mistrial is going to be up to Judge Harpman.

As he sat at his kitchen table eating some scrambled eggs and toast for dinner, along with some Macallan scotch, Dillon looked over to the photograph of his wife above the kitchen desk. "God, I wish I could talk with you right now. We are in real trouble on Mark's case. We have a badly divided jury and, as you know, they can be totally unpredictable. I have this desperate fear that at some point I'm going to be forced to look at Mark and his wife and try to answer their inevitable question, 'Why did we lose?.' And I just may have no answer."

CHAPTER 18

Trial – Day Eleven
(Monday, January 18)
(Final Arguments on Damages)

On Monday, Dillon arrived at court early and for a second time he told the clerk, Charmaine Parker, that he wanted to talk with the judge. "Tell him we need a conference regarding what to do with the juror with the note."

When Dillon and Haverley arrived at Judge Harpman's chambers, Dillon got right to the point. "Your Honor, Mr. Jordanson has indicated quite clearly that he has made up his mind even before we finish the evidence on damages. He just wants to get it over with and go home. So reluctantly, I now request that you dismiss Mr. Jordanson and seat the alternate juror in his place."

"Not so fast," Haverley said quickly. "There are no grounds to dismiss this juror. Last time I looked, being impatient does not disqualify a juror."

Judge Harpman had been giving a lot of thought to Mr. Jordanson and had actually done some research himself. It was no surprise that the law said he had broad discretion to make sure each party got a fair trial. He leaned back in his chair and said, "Gentlemen, this is a close question. I agree with Mr. Haverley that the note itself does not disqualify Mr. Jordanson. But what bothers me is that he was one of the three who disagreed with the liability verdict. When you put these two things together, I think it is best

275

to let the alternate step in to finish the trial." Looking at Dillon, he added, "Anything further, Mr. Clark?"

"No, Your Honor," Dillon replied. "I think this is the correct thing to do."

When everyone was again seated at counsel table, Judge Harpman told the bailiff to bring the jurors in. When they were all seated, he had intended to explain his ruling, but before he said anything, another juror raised his hand and said, "Your Honor, I also have a question. I have it here in writing."

Judge Harpman noticed that it was juror number ten, Mr. Hughes, who spoke. "Yes, of course," Judge Harpman said with a tone of disapproval. "Please give your note to the bailiff.

When Judge Harpman read the note, there was a flash of irritation that crossed his face. The note said "Your Honor. We have been sitting here day after day and the attorneys keep going over the same thing. Is there a way you can bring this case to an end?"

Judge Harpman looked over at the jury and said, "Ladies and gentlemen, with a second question, we are going to have to take another short recess. The bailiff will take you back to the jury room until we are ready."

When Dillon and Haverley again entered Judge Harpman's chambers, they saw that he was pacing back and forth. "I have never seen questions like this in all my life as a judge," he finally said in frustration. "What do we do now?"

Dillon was also stunned by the question from a second juror. The juror, Mr. Hughes, was also one of the three who protested the liability verdict and this was grim news at best.

A trial lawyer must make hundreds of instant decisions during a trial, and this was Dillon's turn. He knew that with only one alternate juror, they could only replace one the two disgruntled jurors.

But what affect would dismissing one have on the other? Would he get even angrier seeing a fellow unhappy juror being dismissed?

With great reluctance, Dillon said, "Your Honor, I must now renew my request for a mistrial. We have two very unhappy jurors and replacing one is not going to cure the problem. Granted, we don't know what they talked about in the jury room, or why they so strongly disagree on the liability verdict, but their bias can taint the whole jury. I don't like trying this case again any more than you do, Your Honor. But the reality here is that we have three jurors who are out of control and that can now spill over to the deliberations on the damage phase."

Haverley was now on the edge of his seat and said vehement-ly, "Your Honor, this is craziness. The plaintiff wins the liability phase and he now wants a mistrial? And more to the point, look at the facts. All we have are two jurors who may be getting impatient. Nothing more. There is not a shred of evidence that they won't listen and do their job as jurors."

Judge Harpman sat silent for a moment and then stood and walked over to the counter in the corner of his office and absently poured himself a glass of water. He returned to his desk and as he sat down he took a sip of water and said, "No. I'm not going to grant that, Mr. Clark. We're about at the end of this case and I want the jury to do their job. No mistrial. But I will replace Mr. Jordanson if you want?"

"That could just make matters worse," Dillon said with disap-pointment. "Dismissing one could very likely irritate even the oth-ers who seem to be getting along. But I do need to make my request for a mistrial on the record."

Judge Harpman called Charmaine Parker and asked her to have the court reporter come in with her equipment. When Dillon put his request for a mistrial on the record, Judge Harpman said, "OK, gentlemen. Let's go out and finish this trial."

When the bailiff brought the jurors back into the courtroom and they were all seated, Judge Harpman explained, "Ladies and gentlemen, as you know we have had questions from two jurors. I have discussed the questions with counsel, and I have concluded that it is best to not reply now. I want you to all listen to the rest of the evidence and the arguments of counsel, as well as the final jury instructions that I'll be giving you before you retire to deliberate on this damage phase of the case. If by then you still have questions, let the bailiff know and I'll consider them at that time."

Looking down at Dillon, Judge Harpman said, "Mr. Clark, are you ready with your next witness?"

"I am, Your Honor. Our next witness will be our expert psychologist, Doctor Howard Erickson," Dillon replied.

Doctor Howard Erickson worked for the Veteran's Hospital in Los Angeles and specialized in emotional trauma. He also taught at the UCLA Medical School. Doctor Erickson was on the chubby side, around sixty years old with a distinguished beard that was peppered with gray. And he was totally bald.

After Doctor Erickson was seated and given the oath, Dillon asked him the standard questions so the jury could learn about his expertise in trauma cases. When the background information was done, Dillon asked, "Doctor Erickson, did you at my request examine and test Mark Austin for emotional trauma that he may have suffered because he was fired?"

"I did," Doctor Erickson replied. "Mark is an unusually strong masculine individual, but this only operates as an outer defense. When he was fired, the whole image of himself as a man was shattered. When he was fired, he perceived himself as a loser who could no longer support his family."

This was getting dangerously close to violating the stipulation that Dillon had reluctantly agreed to which forbids any claim for emotional distress because of any adverse effect the firing had on Mark's sex life with his wife.

Dillon saw Haverley look in his direction, so he raised his hand and said, "Doctor Erickson, focusing just on how Mark viewed himself, could you tell the jury if his distress was mild, middle road or strong? Use a scale of one to ten."

"On a one to ten scale, Mark's distress level was a solid ten," Doctor Erickson replied. "You see, when a man sees himself as smart, successful and has a beautiful family, and that image is shattered, it is a terrible blow. It is not unlike veterans who come home from a war with no legs. They just don't see themselves as a man any more. They see themselves as not able to care for their family. And that is how Mark felt and still feels to a lesser extent. He is not the man he was because he was fired and his image and dreams about his future were left in tatters."

"Does Mark still suffer from emotional distress?" Dillon asked.

"Yes, he does," Doctor Erickson replied. "While it may now be at the eight level at this time, he will continue to suffer for many years to come. It is not easy to regain self-confidence and to get back to seeing yourself as you did before being fired."

"Thank you, Doctor Erickson. I have nothing further," Dillon said as he glanced at the jury to see if they were listening. Not a single juror took notes.

When Dillon finished his questions, Haverley stood and walked over to the speaker's podium. He cleared his throat and asked, "Doctor, did Mark Austin tell you he was in pain?"

When he heard this question, Dillon's head snapped up and his tongue suddenly felt like sandpaper. The jury already saw that Mark cannot talk about his private feelings and if he told anything to Doctor Erickson, the jury would conclude he was faking before. But if he didn't explain his pain, Doctor Erickson was then depending on his own analysis and tests, and this is where Haverley was headed.

Dillon held his breath waiting to hear the answer.

"Doctor Erickson smiled as he answered. "Not directly. Mark is a typical man who doesn't talk about private matters, and certainly not about feeling emotional pain. I spent hours with him and he just could not say directly what he was feeling."

"Well, then, Doctor, how do you know he is suffering any emotional distress. Are you just guessing?" Haverley asked aggressively.

"We gave Mark a whole battery of psychological tests designed to detect emotional issues. You probably know them. They are routine. To give you one illustration, Mark was asked to draw a picture of himself and his family. What he drew was a picture of his wife and daughter standing together, but he placed himself far away in a corner. This tells us he sees himself remote and disconnected from his family," Doctor Erickson explained.

"But how are we to know he is suffering distress?" Haverley continued.

"This is where our training as psychologists comes into play," Doctor Erickson replied. "We take the information from the tests and then explore the answer directly with the patient. In this case, using the drawing for example, when I asked Mark to tell me why he put himself off in the corner, he just shook his head and said he didn't know. But when he said this, his eyes welled-up with tears and he turned away from me until he composed himself. This is pain. It is the kind of pain that really no words could describe. You see it on his face."

Haverley could tell he was getting nowhere with Erickson, so he returned to his key defense. "Doctor, you said this emotional distress was caused by Mark being asked to leave the Baukus & Johnson firm. Correct?"

"Yes. It was that event that caused him to lose his self-esteem and the image of himself as the bread-winner in the family," Erickson replied.

"We are now at an important point here Doctor, so listen carefully," Haverley said slowly yet loud enough for the jurors to all hear. " If the law firm, for whatever reason, decided not to make Mark a partner in say six months or a year later and suggested he leave the firm, would this so-called emotional distress have been the same?"

Doctor Erickson leaned forward slightly in the witness chair and said, "Yes, I think it would be the same. Maybe not as severe in that being fired is a lot more demeaning than not being made a partner, but essentially the same. His image of himself as a successful attorney with a bright future would have been shattered."

Haverley smiled as he asked, "Doctor, I assume you would agree with me that it was the fact that Mark Austin was asked to leave, fired or not made a partner and then asked to leave, however you want to put it, that is what caused his distress? It was the fact that he lost his position. Am I correct?"

"Yes, indeed," Erickson answered. "The distress comes from being asked to leave the firm. That is the cause."

"Would you then also agree with me that the Baukus & Johnson law firm would not be responsible for this so-called distress if they had a legitimate business reason for asking Mark to leave?" Haverley quickly asked.

Dillon stood and angrily said, "Objection. He is asking this expert a legal question. It is for the jury to decide if the defendant was responsible."

Haverley raised his hand in surrender and said, "I'm sorry Your Honor. Mr. Clark is right. It is a legal issue and I withdraw my question. I have nothing further. Thank you Doctor Erickson."

Dillon had discussed with Mark the option of putting him back on the stand to testify about his emotional distress, and decided it was best to rely on Doctor Erickson. The same conclusion applied to Suzzi. The heart and soul of Mark's pain was how his firing played havoc with their sex life, but they were prohibited from going into that because of the earlier agreement. Even if Mark could not say out-loud how he felt, Suzzi could have been a terrific witness. She was an eye witness to Mark freezing-up at night and not even touching her for months at a time. Dillon had explained all of this to Mark and Suzzi, but Suzzi refused to let anyone ask Mark more questions about their sex life, regardless of the consequences.

All of this was flooding through Dillon's mind as he now stood and announced, "Your Honor, this concludes the plaintiff's case. We rest subject to final argument."

Judge Harpman turned to Haverley and asked, "And you, Mr. Haverley? Any further evidence?"

"The defense also rests, Your Honor," Haverley replied.

Judge Harpman let the jurors go to an early lunch and had told them to return at 1:00 p.m.to hear the final arguments from counsel. Kelly took Mark and Suzzi up to the cafeteria for lunch. Dillon apologized and said he was going for a walk and would see them back in the courtroom.

Dillon was worried. Try as he might, he couldn't shake off the ever increasing dark mood that seem to hang over his head whenever he thought of the three dissenting jurors. A thousand questions kept running through his head. "What in the world are they thinking? What caused them to be so against Mark? Are they opposed to anyone filing a lawsuit when they get fired? What will Mr. Jordanson, Hughes and the others be saying to the other jurors? Will they convince one more juror to vote their way?"

As he walked, Dillon was also thinking about the other nine jurors who he desperately needed on his side. If they accept Alison Craft's testimony and believe she would have criticized Mark no matter what and that she would not have voted to make him a partner, the damages could be only the difference between what Mark would have earned as a junior partner at Baukus & Johnson and what he made with his current firm. This could be one of those famous verdicts where the jury finds liability but awards a token amount in damages. Dillon had actually been on the winning side of one of those verdicts many years ago. He was defending a client in a federal lawsuit where the plaintiffs were alleging a violation of due process. It was a trial before a federal judge who, in the end, found a violation but only awarded the plaintiffs $1.

Dillon feared this might happen to Mark. The disgruntled jurors, having lost their fight on liability, could now convince the other jurors to award $1.

"Mr. Clark, are you ready for your final argument?" Judge Harpman asked after the jurors were all seated.

"Yes, Your Honor," Dillon replied as he rose and walked over to the speaker's podium.

Dillon, with a gracious smile, said, "Ladies and gentlemen, you have been very kind and attentive to all of us throughout this trial, and I want to thank you on behalf of my client, Mark Austin," He had made a tactical decision during his walk. The only issue now was one of damages, and he needed to remind the nine jurors who voted for liability that this was not the time to revisit that issue. The only issue was damages.

"As you all know, this trial was bifurcated. You already decided that the Baukus & Johnson law firm wrongfully terminated Mark Austin and in doing so they intended to cause him emotional distress. This was your verdict on liability," Dillon explained.

Looking now more serious, Dillon continued. "As Judge Harpman will explain in his final instructions, your task now is to decide how much to award Mark Austin for damages. Damages in this case are divided into two categories. One is what Mark lost in wages and what he is likely to lose for a reasonable time in the future caused by his termination. This is really just a mathematical calculation based on how much you find he lost and will continue to lose. The second category is emotional distress damages. Judge Harpman will explain that in this area, the law does not give you any standard to use. Mark is entitled to receive compensation for the emotional distress the Baukus & Johnson firm caused him in whatever sum you believe is reasonable. Jerry Keller and Alison Craft, in what they did to Mark, showed intent to harm Mark, or at best a reckless disregard for what he would suffer. This presumably is why you found the Baukus firm liable."

Dillon had Kelly prepare a chart on damages using the numbers from professor Sarah Connery. He walked over to the counsel table and Kelly, who was now seated next to Mark, handed him the chart. It was four feet by three feet and Dillon placed it on an easel that Kelly had brought to court.

"The evidence on lost wages is simple yet staggering, depending on how you view the evidence. As you see, Professor Connery calculated out for all of us what Mark lost in income just as an associate or junior partner," Dillon explained as he pointed with his pen to the number on the chart. "But the real number is what Mark would have made as a senior partner, assuming you find he would have been made a partner except for the outrageous conduct of Jerry Keller and Alison Craft. To reach this number, you have to decide how many years are reasonable to reach a just award. As you can see, Professor Connery calculates this out for ten years and her total is $ 8,440,000. We can just call this $8.5 million."

Dillon returned to the speaker's podium and continued. "Folks, I can't really help you on the emotional distress damage issue, so I won't even argue this one. You have to pick a number you think is reasonable. But I will remind you that the Baukus & Johnson firm is responsible and liable for the actions of both Jerry Keller and Alison Craft. They were both partners. It may very well be that the Executive Committee at the firm terminated Mark in good faith because they believed the memo from Alison left them no choice. But the firm is nevertheless liable for the damages caused by these two partners who clearly conspired to get Mark fired. They both knew he would be fired as soon as the Committee got the memo. And, I might add, the memo with a fake date! "

Dillon took a sip of water and said, "I suppose there are many ways to look at the facts, but I'm going to tell you my version. Mark Austin was fired because Jerry Keller wanted to get rid of him. He was greedy and wanted all the credit and money for the Gibbons's accounts, and to get that he had to get rid of Mark. He made that decision as soon as he got a copy of Mark's own memo asking for a bonus for originating the new accounts. And this is why Craft back-dated it. To let others think she had been thinking about this for a long time, when the truth, and I emphasize the truth, was that Jerry Keller got her to write the memo in December when he first saw Mark's bonus request."

"Why is all of this important for damages?" Dillon asked as he held his arms out and shrugged his shoulders. "It is important because, but for the interference by Jerry Keller and Alison Craft, Mark Austin..." And at this point Dillon paused and walked over and stood behind Mark. "But for the interference of these two partners, Mark Austin would have surely been made a senior partner. If you believe this, then his damages are staggering. Only you can decide how many years of lost partner income can adequately compensate Mark for this loss. I certainly think the ten years used by Professor Connery is fair."

Dillon walked back to the speaker's podium and let the silence settle in before he added, "You will no doubt hear from Mr. Haverley, that Alison Craft said her comments about Mark were true and she would not have voted to make him a partner. He will say this means Mark would never have been made a partner and what he might have made is not relevant. Only you can decide if she told you the truth. I can only remind you that she lied under oath when she first testified and only told you Jerry Keller asked her to write the now famous memo when she slipped-up on cross examination. And she still kept secret the fact that she back-dated her memo. Is this someone you want to believe?"

"As I said at the start, this is really a simple case. Yes, the damages are potentially large, but that is now your decision. Thank you for your courtesy and time," Dillon said by way of concluding his argument.

Haverley was a clever defense lawyer and had thought out his pitch to the jury very carefully. He wanted to do two things: help the disgruntled jurors convince the others to change their mind; and to keep damages to a token number.

"Mr. Clark, as you can well see, is an excellent lawyer," Haverley said as he started his final argument. "But, as Judge Harpman will instruct you, his oratory is not evidence. His words, no matter how eloquent they are, are not evidence. And this is critical, because there is no evidence, either direct or circumstantial, that shows that

Alison Craft was not truthful when she said her comments about Mark were true and she would not have supported him as a senior partner. Why is this so critical? It is critical because Mark Austin would never have been made a senior partner and all of the damage numbers you have been hearing about are just smoke and mirrors."

Haverley was watching the three dissenting jurors carefully and he saw one write down notes as he was speaking. Looking right at juror number eight, Mr. Jordanson, he said slowly so every juror would hear every word, "If Mark Austin would never have been made a senior partner, his damages are limited to what he would have earned for maybe a year at the Baukus firm less what he earned where he is now. Professor Connery gave you the numbers. They come out to less than $100,000. This is the maximum damages that you should award Mr. Austin on his wrongful termination cause of action. Anything beyond this number would be indulging in gross speculation and the law does not permit you to do that."

Haverley stepped back from the speaker's podium, allowed a small grin to creep across his face and said, "But this doesn't end your job. Mr. Austin also threw in a second cause of action. This is the one for emotional distress, and I would like to briefly discuss this. I agree with Mr. Clark in that we don't know why you found liability, but we do know there was disagreement. You can't change the liability verdict, but you can..."

"Objection," Dillon shouted out. "Mr. Haverley is about to suggest a way for the jury to ignore the liability verdict and that is grossly improper."

Judge Harpman looked over at Haverley and motioned for both counsel to approach the judge's bench so that what they said could not be heard by the jury. "I don't know what you were about to say, Mr. Haverley, but you can't argue the liability verdict was an error."

"That was not my intent, Your Honor," Haverley explained. "But damages for intentional infliction of emotional distress, as the jury instruction says, calls for the conduct to be outrageous and a substantial factor in causing the distress. There is no standard to measure an award, so I am entitled to discuss the outrageousness of the conduct because that is the only guideline the jury has."

Judge Harpman hesitated for a minute as he considered Haverley's argument. Finally he said, "I have to agree with you, Mr. Haverley. The degree of the outrageousness is one way for a jury to look at damages."

When counsel returned to the counsel tables, Judge Harpman said, "Your objection is overruled." He turned to the jury and added, "Because you found liability on the emotional distress cause of action, counsel is entitled to discuss the outrageousness of the conduct." Turning back to Haverley, he said, "Proceed counsel."

Haverley turned toward the jury and said, "As I had been saying, you can't change the verdict on liability, but you can again consider what the jury instruction calls outrageous conduct. In this case, what Alison Craft said about Mark Austin in her memo was true from her perspective. The point is that Mark would never have been made a partner. So it would be unreasonable for you to now award some large damage number for distress."

Haverley now leaned over the podium and again said slowly, "The key here, ladies and gentlemen, is that Mr. Austin would always have suffered some distress when he was not made a partner. This is not a technical or crafty statement from me as the defense attorney. It goes to the heart of the case. This has always been a lawsuit where the plaintiff has been reaching far beyond the facts to grab the golden ring and you should now end this case with a nominal damage award. It is your decision. The number can even be $1. Thank You."

This was Haverley's appeal to the disgruntled jurors. He had now given them the ammunition to use to get the whole jury to bring reality to the final verdict. If his instincts were correct, the jury would likely come in with a verdict in the low thousands that would satisfy all of the jurors.

It took Judge Harpman about thirty minutes to give the jury their final instructions. Dillon and Kelly had prepared a brief supporting the instruction they wanted on future wage losses. Haverley had fought to keep it out but the Judge Harpman finally agreed. Dillon now listened carefully as he read the instruction.

> **"In determining the period that Mark Austin's employment with the Baukus & Johnson firm was reasonably certain to have continued, you should consider, among other factors, the following:**
>
> 1. **Mark Austin's age, work performance, and intent regarding continuing employment with Baukus & Johnson;**
>
> 2. **Whether it is reasonable to conclude that Mark Austin would have been made a senior partner with Baukus & Johnson;**
>
> 3. **The average earnings of senior partners at Baukus & Johnson; and**
>
> 4. **Any other factors that bear on how long Mark Austin would have continued to work at Baukus & Johnson.**

As he sat with Mark listening to the instructions, Dillon's doubts about the jury again crept back into his mind. He carefully watched the three disgruntled jurors to see if he saw any sign of what they were thinking. They each sat like statues staring out into space. For all Dillon could see, they weren't even listening. And even more alarming, so did all of the other jurors.

It was almost 4:00 p.m. by the time Judge Harpman finished and he told the jury to go to the jury room and select a foreman and then they could go home for the day. "We can all get an early start tomorrow. I'll see you all here at 8:30 a.m."

When the bailiff finally escorted the jurors to the jury room, the jurors had to walk within a few feet of where Dillon was seated at the counsel table as they exited the courtroom. Most jurors try their best to be neutral, but human nature usually comes into play and they look at the party or counsel they are favoring, and sometimes even smile. Not this jury. They were all stone-faced and even a bit agitated. "Maybe they don't like any of us?" Dillon pondered to himself.

After the jurors left the courtroom, Dillon took Mark, Suzzi and Kelly outside in the hallway. Suzzi looked terrible and Mark didn't look any better. "Well, folks, it is now up to the jury. Any questions?" Dillon asked.

When Mark and Suzzi said nothing, Kelly asked, "Do you want me here tomorrow?"

"No. I think you can stay back at the firm," Dillon replied. "I have a feeling we are going to get a quick verdict. I'll sit it out with Mark and Suzzi."

It was night by the time Mark and Suzzi got home and their mood, dark and gloomy, matched the night sky. Suzzi offered to fix dinner, but Mark was not interested in food. He sat down on the couch in the living room and finally the emotions of the trial caught up with him. He had been holding it all back in a valiant effort to be tough and resolute, but now he was just worn out and scared. Suzzi saw the tears running down his cheek and she went over and sat next to him, put her arms around his neck and just held him tight. They sat that way for hours.

Kelly tried to call Mark and Suzzi later that night, but no one answered the phone.

Dillon had sat waiting for a hundred or more juries over the years and it was never easy. It is one thing to come home after an exhausting trial and talk it over with your spouse, but when Dillon got home, he faced an empty house. He poured himself a healthy amount of Macallan scotch and sat at the kitchen table pondering the mysteries of the jury. Never in his career as a lawyer had he ever seen even one juror say they had heard enough before they had heard all of the evidence.

When he went to bed later that night, Dillon fell asleep asking himself, "Do we have a run-away jury? Can those three stubborn jurors take control and get their way in the end?"

CHAPTER 19

Trial – Day Twelve
(Tuesday, January 19)
(The Jury Revolt)

Ironically, it was almost two years to the day from when Mark had been fired, and Dillon was up early. He had had a miserable night thinking about what to expect from the jury.

Dillon showered, shaved and put on his traditional blue trial suit with his lucky straps and a light yellow tie and was at the courthouse before the bailiff even unlocked the door to the courtroom. He had told Mark and Suzzi that he would meet them in the cafeteria, so when the courtroom door finally opened, he walked in and told Charmaine Parker that he would be upstairs and to call him on his cell phone.

He rode the elevator up to the top floor, and as he entered the cafeteria, he saw that Suzzi was there alone. She looked flustered and when she saw Dillon, she ran over and threw her arms around Dillon's shoulder and stood there for a moment shaking. She finally said in a panicked voice, "Mark's not coming. He just can't take the ups and downs anymore."

Dillon stepped back and took Suzzi's hands into his own and said reassuringly, "It's OK, Suzzi. He doesn't have to be here. Whatever the jury decides, I can take care of things, so why don't you go home and stick close to Mark. He's going to need your help."

"I sorry, Mr. Clark," Suzzi said as she took in a deep breath. "I've never seen him like this before. He sat on the couch and cried. He looked so defeated. What can we do?"

"Mark needs time. He's a strong man and a fine lawyer, and whatever the jury does, he'll get it together and go on and have a great career. Just give him time," Dillon replied.

After Suzzi left, Dillon called his secretary, Jeanne Davis, and told her how to reach him and he gave a few instructions on other matters. Doing any productive work on other cases as you wait for a jury verdict is almost an impossibility, so Dillon just sat people watching. After several hours, he stood and wandered over to the outdoor patio. It was a clear day and he could literally see all of downtown Los Angeles spread out below.

When his cell phone rang, Dillon was slightly startled until he remembered why he was standing there waiting. It was Charmaine Parker, Judge Harpman's clerk. "Mr. Clark, I'm sorry to say this, but the judge wants the lawyers in his chambers right away."

Dillon walked back into the cafeteria, grabbed his battered old briefcase, and hustled over to the elevators. When he got to the courtroom, Haverley was there. They looked at each other and each shrugged their shoulders to indicate they had no idea what the judge wanted.

When they entered Judge Harpman's chambers, Dillon saw that Judge Dale Bannerman was also sitting in one of the easy chairs in front of the bookcase. While most trial lawyers know Judge Bannerman, not all have actually met him, so Judge Harpman made the introductions.

"I asked Judge Bannerman to join me this morning because we have a serious problem with the jury and I wanted his advice," Judge Harpman explained.

There was a moment of tense silence before Dillon asked, "What's happening, judge? Is someone ill?"

"I wish it were that simple," Judge Harpman replied. "The truth is I really don't know what is wrong. The bailiff told me they were screaming and yelling at each other so loudly that he could hear them from where he sat down the hallway. He knocked on the door once and one of them shouted at him to go away."

Judge Harpman glanced over at Judge Bannerman and added, "What concerns me is the three jurors who opposed the liability verdict. They could well be demanding that the others now join with them. We could have a change in the verdict even though I told them they can't do that. Or we have a dead-locked jury unable to agree. Judge Bannerman and I have been talking this over and we thought you should be involved. Any ideas?"

Judge Bannerman interjected, "As you know, I was once a partner at the Baukus & Johnson firm so my role is limited. But if you want my suggestion, I would have Judge Harpman conduct an interview with whoever they chose as their foreman and see what is going on. Sometimes the re-reading of jury instructions can help square away disputes. You won't know until you find out why they are arguing."

Dillon was skeptical of any suggestion from a former partner of Harlan Cross, but it was a reasonable idea and he said, "I have no problem with that approach. I would like to hear what the foreman says before you do anything more."

"OK by me," Haverley added.

Dillon and Haverley excused themselves and walked out into the courtroom to wait. When the bailiff brought the foreman to Judge Harpman's chambers, he was dismayed to see that it was Mr. Jordanson who appeared. He was not the foreman who handed the clerk the verdict on the liability phase. "Why in the world would the jury select a foreman who disagreed with the first verdict? This can only mean one thing. He's taking over the jury," he thought to himself irritably.

"Mr. Jordanson, may I assume you were elected the foreman?" Judge Harpman asked.

"Yes, sir," replied Mr. Jordanson.

"The bailiff tells me he can hear loud shouting going on. Is there a problem that I can help with?" Judge Harpman asked.

Mr. Jordanson was calm and a small smile appeared at the corner of his mouth. He shook his head and said, "No, Your Honor. We're having a serious debate, but I think we are making progress. I guess I can try to keep them quiet, but I'd hate to do that because some are very animated and well, yelling is just how some communicate."

"No, no," Judge Harpman quickly replied. He didn't want to interfere in the jury deliberation process and he added, "As long as you think the jury is making progress, I guess we can stand some shouting."

When Judge Harpman advised Dillon and Haverley who was elected foreman and what he said, Dillon was even more stunned and alarmed. If the jury were to now change their mind on the liability verdict, this would no doubt result in a mistrial. But neither Dillon or Haverley could actually think of any law that said they couldn't change their mind. So tactically, a change in the verdict would be a total victory for the Baukus & Johnson law firm, and Dillon now realized why Judge Bannerman had been present. A hung jury would help the Baukus & Johnson firm because, while it would result in a new trial, Haverley would now have no surprises and could have time to work with Alison Craft and other key witnesses. And Dillon knew he may not have a client willing to go through another trial.

The implications were all favorable to Haverley and he wisely said nothing. The implications to Dillon were disastrous but he had no way to head off the bad ending before the jury reached a verdict or threw up their hands in defeat.

With considerable effort, Dillon repressed what he was really feeling and instead said, "Your Honor, you did what you could. Yelling and screaming usually means a bitter division among the jurors, but we won't know until they decide."

At 4:30 p.m. Judge Harpman let the jury go home for the night. The bailiff continued to report loud shouting among the jurors, but they seemed friendly to each other as they left the jury deliberation room and departed on their way home.

Dillon hustled back to the firm and Laurel Kennedy and Kelly Parks were waiting for him in his office. "Jeanne told us what happened," Laurel said. "What is your take on it?"

"Not good," Dillon answered with a grimace. "If they change the first verdict or get hung-up and can't decide, we lose. There is no way we're gonna get Mark to go through another trial. He wouldn't even come to court today."

"Yes, we heard that," Kelly said. "Suzzi called me after she had spoken with you. I offered to go to their home, but she thought it best to leave Mark alone for now."

"I can't tell you how sorry I am," Laurel said in a sad voice. "Is there anything I can do?"

Dillon just shook his head. He could feel his heart pounding and that dreaded fear of loss enveloping him, and he felt powerless to do anything to stop the train wreck that he saw coming right at him.

As Dillon left his office to go home, Jeanne Davis turned her head aside as he walked by her desk. She didn't want him to see the tears in her eyes and have him guess her feelings that the case of Austin v. Baukus & Johnson was lost.

For the first time in his legal career, Dillon was unable to think of a way around the train wreck. Even opening a special twenty-seven year old bottle of Macallan scotch that night failed to take away the ache deep inside his stomach. He actually only sipped one glass and went to bed. His last conscious thought as he drifted off to sleep were Laurel's words, "I can't tell you how sorry I am."

CHAPTER 20

Trial – Day Thirteen
(Wednesday, January 20)
(Jury Deadlock)

Dillon got to the courthouse before 8:00 a.m. and sat drinking coffee until almost noon when Charmaine Parker called. "The judge says they're still arguing. The bailiff can't tell who is the loudest, but it is a man who keeps saying 'That's bullshit,' over and over. He's going to let them break for lunch and if they're still arguing by mid-afternoon, he's going to send them home early. He thinks some more time off might help break the deadlock."

Charmaine Parker's message caused the excessive coffee he had been drinking all morning to start fighting back and Dillon reached down into his briefcase and pulled out a bottle of Tums and threw several into his mouth and started chewing. "Damn it all to hell," he said to himself in anger as he threw the bottle back into his briefcase and slammed the cover shut. "Those three hard-asses have obviously managed to convince at least one other juror to go their way and now they can't get the required number to get to a verdict. Or they have convinced most of the others to change their mind. Why else would Jordanson have been chosen as the foreman in place of the prior foreman? Who would have figured?"

Haverley had selected one of the attorney lounges to work in and when he heard the news from Charmaine Parker, he immediately called Harlan Cross. "You know, Harlan, I think the three holdout jurors are finally getting their way. I think they are trying to change the first verdict. I don't know if that's legal, but I sure do like it. We either win or the judge will have to declare a mistrial and we will win the second time around."

"I talked with Derrick Warner about this," Harlan Cross replied. "He hasn't heard of a jury changing its mind either. We're gonna do some research, but he thinks since the full verdict is what counts, it likely will be upheld."

Haverley was feeling very good about the case and just laughed. Even Cross, who was not known much for his humor, chuckled a little. It is always good to be on the winning side.

Dillon and Haverley were both seated at their respective counsel tables when Judge Harpman buzzed Charmaine Parker and told her to let counsel know he was sending the jury home for the day. Charmaine hung up her telephone and said to both counsel, "They're on the way home for the day. Sorry."

As he walked through the tunnel from the courthouse to the parking garage, Dillon called Jeannie, his secretary, and told her the bad news and that the judge had sent the jury home. When he arrived at the office, no one said a word to him as he walked past the reception desk and down the hallway to his office. Even Jeannie made herself busy typing as he walked by her desk.

Jeannie Davis had passed on the bad news to Laurel Kennedy and Kelly Parks and they were in Laurel's office. "I've never seen anything like this," Laurel said bleakly.

"I don't think Dillon has any choice now but to push again for a mistrial," Kelly said as her voice cracked slightly.

They sat in Laurel's office without talking for some time. Gloom hung over the room as they each pondered the same disaster they saw happening. Mark Austin would not agree to another trial.

Finally Laurel said very softly, "Let's go down and see Dillon. He must be feeling terrible right now."

As they approached Dillon's office, Laurel saw that the door was open. She carefully stuck her head partially through the doorway and actually knocked gently on the door frame to make sure they could enter. When he looked up and saw the two of them standing in the doorway, Dillon waved his hand for them to come in.

He knew why they were there and Dillon said unconvincingly, "Look you two, things could be worse."

"I don't see how," Kelly blurted out before she caught herself. She hesitated and added, "I'm sorry Dillon. But we all know Mark will never go thru another trial. Doesn't that mean you have to just roll the dice and see what happens with the current jury?"

Dillon leaned back in his chair and said thoughtfully, "Yes, you're probably right. But only Mark can make that call." He reached over and grabbed his cell phone and dialed Mark's number.

It was Suzzi who answered. When Dillon told her what they were discussing, she said, "Mark doesn't want to talk about the trial any more. It's over as far as he's concerned."

"I understand," Dillon said trying to be encouraging, "but Mark has to agree to let me try to get a mistrial or let this jury do whatever they are going to do. I can't make that decision without his input."

"Hang on. I'll see if he'll talk to you," Suzzi said.

A few minutes later Mark was on the telephone. "Dillon, this has nothing to do with you. I want you to understand that," he said hesitantly.

When Mark said nothing further, Dillon said, "Mark, we have to make a decision. There are only two things to do at this point. I can push again for a mistrial, and that means another trial in six or ten months down the road. Or, we can just hold our breath and see what the jury decides. It's your decision, Mark, but I want you to know I think we should try for the mistrial. For whatever damn reason, Mr. Jordanson, the first juror to complain about the liability verdict, is now the foreman. This can only mean one thing. He and his two buddies who opposed the first verdict have managed to win over some of the other jurors. I don't have the foggiest idea if they can legally change the first verdict at this point, but they sure can make sure you get next to nothing!"

There was a long pause before Mark replied. Dillon could literally feel the pain in his voice when he said, "No more trials. Just let them get this over with."

Mark hung up the telephone before Dillon could reply.

Laurel and Kelly could not hear Mark's comments and they were anxiously looking at Dillon as he turned off his cell phone. "He doesn't want another trial." As he said this, Dillon stood and added, "It's out of our hands at this point."

Kelly shook her head in denial and said in anger, "There has to be something you can do! If the jury changes their mind or just gives Mark a dollar, this would be the biggest injustice that I've seen since I started working as a paralegal. I can just see that bastard Keller and his lady friend gloating over the verdict. And hell, I have no doubt that Harlan Cross is already celebrating. He offered $1m and we turned him down. It's a crappy system that can allow something like this to happen."

Laurel had a lot more trial experience than Kelly and Dillon saw that she was deep in thought. "Any ideas?" he asked.

"Maybe," Laurel answered. "With Mark refusing to seek another trial, we have to do the best we can with this jury. So what I'm thinking is to ask Judge Harpman to give some additional instructions to the jury. Tell them they have already decided the liability issue and their job now is to decide on how much Mark should receive for damages. Try to get them to understand that their duty at this point is limited to that one issue."

"I've been thinking the same thing," Dillon said. "Even with a hostile jury, the judge might be able to appeal to their conscience and get them to see that Mark really has been harmed."

Laurel was now excited and said, "OK. I'll draft an instruction that you can give to Judge Harpman. At this point it can't get any worse."

By the time Dillon got home that night, he was exhausted. When you are in a trial, you can spend ten or twelve hours a day working and preparing and you actually feel great because your brain is flying a mile a minute and you are oblivious to the hours. But when you are faced with nothing to do and can find no way to avoid the train wreck, emotions weigh you down and fatigue sets in. All you want to do is sleep. And that is what Dillon did that night.

CHAPTER 21

Trial – Day Fourteen
(Thursday, January 21)
(The Verdict)

Both Laurel and Kelly were waiting in the hallway when Dillon reached Judge Harpman's courtroom the next morning. Laurel handed him the jury instruction and said, "I laid it on a little thick, but the judge will see the point. He may want to do his own instructions, so it is written as a draft. I also drafted a special jury verdict form. It might help the jurors focus on the issue of damages."

Dillon opened the file folder that Laurel had handed him and took out the instruction. It said:

> "Ladies and gentlemen, Mr. Jordanson has advised me that he has been selected as the jury foreman for the damage phase of this case. This is most unusual in that the initial foreman in a bifurcated trial remains the foreman in the damage phase as well. But that is a decision I think you as the jury have the discretion to make.
>
> With this in mind, I want to remind you that you have already decided the liability phase and in doing so, you have found that the Baukus & Johnson law firm wrongfully terminated Mark Austin and intentionally

caused him emotional distress. This is your decision and you must follow that decision in deciding the damage phase. This means you need to follow the instructions I read to you on damages. Mark Austin is entitled to receive an award of damages for what you think he reasonably lost in income and for any emotional distress he suffered as a result of being wrongfully terminated.

So to help you at this point, I will have the bailiff bring you copies of the damage jury instructions. You must consider and follow these instructions. A set will be made for each of you."

"I like it Laurel," Dillon said. He then flipped to the Special Jury Verdict form and read it quickly. In most trials, the jury is given a general form that just asks the jury to specify the damages awarded. But a court can instead use special forms that asks the jury specific questions. In this case, Laurel set out the two questions"

"1. *How much do you find, if any, that the Plaintiff Mark Austin will lose in compensation as a result of the wrongful termination by the Baukus & Johnson law firm?*

ANSWER [Insert the dollar amount]: $_____

2. *How much do you find, if any, that Plaintiff Mark Austin reasonably suffered in emotional distress damages as a result of the wrongful termination by the Baukus & Johnson law firm?*

ANSWER [Insert the dollar amount]: $_____."

Dillon took the instruction and special verdict form and gave them to Charmaine Parker and asked her to tell the judge he would like to have a brief conference in chambers before the jury is brought in. He also handed a set to Haverley.

When Dillon and Haverley were seated in Judge Harpman's chambers, Haverley spoke first. "This is totally improper, Your Honor. We agreed on the instructions several days ago and now Mr. Clark wants you to add another instruction. And, I might add, an instruction that is designed to favor his case."

"Your Honor, I had this instruction and special verdict form prepared in light of the clear animosity of some jurors to the liability verdict and because we now have Mr. Jordanson as the foreman. He was the most outspoken of the jurors. It is intended to help clarify any confusion the jury might have. They have already decided liability and they need to be reminded of that by the court," Dillon replied with intensity.

"Your Honor, I must still protest," Haverley replied. "The instructions were decided on before we gave our final arguments. We had no chance of knowing of this new surprise instruction so we could comment on it."

Judge Harpman had a worried look on his face. He, too, may have had difficulty sleeping, thinking about what was happening with the jury, especially when they selected Mr. Jordanson as the foreman. As he studied the papers he reflected back to the words of Judge Bannerman that cautioned about favoring one side or the other. But his instincts told him he was dealing with jurors who are unhappy and might just change their minds.

Judge Harpman finally turned to Haverley and said, "I agree with you in general, Mr. Haverley, but we have a very unusual circumstance with this jury. I will let them use the Special Verdict form but I won't give the instruction requested by Mr. Clark. But I will remind them that they have already decided liability and their only task now is to decide whether Mr. Austin suffered any damages and if so how much."

When Dillon returned to the courtroom he noticed that both Mark and Suzzi were absent.

After the jurors were all seated, Judge Haverley entered the courtroom and took his seat. He looked over at the jurors and said, "I apologize for the delays that we are having and I'm going to let you go back and finish your deliberations after a brief comment. Please remember that you have already rendered your verdict on liability. Your only task now, in this damage phase of the case, is to decide whether Mark Austin suffered any damages and if so the amount. I'm also going to give you a Special Verdict form for you to fill out. It asks two questions for you to answer on damages. Again, thank you for your patience. The bailiff will now take you down to the jury room."

It was 8:45 a.m. when the jury began their further deliberations. Dillon, Laurel and Kelly all went up to the cafeteria to wait. Neither Laurel nor Kelly wanted to leave Dillon to wait alone. "I don't care if I live to be a hundred," Kelly said in frustration, "but I'll never learn to just sit and wait for a jury. My stomach is killing me already. How do you do it?"

Dillon laughed but it was plain to see that he too was tense and feeling the stress. "It may never get easy," he finally replied. "but, with all of its faults, and we are seeing one of those in this case, it is still the best system around."

Leaning forward in his chair slightly, Dillon said reflectively, "You know, we have to remember that Mark has done some things that a jury might not like. I suspect they bought Haverley's defense that Mark would not have been made a partner. Mark even admitted this on cross examination and that hurt big time. If I'm correct, that will knock out most of the damages."

"But what about emotional distress?" Laurel asked.

"That, too, is in jeopardy. If the jury believes Mark would not have been made a partner, they can easily conclude that any distress he suffered would have been suffered anyway when he left six or ten months later and that can't be blamed on the law firm," Dillon explained with sadness written all over his face.

"God, I can't take this," Kelly said in exasperation. "I think I may become a corporate law attorney or anything but a trial lawyer."

Dillon and Laurel just looked at each other and were thinking the same thing. If you can't stand the fire, stay out of the kitchen. You have to love the law and have thick skin to take the sudden ups and downs, and the wins and losses, which go hand in hand with being a trial lawyer. It can otherwise destroy you.

At 3:45 p.m., just about when Dillon, Laurel and Kelly were ready to throw in the towel for the day, Dillon's phone rang. It was Charmaine Parker and she said, "They have a verdict."

They all looked at each other and said nothing as they walked to the elevator and went up to Judge Harpman's courtroom. The judge was already sitting on the bench. Haverley arrived a minute later.

Judge Harpman said to Charmaine Parker, "Call the bailiff and have him bring in the jury."

It took another few minutes for the jury to begin to file into the courtroom. The jury room is down the hallway behind the courtroom so they enter from the back door. As each came through the door, they all locked eyes with Dillon. This was a terrible sign because jurors tend to look at who they are favoring when they enter a courtroom to render their verdict, but they do so with a smile or some indication that they like the person. These jurors were frowning and had a cold stare. Many actually looked upset.

When the jury was seated, Judge Harpman asked, "Mr. Foreman, do you have a verdict?"

"We do, Your Honor," Mr. Jordanson said.

"Please hand it to the bailiff," Judge Harpman said.

The bailiff walked over and took the Special Verdict form from Mr. Jordanson and walked over and handed it to Judge Harpman who read it quickly and handed it back to the bailiff. The bailiff then walked over and handed it to Charmaine Parker.

"Please read the verdict," Judge Harpman told Charmaine Parker.

Dillon sat watching the jurors trying to figure out what went wrong. Kelly actually stopped breathing as she heard Charmaine read the verdict.

"Question one. How much do you find, if any, that Plaintiff Mark Austin will lose in compensation as a result of the wrongful termination by the Baukus & Johnson law firm? Answer. $ 4,500,000.00."

There were only a few spectators in the courtroom but you could audibly hear each of them suck in air. Laurel and Kelly were at first confused and thought they had not heard what Charmaine Parker said correctly, until they saw the jurors begin to smile.

Charmaine Parker continued. **"Question Two. How much do you find, if any, that Plaintiff Mark Austin reasonably suffered in emotional distress damages as a result of the wrongful termination by the Baukus & Johnson law firm? Answer: $ 9,000,000.00. Signed, Walter Jordanson, Foreman."**

Haverley went pale as he heard the verdict. He raised his hand half-heartedly and stuttered, "Poll the jury please."

This time every juror confirmed it was their verdict. It was unanimous.

Judge Harpman thanked the jury and told them they were now free to leave. He added, "Counsel may want to ask you some questions. You are free to talk with them now or just leave. It is your choice."

When Judge Harpman left the bench, Mr. Jordanson and seven or eight of the jurors came over to Dillon. Mr. Jordanson said, "I know you must have been concerned about what the hell we were doing, but we were all really for you and Mark from the beginning. We just couldn't find a way to let you know."

"But what was the big argument about? Why the shouting?" Dillon asked.

Mr. Jordanson and several jurors laughed and one of the other jurors who opposed the liability verdict explained, "Walter and I felt that the real bad guys were Jerry Keller and Alison Craft. We wanted to hold them personally liable. The others all agreed they were the culprits but as partners, it was the firm that was responsible. We disagreed. We almost asked the judge if we could add them to the complaint, but decided that might not be proper. Anyway, it was clear who did what and why and that is why we just wanted to get on to end the case."

Haverley by now had walked over to the group of jurors and asked, "How did you get to $4.5 million on compensation?"

Mr. Jordanson replied, "It was pretty clear that Mark was having trouble getting another position with a major firm, so we felt he might not ever really get with another one like Baukus & Johnson. So we took the damage calculation out for twenty years and then took the present value of that figure. It was really all on the chart presented by the economist. She used ten years but she had actually done the calculation for twenty years so we had the number right there."

With this Haverley just shook his head and walked away.

It was Kelly who, after she got over the shock of the verdict, said, "We were so concerned that you were going to find that any emotional distress would have been suffered anyway when Mark didn't become a partner."

Another juror said, "We thought Mark would have been made a partner. It was only because of Keller and Craft and their little conspiracy that he was asked to leave. So whatever Mark suffered, it was from what they did."

Dillon wanted to know more about the emotional damages so he asked, "As you know, we had to stipulate to exclude any emotional distress that Mark suffered because of what the firing did to his relationship with his wife. How did you calculate the damage here?"

"Mr. Clark," another juror said, "we are all sorry about what happened to Mark. We could see the pain on his face when he was questioned. We didn't have to hear him say it. I wouldn't go through the hell they put him through for fifty million!"

"Where are Mark and his wife?" one of the female jurors asked. "I was hoping to congratulate them. We could all see how hard it was on the wife and, well, I want her to know I thought she was very brave when she jumped up and defended her husband when he was being cross-examined."

Dillon took some time explaining to the jurors how hard it had been for Mark and that he could not emotionally bring himself to come back to court. He then smiled and said to Mr. Jordanson, "We were so concerned about your questions that we all decided you were angry that the jury found liability. When we then got a second question showing impatience, I was going to ask the judge to declare a mistrial. But Mark said he just couldn't go through another trial. Boy, am I glad Mark resisted."

Juries often want to celebrate with the winning parties, and this jury was no exception. They stood around talking for over an hour before they all departed for their homes.

When the jurors had all gone, Laurel finally let her own feelings out. "I don't know about you Dillon, but I was convinced we were going to lose the whole case. When Charmaine started reading the verdict form, I felt a thousand prickly needles running up and down my spine. I think I'm still a little numb. The change from the gloom of losing to the thrill of winning has not really sunk in yet."

"Double that for me," Kelly chimed in. And she then hurriedly said, "We have to call Mark and Suzzi. They're probably sitting at home thinking they have lost."

Dillon reflected for a few seconds and said, "I'll tell you what. This is not something to say over the telephone." Turning to Kelly he added, "Give them a call and say we need them to come to the office asap. But tell them you'll pick them up. I don't want either one driving right now."

It was a little after 6:00 p.m. when Kelly arrived at the firm with Mark and Suzzi and ushered them into the firm's main conference room. Dillon and Laurel were there waiting.

Mark looked subdued when he said, "Thank you, Mr. Clark. You did your best. But I'm ok with whatever the jury decided."

Kelly by now was busting her seams but kept quiet. It took all of her willpower to keep from telling them they had been awarded $13.5 million dollars.

Suzzi was staring hopelessly at the floor when she asked, "I know you wanted a mistrial, but, well..." Her words trailed off before she finished her thought.

Dillon saw that both Laurel and Kelly were nodding in his direction to get on with the story. He had asked Jeanne Davis to make him a copy of the Special Verdict form and he had several copies in a file that was sitting on the table in front of him. He was going to string them along a bit further but decided they had been through enough trauma. He looked at Mark and Suzzi, who were both seated at the conference room table looking miserable. Suzzi's lower lip was trembling and they were clearly bracing themselves for the bad news.

Dillon cleared his throat, smiled and said as he passed a copy of the Special Verdict form to each of them, "The jury actually reached a verdict this afternoon. Here is their decision."

There was tense silence as Mark and Suzzi read the verdict. As he read the verdict, a frown formed on Mark's forehead as if he could not understand. Everyone sitting at the table then saw a look of amazement cross his face as he realized what he was reading. He looked up at Dillon and nervously asked, "Is this for real?"

"It is indeed," Dillon said as he slammed the palms of his hands on the table in celebration. "They were with us the whole way. We just misinterpreted the questions from the two who showed impatience. What they really wanted was to add Jerry Keller and Alison Craft as defendants so they would be personally liable. Amazing. That was what they were upset about!"

Kelly saw that Suzzi now also understood and she walked over and gave her a big hug and said, "The jury wanted you to know they were proud of you standing up for Mark. It is now really over."

Suzzi looked over at Mark and tears began to run down her cheeks and she finally burst out with sobs as she flung her arms around Mark.

As Dillon sat watching Mark and Suzzi hug each other, he thought back to the day when Mark and Suzzi held each other in the firm's reception area. "Justice has finally found her mark," he said to himself with satisfaction.

Mark finally let go of Suzzi and, while happiness was written all over his face, he still asked hesitantly, "It this really it? Are we really going to get all this money?"

"Oh, they'll probably try to get a new trial, and they may even appeal, but I think it is really over. You may have to wait a year or so to get paid if they appeal, but what the heck, the judgment will run at 10% interest until you do get paid!" Dillon explained

Dillon stood and walked over to the bar and opened the cupboard. "I think it's time we all had some cheer. He opened the refrigerator and pulled out a bottle of champagne. He carefully opened the bottle and poured a glass for each of them.

As they all began to relax, Dillon proposed a toast. He tipped his glass toward Mark and said, "To the Baukus & Johnson firm. They have been kind enough to make life very pleasant for Mark and Suzzi." He paused and added, "And you know Mark, I've been thinking. With that kind of money, you could open your own law firm and maybe even hire the attorneys that Keller took with him. I'm thinking specifically of the ones who work on the Gibbons's accounts. We know Gibbons likes you and it would be no interruption for him because he would be working with the same lawyers. Except, of course, for Jerry Keller. I bet the old guy would be amused at the justice of that!"

Harlan Cross was in total disbelief when Haverley called and told him what the jury had decided. "What the hell went wrong?" he demanded.

"There are no guarantees with a jury," Haverley said unconvincingly.

"Can this get reversed?" Cross asked in a critical tone.

"We'll have to research that, Harlan. But with the crazy testimony of Alison and her back-dating her memo, I doubt that a court of appeal would want to touch it," Haverley explained.

"Get over here to the firm. We need to figure out how to get this thing turned around," Cross replied.

By the time Haverley got to the Baukus & Johnson firm, Harlan Cross was already in deep discussion with Derrick Warner and Wayne Bailey. He was visibly upset.

"If we don't get this reversed, and I mean quickly, this firm is going to go under. I assume you all know and understand this?" Cross said with steel in his voice.

As Haverley took his seat at the conference room table, Cross turned to him and snapped, "I thought we were sitting pretty. It sounds like we were sandbagged by the jury!"

"Harlan, all I know is what the jurors said when we talked with them. They saw right through our defense and didn't believe a word that Alison Craft said once they learned Keller put her up to it," Haverley explained with a sigh.

"What about switching the jury foreman?" Derrick Warner asked. "I've never seen this happen in thirty years of practice. Can't this be grounds for appeal?"

"The jury was unanimous," Haverley replied. "If they had been split, we might have a chance. But I just don't see how we can argue we were prejudiced."

Wayne Bailey had just been listening, but he now directed himself to Haverley and cautiously asked, "How much of this judgment is covered by insurance?"

Haverley took a deep breath and hesitated before he answered. The Baukus & Johnson firm, as most large law firms, carried a lot of insurance. The main policy was for $50m with an extra umbrella policy for another $100m. But it was not clear whether the policies would cover a judgment where the firm was found guilty of intentionally causing emotional distress. The wrongful termination portion would be covered because there was a rider for employment matters. But that still left $9m in doubt. And this was no small change even for the Baukus firm.

Clearly looking nervous for the first time, Haverley said, "You may have a fight on our hands on the emotional distress damages." He had a serious conflict on any issue of insurance coverage. While he was the law firm's attorney, he was hired and paid for by the insurance company and he would be jeopardizing getting future work from the insurance company if he took an adversarial position against them.

"What the hell is that supposed to mean?" Harlan asked in a tone of disgust. "You just said 'you' might have a fight. Don't you mean 'we'?"

"You've been through this before, Harlan. I can't represent you on an issue of insurance coverage. You'll have to have your own lawyer handle that if the company denies coverage," Haverley explained.

"That's bullshit," Cross said angrily. "We pay a fortune to that damned company, and they better well step up to the plate and get this thing over with."

They discussed filing a motion for a new trial based on jury misconduct and decided that would be their best chance. Judge Harpman would be the one to decide the issue and maybe, just maybe, the Honorable Dale Bannerman could lend them a hand.

When Haverley excused himself and left the meeting, Cross, Derrick Warner and Wayne Bailey continued. At this point, the verdict was the least of their worries.

Wayne Bailey asked, "Harlan, have any more partners or associates said they were leaving?"

"Not yet, but I'm sure they will," Cross snapped in frustration. "They can see the empty offices just like we can, and no one wants to be the last one out the door."

"What a mess," Derrick Warner said as he walked over and helped himself to some of Harlan's fine liquor. Cross and Bailey joined him.

They sat sipping their drinks for several minutes, each seething inside over the bloody mess Jerry Keller caused because of his greed for more money.

It was Derrick Warner who finally broke the silence. "Harlan, I think we should re-think suing Keller for soliciting clients. If the firm does go under, and we don't get insurance coverage for the emotional distress part of the judgment, we're gonna have to pay that out of income and Jerry should bear the burden of that. We can sue him for breach of fiduciary duty as a partner. I wouldn't add Alison. She was just stupid to go along with him. But Jerry is the one who started the conspiracy with her, all in an effort to get more of the Tier Two bonus money. And when he encouraged Alison to write a critical memo, knowing it was to get Mark fired, that's where he breached his duty to the firm."

"I think you're right," Cross replied. "But let's wait until we see if Judge Harpman grants the new trial motion."

When Mark received his copy of Haverley's new trial motion, his hands began to shake and his fear of going thru another trial was overpowering. He was sitting at the kitchen table holding the motion in his hands, but his mind was so paralyzed that he could not read past the title of the motion. "No. Never again," he kept saying to himself over and over.

Once the motion for a new trial was filed, Harlan Cross called his old partner, Judge Dale Bannerman.

"I was half expecting you to call, Harlan," Judge Bannerman said in a consoling manner. "I'm truly sorry about the verdict. I've already talked with Harpman and he has read the motion for a new trial and is giving it some serious thought. He's actually got two of our research clerks researching the change in jury foremen."

"Dale, Derrick tells me a new trial motion is one of those things that are within a trial judge's discretion and is almost never reversed on appeal," Harlan said. "We have to get this verdict knocked out somehow and quickly. We won't find a firm to merge with if more partners leave and the rest have to pay a part of the judgment."

"But aren't you insured?" Judge Bannerman asked.

"We are, but Haverley says the insurance might not cover the emotional distress damages," Harlan explained. "If it doesn't, partners are going to be putting on their running shoes to see who gets to the door first. We might be able to hold them liable if we have to pay, but you know as well as I do that they'll fight like hell."

There was a moment of silence before Judge Bannerman said, "Harlan, what happened? Harpman told me the jury found a conspiracy between Keller and Craft to get Austin fired, but I find it hard to believe he would do something like that."

"Well, between you and me, he did," Harlan replied. "He always wanted to make the most money and he thought Austin was going to get a portion of the bonus money, so he wanted to make sure he wasn't around at the end of the year. Hell, he even had a client hold back paying hundreds of thousands of dollars until the following year!"

Judge Bannerman said quietly, "I'll talk with Harpman and see if I can nudge him to grant the new trial."

EPILOGUE

The law partnership of Baukus & Johnson eventually dissolved when the remaining partners learned that the firm's insurance carrier refused to pay the emotional distress damages. The firm is still in litigation with the insurance company.

The Baukus & Johnson firm eventually decided to sue Jerry Keller for breach of his fiduciary duties to the firm. They left Alison Craft out of the complaint in part because they needed her testimony. In depositions, she told them that she had actually expressed concern to Keller about soliciting clients and he reassured her he knew what he was doing. Trial was not expected to take place for another year.

The law firm of Keller, Craft & Anderson also dissolved. And what had been a budding relationship between Jerry Keller and Alison Craft went the same way.

When Keller, Craft & Anderson dissolved, the attorneys scattered and joined other law firms in the Los Angeles area. By then Boyd Gibbons had had enough of Jerry Keller and when Mark joined another law firm, it was easy for him to move most of his legal work to Mark Austin's new firm. Instead of opening his own practice, Mark was actually solicited by Roscoe, David & Turner, a law firm which had been the main competitor of Baukus & Johnson, and he joined them as an equity partner. And yes, Mark became the billing attorney for the Gibbons's accounts.

Judge Gerald Harpman took Haverley's motion for a new trial seriously. He knew he had broad discretion and that whatever decision he made would no doubt be upheld on appeal. There was simply no law about a jury picking two different foremen for different phases of a trial. But he got irritated when Judge Dale Bannerman wandered into his chambers and subtlety tried to convince him to grant the motion. When Judge Bannerman left his chambers, he called Charmaine Parker and said, "Do a minute order denying the motion for a new trial."

It took almost a year before Mark Austin received final payment on the judgment. The Baukus & Johnson firm, which was in the process of dissolving, sent their check for nine million to Dillon Clark's office when Dillon had called Haverley and threatened to send a Los Angeles County sheriff deputy to execute on their bank account. The insurance company had sent their check for four million five hundred thousand dollars plus interest, as soon as the decision was made not to appeal the judgment.

Dillon had deposited both checks into his firm's trust account and arranged for Mark and Suzzi to come over to the office to celebrate. Laurel Kennedy, Kelly Parks along with Dillon's secretary, Jeannie Davis, were present in the firm's conference room when Mark and Suzzi arrived.

Mark was wearing blue jeans and a blue and white striped long sleeved shirt open at the neck with the sleeves rolled up above his elbows. He was tanned, relaxed and his body language emoted happiness. He was the old Mark Austin.

As Mark and Suzzi entered the conference room, Suzzi ran over to Dillon and threw her arms around his neck and gave him a big kiss. "I don't know how we could ever pay you for what you've done," she said excitedly, with a small tear running down her left cheek, a tear of happiness and not sadness or fear.

"Well, I think you all know how we feel here at the firm," Dillon replied with a little emotion of his own. His words slightly caught in his throat as he added, "I've practiced law for a long time now, and I can say quite honestly that I've never enjoyed representing anyone more than I have the two of you. It was a tough road, but you stayed the course and deserve all the best in life."

It was a touching scene and Laurel and Kelly just clapped their hands and said in unison, "Double that from us!"

Looking at Suzzi, Kelly said, "Suzzi, I have to tell you. I'll never forget the day you stood up in court and shouted, 'Leave him alone!' That was one of the bravest things I've ever seen. You weren't thinking of winning or losing. You just wanted to protect Mark."

Mark turned and faced Suzzi. He stared deep into her eyes, smiled and said, "I'm proud of you, too. And I think you can now give up your teaching job!"

Despite Dillon's protest, Mark and Suzzi insisted that he take his full contingency fee. After giving generous bonuses to Laurel, Kelly and the rest of the firm, Dillon reflected on the trauma of trial work and was actually giving serious thought to retirement. He then mused to himself, "But I really do like being a lawyer."